CANADA
Indian wars
in the Black Hills
Boston Tea Party
Cornwallis'
surrender
1781
Battle of
Bunker Hill
Great
Chicago Fire
1871
Abraham
Lincoln
President
Lewis and Clark
Oregon bound
Pickett's charge
at Gettysburg
Stars
and Stripes
born
The rush
to the West
Lincoln's
birthplace
1809
Daniel Boone
in Kentucky
Fort Sumter
1861
Sherman's
march through
Georgia—1864
Andrew Jackson
at New Orleans
Jefferson Davis
and the Confederacy
"Remember
the Alamo!"
1836
Seminole
wars in
Florida

# History of Your

# America



TRACING THE MOVING STORY OF AMERICA'S STRUGGLES, TRIUMPHS AND GROWTH FROM COLONIZATION TO PRESENT GREATNESS

## AUTHORS AND CONSULTANTS

**Edward F. Brufke, M.A., M.Ed.**
Chairman, Social Studies Department, Niles Township High School, Skokie, Illinois. Instructor, United States History, Advanced Placement and Basic Learning program.

**Vivian Malczyk, B.S.**
Instructor, Public School System, Washington, D.C.

**Walter J. Kelly, M.A.**
Supervisor of Student Teachers in History and Social Studies, Chicago State College, Chicago, Illinois.

**John J. Lambert, B.S.**
Chairman, Social Studies Department, Alain LeRoy Locke High School, Los Angeles, California.

**Caryl Kurtzman, B.A.**
Speech and Language Specialist, San Anselmo School District, Marin County, California.

**William M. McCarthy, B.S.**
Specialist in American History



UNITED STATES HISTORY SOCIETY INC.

# table of contents

## PART 8. THE WINNING OF WORLD WAR II



## PART 9. COLD WAR AND THE ATOMIC BUILD-UP



## PART 10. COMMUNIST WARS AND MEN IN SPACE



## PART 10 (continued)



### SUMMARY-GRAPHICS



### MAPS AND DIAGRAMS

# Why you should take a deep interest in the History of Your America

The people and events you will see and read about in this book are very important to you. Just as a tree needs deep roots to give it strength and help it continue to grow . . . you, as a young citizen of America, need to know of your own country's roots so that you, too, can continue to grow.

Today you enjoy many benefits and privileges as an American. You can speak your mind without being thrown into jail. You can disagree with the way your government is running things. You can belong to a labor union, or even go out on strike, without fear of being fired from your job.

Nobody can force you to attend a church that you don't want to attend. You sleep peacefully at night. No policeman can carry you off to jail because someone doesn't like the way you worship, or the color of your skin.

How did all of these freedoms and privileges you enjoy come about? As you read through this book, you will see that they were no accident. To win all these wonderful benefits that you enjoy today, other Americans, for 200 years, have struggled, triumphed, and died.

Your America is a land where people came from many other countries. Some came for religious freedom. Some came for adventure. Some came for riches. Some came in chains. But most came because they were dissatisfied in the country where they lived. Here, in your America, they dreamed of a better way of life for themselves and their children.

The History of Your America traces for you this most interesting and dramatic story. Compared to the age of other nations, America is only an infant. Yet in four overlapping lifetimes, America has become the leader among all nations.

More young Americans go to school than young people of any other country. More young Americans stay in school longer and step out of their schools trained to make a better living for themselves and their families than young people from other countries.

As you read through this book, and learn more of your American roots, you will see how knowing of your past will help you to understand your country and how this knowledge will help you to guide your country in the future.

Reading the History of Your America is witnessing the life story of your country.

In this story you'll meet people and events of all kinds. You'll read how Christopher Columbus, a brave sailor with three small ships, ventured across an uncharted ocean. He reached a continent which few, if any, in Europe knew existed—America.

Adventurers and settlers next set foot on American shores and suffered disappointments and hardships. The Pilgrims and Puritans came to make a new home for themselves where they could practice their religion in peace.

You'll see and read about the struggles of the colonies—from Jamestown to Georgia. You will watch them grow in size and strength. You will note the rising spirit of freedom and independence.

The History of Your America will tell you about the brave patriots of this young land, who fought England with all her strength and resources. You will march with George Washington through the Revolutionary War to victory—and independence—at Yorktown.

You will have your own seat at the convention in Philadelphia, where wise leaders of the new nation adopted the constitution. This is your Constitution . . . the law of your land. And included in it is the Bill of Rights, which protects your personal freedoms as an American.

How the United States won the War of 1812 and upheld freedom of the seas will unfold before your eyes.

The History of Your America carries you on through the bitter War Between the States. From pictures and stories, you will realize the struggles the Civil War generation went through. As an American, you will rejoice as the American slaves are set free after the end of the war.

With the History of Your America, you will travel on through the Nineteenth Century. This will carry you through Reconstruction, Presidential administrations both stormy and progressive, the winning of freedom for Cuba, and the great gains which marked America's miracle century.

As the Twentieth Century opens, you will see America entering a new period as a great world power. The History of Your America tells about Theodore Roosevelt's swinging of the "Big Stick," as his world policies were called. It tells of America's bravery in World War I.

After World War I, you will learn how inflation, high prices and stock market gambling bring on the Great Depression. Franklin D. Roosevelt and the New Deal fight this depression through two of his four terms.

Then you will watch the rise of the dictators, Hitler and Mussolini, bringing on World War II. Still another new period unfolds–the Cold War and the atomic age. You will stand by as the United States and Russia meet face to face on the problems of post-war German rule. You will see them influence other countries as the two strong nuclear powers, and you will see America become Free World leader.

You will follow the progress of Americans in Communist wars in Korea, Vietnam and Cambodia. Then men blast off into space–and Americans land on the moon!

You will become a part of the age of dissent, or disagreement, on one side or the other, beginning in the 1960's and moving on into the 1970's. You will observe the Revolution for Civil Rights, antiwar movements, young Americans joined in a youth crusade headed by student protests and demonstrations, and advances of the fight for equality and minority causes. And you will see, too, an age of civil disorder, with crime on the streets.

In the History of Your America you will see that underlying America's growth has been the strength and backbone of every American patriot of the past–citizenship responsibility. He knew that inequalities would be unearthed in the future .

But, as a responsible American, he knew that only through the framework of the Constitution and Bill of Rights could inequalities be wiped out permanently without destroying precious freedoms.

Now read on for yourself . . . this is your America and this is your history.

# PART 1

# CHANGES IN THE OLD WORLD LED TO FINDING OF A NEW WORLD

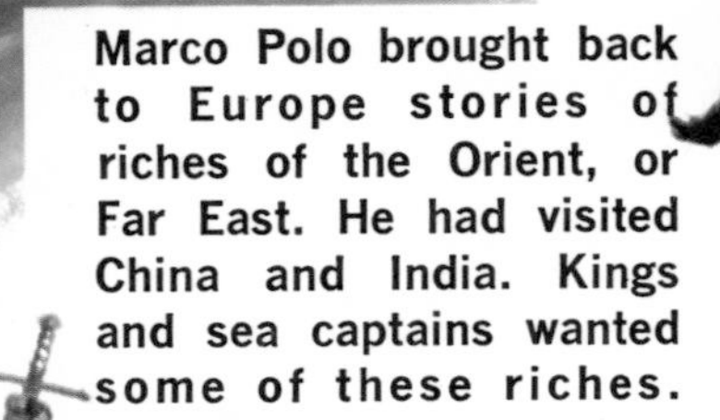

Marco Polo brought back to Europe stories of riches of the Orient, or Far East. He had visited China and India. Kings and sea captains wanted some of these riches.

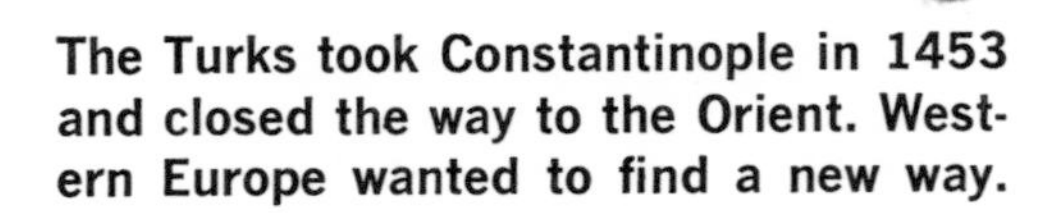

The Turks took Constantinople in 1453 and closed the way to the Orient. Western Europe wanted to find a new way.

Christian Crusaders, or religious knights, went to the Holy Land to fight the Moslems, who were not Christians. They also told of the Far East's riches.

A change came in the ways of making a living. Owners of big farms became merchants, who sold things. The farm workers got jobs in cities.

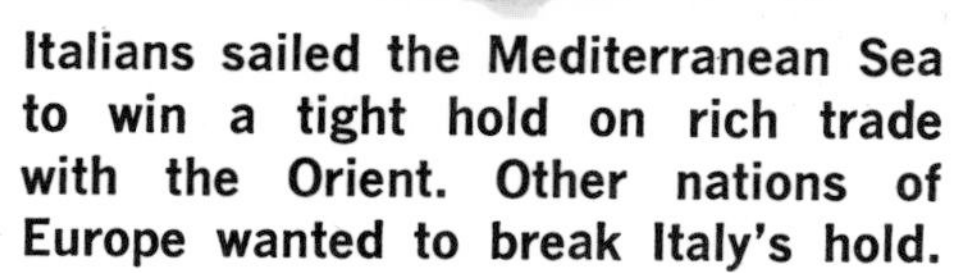

Italians sailed the Mediterranean Sea to win a tight hold on rich trade with the Orient. Other nations of Europe wanted to break Italy's hold.

Spreading Christianity into heathen, or non-Christian, lands was a goal for many religious men. They carried the cross to faraway lands.

Teachers and students began to learn more about the world. The Fourteenth Century saw a big gain in the study of ocean travel.

Study of navigation, finding one's way on unknown seas never sailed before, made such trips safer. The goal—"Find a new way to India"—led many explorers to the new world.

# A CONFIDENT COLUMBUS REACHES A NEW WORLD

**Christopher Columbus** and his men looked with joy as an island came into view. The long hunt was ended. All fears were gone. Columbus had landed in the New World.

LAND AND A NEW WORLD! Soon after dawn on October 12, 1492, a cannon aboard one of three little ships was fired, telling Christopher Columbus that land had been seen. He had been right! Great things were to be found by sailing west. But Columbus had not reached India, as he thought. He had reached America. The tall son of an Italian merchant from Genoa had studied the lessons of Prince Henry the Navigator. King John II of Portugal and King Henry VII of England refused to back a voyage by Columbus. He won the help of Queen Isabella of Spain, and she put up the money to pay for his voyage. Three small ships, the *Nina*, *Santa Maria* and *Pinta*, were bought for Columbus. He sailed from Palos, Spain, on August 3, 1492. After a month's stop in the Canary Islands, the voyage west continued. Five weeks passed. Columbus' crew became frightened and planned to mutiny, or disobey, Columbus. Then birds flew overhead and tree branches floated by. All of the sailors were excited and they forgot their fears. These were signs of land nearby—and then the land was seen. It was an island known today as Watling Island in the Bahamas. Columbus landed and went ashore. Wearing a red coat and carrying a holy banner, Columbus said the island now belonged to Spain. He called it San Salvador (Holy Savior). Columbus sailed on and discovered Cuba and Haiti. He returned home and was called a hero. But he died a poor and unhappy man.

## *THE NEW LAND IS NAMED AMERICA*

ENGLAND JOINED IN the race for New World lands when her flag was taken to North America in 1497 by John Cabot. An Italian sailing for England, Cabot reached Newfoundland's coasts. He claimed all of his discoveries for England. Cabot had heard Bristol fishermen tell of North Atlantic trips. He asked King Henry VII to help him make a voyage and the king put up the money. Cabot and his son, Sebastian, sailed in May from Bristol with eighteen other sailors in his crew. On a second voyage, Cabot reached waters off Maryland. England later said that all the lands found by Cabot belonged to her.

THE NEW LANDS WERE NAMED not for the man who found them—Columbus—but for Amerigo Vespucci, an Italian merchant. Vespucci had studied navigation and learned much about the art of seamanship. He headed out to sea and sailed for the New World. Starting in 1499, Vespucci made four trips along the coast of South America and reached Brazil. He wrote a book which he called *The New World*. A German professor, Waldseemuller, printed a geography in 1507 and said America should be the name of the New World. Waldseemuller took this from the Latin word for Vespucci's first name—Americus.

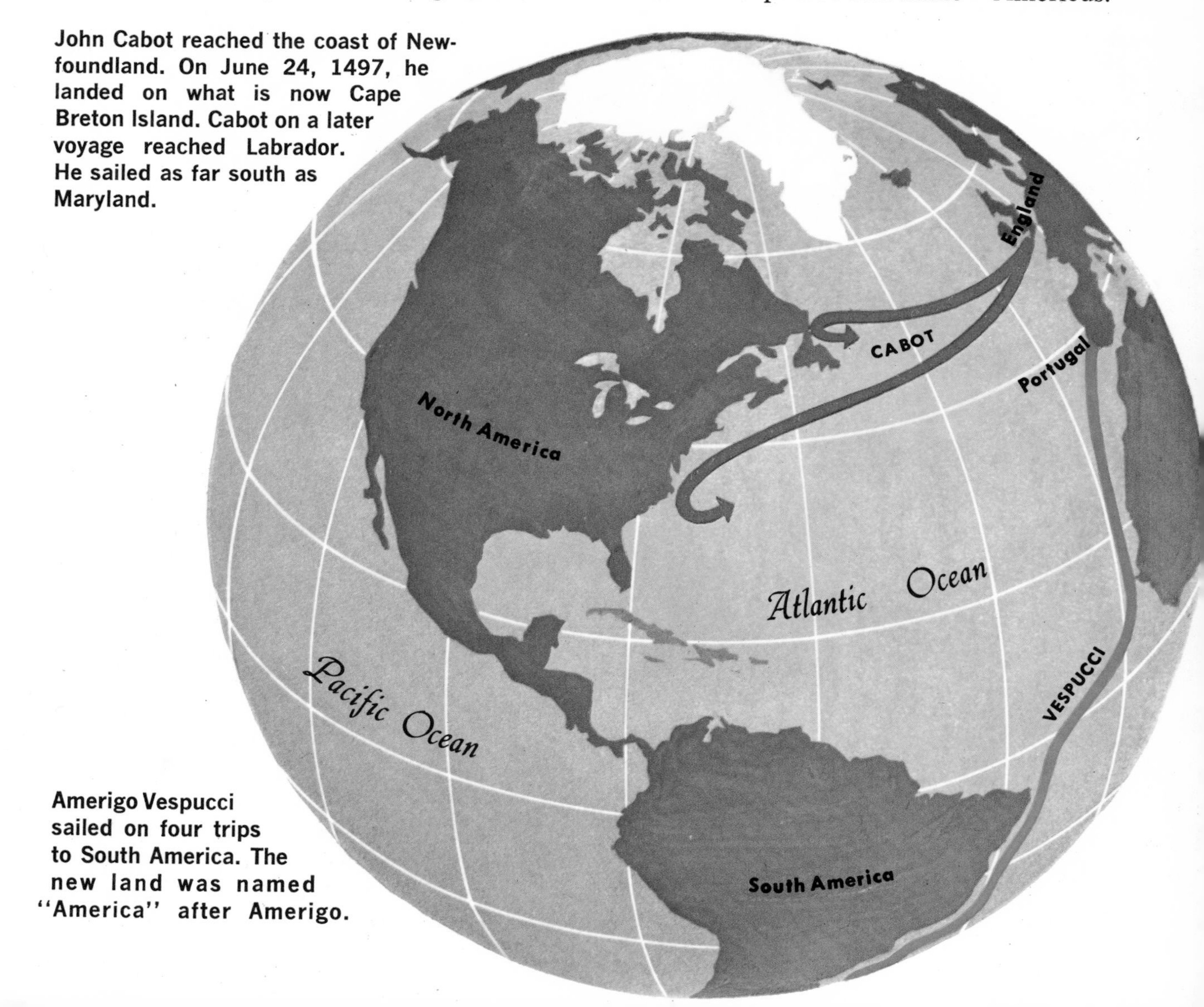


**John Cabot reached the coast of Newfoundland. On June 24, 1497, he landed on what is now Cape Breton Island. Cabot on a later voyage reached Labrador. He sailed as far south as Maryland.**

**Amerigo Vespucci sailed on four trips to South America. The new land was named "America" after Amerigo.**

**Balboa** waded into the water and gazed in wonder upon the great ocean stretching out of sight. He had crossed the Isthmus of Panama and reached the mighty Pacific.

SPANISH EXPLORERS and soldiers spread over the New World and founded a strong New Spain. They discovered new lands and some found much treasure, gold and silver. This treasure was taken from the Indians who lived on the land and was sent home in big Spanish ships called galleons. Ponce de Leon hunted for a Fountain of Youth, which was only a dream, and found Florida instead (1513). Vasco Nunez de Balboa crossed the Isthmus of Panama (1513) and became the first white man to see the Pacific Ocean from the American side. Alvar Nunez Cabeza de Vaca and several friends walked from what is now the Texas coast to the Gulf of California. It was a hard trip taking nine years and only four men lived to return to Spain. Hernando de Soto discovered the Mississippi River (1541) and later died and was buried in the great river which he had found. De Soto traveled in seven states.

FRANCISCO VASQUEZ DE CORONADO, on another Spanish hunt for gold, discovered the Grand Canyon, one of the world's wonders and a place of great natural beauty. Coronado explored widely in Southwest North America while he hunted for the imaginary "Seven Cities of Cibola." None of these explorers found treasure, but two others did—Hernando Cortez and Francisco Pizarro. Cortez defeated Montezuma, emperor who ruled the Aztec Indians in Mexico (1521), and took much gold and silver. Pizarro defeated and robbed the Inca empire in Peru (1531-1536). Atahualpa, the Inca emperor, was killed.

ST. AUGUSTINE, the first city north of the Mexican border, was built in Florida by Spain. It was begun in 1565 by Pedro Menendez, on orders from King Philip II. Menendez was sent to drive out a group of Frenchmen who had built camps which they used as bases on the northeast coast of Florida. Spanish treasure ships were raided from these bases. Menendez arrived with 19 ships and 1,500 men. On landing, he had nearly all of the Frenchmen killed. Menendez then carried out the second part of the king's orders—to build a fort to hold the town. This fort was St. Augustine, which rose on a finger of land, or peninsula, south of where the French camp had been. For many years, the Spaniards fought to hold St. Augustine. After Menendez's killings, France sent ships and soldiers, and St. Augustine was nearly ruined before the French were driven off.

ST. AUGUSTINE was burned twice by English raiders, one of whom was Sir Francis Drake. It was not until the late 1590's that St. Augustine began to enjoy peace. Many missions, or churches, were built to spread religion among the Indians. After Spanish soldiers based at St. Augustine won control of the southeastern coast, all of New Spain began to spread out. Cuba, the West Indies, Mexico and parts of South America grew into large colonies. A fort was built on Haiti, and Darien became a large city on the Isthmus of Panama.

NEGROES TOOK PART in New Spain's explorations and expansion. Thirty Negroes traveled with Balboa to the Pacific Coast and helped build the first ships there. Negroes dragged Cortez's cannon into Mexico and set them up for battle. Negroes also fought for Pizarro in his conquest of Peru. Among the best known Negro explorers of Latin America was Estevanico, who was an advisor on Cortez's invasion of Mexico and an advance scout on one of the Spanish parties seeking the "Seven Cities of Cibola." Indians killed Estevanico.

**St. Augustine,** oldest city in the United States, was founded by Spaniards in 1565.

**The Pilgrims,** seeking religious freedom, founded England's second American colony. Miles Standish helped select Plymouth as the Pilgrims' new home.

THE THIRTEEN ORIGINAL colonies were founded in America by England over a 126-year period from 1607 to 1733. These original, or first, thirteen were the colonies which later became the United States. The first colony was Jamestown, founded by the London Company under a charter, or written permission, granted by King James I. Captain John Smith led Jamestown through its hard first two years. When a young farmer named John Rolfe found a way to cure tobacco for smoking, tobacco became a crop which earned much money. The need for field workers grew. In 1619, a Dutch ship landed twenty African prisoners in Jamestown. Jamestown farmers bought them to work in the fields, and they became the first Negro slaves in British America. That same year, the London Company gave Jamestown some self-rule, or a government of its own. A law-making group called the House of Burgesses was formed.

THE PILGRIMS founded England's second colony in 1620. They chose Plymouth as the site, or place, of their new home. Captain Miles Standish was a brave and wise leader of the Pilgrims. He made peace with the Indians. The Pilgrims were ruled by the *Mayflower Compact,* an agreement named after their ship. The Compact formed a "civil body politic" as the government and provided for just and equal laws and such officers as were believed best for the good of the colony. Democracy—justice and equal rights for all—had planted its first two roots in America: the House of Burgesses and the *Mayflower Compact.*

OTHER COLONIES FOLLOWED: Massachusetts, founded by the Puritans, in 1629; Maryland, founded by Lord Baltimore, in 1634; Rhode Island, founded in 1636 by Roger Williams, after a religious quarrel in Massachusetts; New York, seized from the Dutch, in 1664; Pennsylvania, founded by William Penn as a home for Quakers, a peace-loving religious group, in 1682; and, finally, Georgia, founded by James Oglethorpe, in 1733. Georgia was a new home where Englishmen would be safe from going to jail because they owed money back in England.

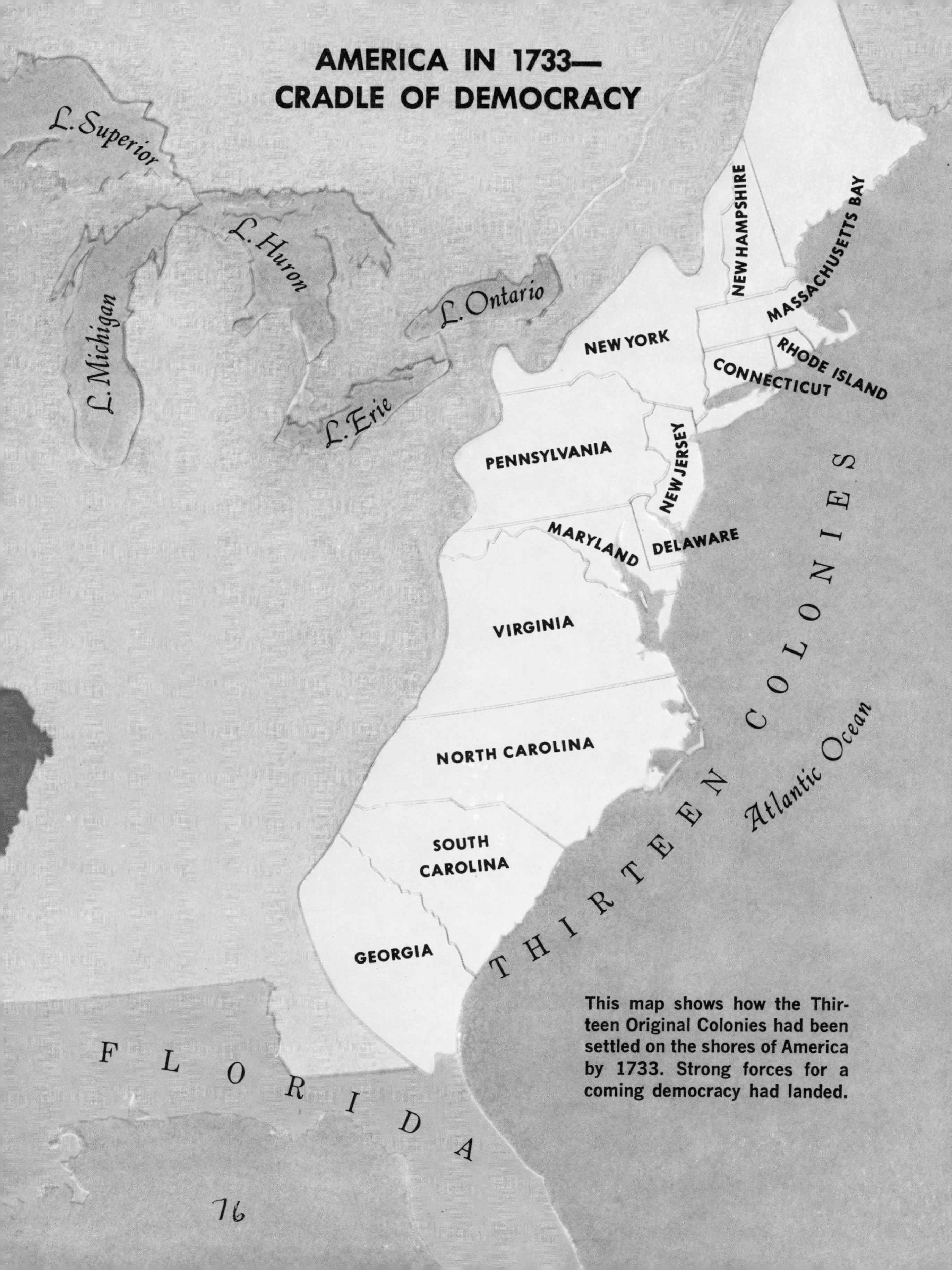


This map shows how the Thirteen Original Colonies had been settled on the shores of America by 1733. Strong forces for a coming democracy had landed.

**Samuel de Champlain,** on orders of his king, founded Quebec on the St. Lawrence River. It was France's first American colony.

NEW FRANCE WAS BORN in America a year after Jamestown, as a result of colonies founded by Samuel de Champlain. Champlain built these colonies for France in what is now Canada. Champlain explored in upper North America from 1603 to 1607. He traveled over much of the land explored and claimed for France 69 years before by Jacques Cartier. Champlain traveled through the Gulf of St. Lawrence and up the St. Lawrence River. He returned to France in 1607 and was sent back by his king in 1608 with orders to found a colony on the St. Lawrence River. Champlain built the colony on the St. Lawrence in 1608 and named it Quebec. This was France's first American colony. The site Champlain chose for Quebec was a high cliff which he believed could be "easily held" against any enemies. Champlain was Quebec's first governor-lieutenant.

CHAMPLAIN SPENT the last 27 years of his life building up Quebec and New France. He led many trips up rivers that flowed into the St. Lawrence. Villages, larger settlements with a few cabins and tents, were built by some of his men who saw the area as good grounds for fur trapping. These villages later became towns. In 1609, Champlain found the lake now named for him. He established Montreal in 1611. In 1615, Champlain discovered Lake Huron and Lake Ontario. He sent brave young Frenchmen to live among the Indians and learn their ways of living and language. The French made many Indian friends, except among the Iroquois, who were still enemies of the French long after a defeat in 1610. After Champlain's death, the French explored and spread south into middle-western America. In 1673, Louis Joliet and Father Jacques Marquette paddled down the Mississippi River to a point where the Arkansas River flowed into the Mississippi. In 1682, Robert Sieur de La Salle made a canoe trip down the Illinois River to the Mississippi. He and a companion, Henri Tonty, traveled on the Mississippi to reach its mouth and the Gulf of Mexico. La Salle claimed all of the Mississippi's lands for King Louis XIV of France. On a second trip, La Salle was killed by a member of his party.

**While exploring** New France, Champlain discovered Lake Huron and Lake Ontario.

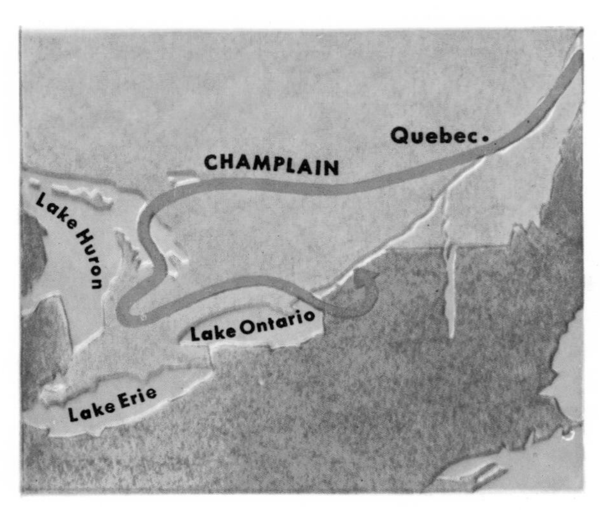

**Peter Minuit** bought Manhattan Island from the Indians for twenty-four dollars. Now worth billions, the island became the site of Holland's New Amsterdam.

THREE GREAT NATIONS had built colonial empires in the Americas—Spain, England and France. Colonial empires were those which were established in foreign lands. This was called colonization. Settlers from these nations were pouring into the new land. For a time the Netherlands—or Holland—owned American colonies. The biggest colony was founded in 1623 on an island now called Manhattan, in New York. For 60 Dutch guilders—worth twenty-four American dollars—Peter Minuit bought the entire island of Manhattan from the Indians. The colony was named New Amsterdam and all of Holland's colonies were called New Netherland. The land bought from the Indians for twenty-four dollars is now worth billions of dollars.

ENGLAND TOOK New Netherland from the Dutch people without a shot being fired. King Charles II of England told his brother, the Duke of York, "I am giving you New Netherland. The land belongs to us anyway. It is yours. Go take it." The Duke of York sent four warships against New Netherland. On a fall morning in 1664, the English ships appeared off New Amsterdam. A letter was sent to Peter Stuyvesant, the New Netherland governor, ordering him to surrender. Stuyvesant was a brave old soldier who had lost a leg fighting for Holland. He refused to give up his colony to the British. He tore up the letter. One of Stuyvesant's men picked up the pieces and pasted them together. He read the letter to the townspeople. They decided not to fight and Dutch officers raised the flag of surrender. Holland's New Netherland then became England's New York. The duke had named the colony for himself when the king gave him the land.

NORTH AMERICA'S last corner was reached by men and ships led by Vitus Bering. In three voyages for Russia (1728, 1729 and 1741), Bering reached the Aleutian Islands and other points off Alaska. Bering and his party found rich fur-trapping grounds. Sea otter furs were worth much money. Bering faced a cruel winter on his last voyage. He died on an island now named for him. Bering gave Russia claims to the lands he had explored in North America.

# COLONIES FOUGHT AGAINST ENGLAND'S TAXES AND LAWS

**James Wolfe** led British troops up the cliffs at Quebec and defeated a French army under Montcalm. After Quebec fell, England won the French and Indian War.

ENGLAND DROVE THE FRENCH from North American lands in a long series of wars. Early fights were King William's, Queen Anne's and King George's Wars. All began in Europe, but spread to America. The British and French each wanted the other's best lands for fur-trapping and fishing. The French pushed into the Ohio River Valley. Governor Robert Dinwiddie of Virginia ordered them out. His letter was taken to the French by George Washington, a 21-year-old leader of Virginia militia, or state soldiers. Washington fought the French at Fort Necessity and lost his first battle.

THE FRENCH AND INDIAN WAR broke out in America as part of the Seven Years' War in Europe. England fought France and Spain in Europe. In America, it was the British against the French and their Indian friends. The British met early defeats. An army under General Edward Braddock was surprised near present-day Pittsburgh by a French-Indian force. Braddock was killed, but bravery by Washington and his Virginia soldiers saved many of the British. The British then won big victories. General James Wolfe led an army up the cliffs at Quebec and took the city (1759). Both Wolfe and the French general, Marquis de Montcalm, were killed in the battle. Montreal surrendered and the war was over.

A GREAT CHANGE in America's map came when England won the Seven Years' War in Europe and the Treaty of Paris was signed in 1763. France gave up to England all of Canada and her lands east of the Mississippi River. Spain was given all French lands west of the Mississippi. A big change also came in England's dealings with her colonies. Her rule became stricter.

## *NEW ENGLISH LAWS TIGHTEN CONTROL ON COLONIES*

AFTER WINNING THE WAR, England tried to force her American colonies to pay heavy taxes and obey stricter laws. Since the early days, England had restricted the colonies with Navigation Acts. These acts told the colonies what goods they could make, where they could sell them outside of America, and what goods had to be sent to England. After the French and Indian War, Writs of Assistance were used against the colonies. The writs let British tax agents search colonists' homes and seize smuggled goods at any time, anywhere. In 1764, a new Molasses Act was passed which hurt the colonies' money-making Triangular Trade. In the "triangle," molasses was brought in from the West Indies and made into rum. The rum was sent to Africa and traded for slaves. The slaves were taken to the West Indies and traded for more molasses. A Stamp Act (1765) called for tax stamps, costing from a half-penny to fifty pounds (British money), on legal papers, newspapers, magazines and many other papers. The Townshend Acts (1767) took the place of the Stamp Act. The Townshend Acts set up new duties, or taxes, on glass, paper, paint and tea.

THE BOSTON MASSACRE was a bloody event in 1770. A mob of colonists attacked a British sentry at a customs house where duties were paid. Eight other British soldiers fired into the crowd. Five Boston colonists were killed, including Crispus Attucks, a Negro, one of the leaders.

**The Boston Massacre** was a bloody tragedy in the colonies' fight against British taxes. British soldiers fired into a Boston mob, killing five American colonists.

**Andrew Oliver,** a British tax stamp agent, was seized by The Sons of Liberty. A straw dummy of him was hanged. He promised to sell no more stamps and was freed.

MOB FIGHTING BROKE OUT as the colonists rose against England's laws which forced them to pay taxes. The Sons of Liberty was formed by Samuel Adams, and at first it was a peaceful group. But soon the Sons of Liberty marched as mobs and riots followed. Many had no jobs and placed the blame on England's taxes. Stormy events took place in all the colonies. Property of British officials was wrecked and the lives of some were in danger. A mob in Boston raided the home of Lieutenant-Governor Thomas Hutchinson. The rioters wrecked his furniture and drank his wine. Andrew Oliver, the governor's brother-in-law who was a stamp agent in Boston, was dragged under an elm tree and was about to be hanged. Oliver was turned loose only after promising he would never sell another stamp. In all the colonies, stamp agents were treated roughly and soon all quit their jobs. At the same time, colonial merchants refused to buy goods from England. The merchants in England begged their government to end the Stamp Act. This was done (1767) but the Townshend Acts then were passed.

RHODE ISLANDERS DISLIKED a British revenue cutter named the *Gaspee*. The cutter was a ship which kept watch on colonial ships to see that they did not smuggle, or slip any goods into the country without paying taxes. The Rhode Islanders also disliked Lieutenant William Dudingston, commander of the *Gaspee*. One day, the *Gaspee* ran aground on a sandbar off Providence, Rhode Island. That night (1772) dozens of Providence townsmen went aboard the *Gaspee*. The hated cutter was burned to the water's edge. No townsman would tell British officials the names of the raiders and nobody was punished.

THE BOSTON TEA PARTY was the colonists' answer to a new Tea Act passed by England in 1772. The act stopped all merchants except the East India Company from selling tea in the colonies. Colonial tea merchants and smugglers were hard hit. Three tea ships arrived in Boston Harbor and Boston planned its "tea party." On the night of December 16, 1773, war whoops rang out and about fifty colonists, dressed as Indians, went aboard the tea ships. They threw 342 chests of tea into the Boston Harbor.

## *COLONISTS CALL FOR LIBERTY AS ENGLAND STRIKES BACK*

THE CRY FOR LIBERTY rose in the colonies as the troubles with England grew. Striking back after the "tea party," England's Parliament, which made England's laws, passed a Port Bill. This bill ordered Boston's port closed on June 1, 1774. The colonists were ordered to pay for the tea which they had thrown into the harbor. An Administration of Justice Act ordered the king's officials to be tried in England when they were accused of serious crimes in America. A Massachusetts Government Act gave the governor full power. A Quartering Act forced Massachusetts citizens to take British soldiers into their homes. The colonists called these laws the Intolerable Acts.

A CONTINENTAL CONGRESS was called as the colonists' anger rose over Parliament's punishment of Massachusetts and Boston. The congress was called by the states five days before Boston's port was due to be closed. The congress, held in Philadelphia (1774), was attended by fifty-five leaders from all colonies except Georgia. The Georgia governor had not let his state elect men to attend the congress. Among the patriot-leaders attending from other colonies were George Washington, John Adams and Patrick Henry. Continental Associations were formed to stop England's sending of goods to America after December, 1774. The congress also decided no American goods would be sent to England after September, 1775.

PATRICK HENRY of Virginia spoke out for freedom of the colonies when Virginia's House of Burgesses met in 1775 to review what had happened. Massachusetts' local government had been barred by King George III, who said the colony was in "open rebellion"—meaning that England's rule had been denied. Massachusetts had formed companies of Minutemen, ready to fight on a minute's notice. The House of Burgesses' meeting was to discuss revolution. Patrick Henry told his countrymen that he believed war with England had to come. In ringing tones, he said: "If we wish to be free, we must fight! I repeat, sir, we must fight! An appeal to arms, and to the God of Hosts, is all that is left to us." Ten years before, Henry had said in a speech against the king: "If this be treason, make the most of it." Henry asked those whom he thought were afraid: "Shall we resort to entreaty and humble supplication? Is life so dear, or peace so sweet as to be purchased at the price of chains and slavery? Forbid it, Almighty God! I know not what course others may take, but, as for me, give me liberty or give me death!"

**"Give me liberty or give me death!"** With this ringing cry, Patrick Henry sounded a call for patriots to seek independence.

PAUL REVERE'S MIDNIGHT RIDE on April 18-19, 1775, spread a warning that General Thomas Gage, British commander at Boston, planned to march on Lexington and Concord. Gage wanted to arrest patriot leaders Samuel Adams and John Hancock at Lexington and seize the colonists' powder and arms supplies at Concord. Revere and another rider, William Dawes, spread the alarm. They were joined on the way by Dr. Samuel Prescott. Revere rode through the night banging on doors and shouting, "The Redcoats are coming!" The Redcoats were British soldiers, who wore red coats. The patriots were ready when the British arrived. Eight Minutemen were killed at Lexington but at Concord fourteen British were killed. Returning to Boston, the Redcoats' ranks were thinned as Minutemen, townsmen and farmers fired on them all along the way. The British lost 273 men killed or wounded, and 93 colonists were casualties. The colonists hit again and took England's Fort Ticonderoga (1775). The British had large stores and many cannon there. Ethan Allen formed Vermont's Green Mountain Boys, and he and Benedict Arnold led them to Ticonderoga. In a surprise attack, the fort surrendered.

## *VICTORY ON BUNKER HILL IS COSTLY TO THE BRITISH*

THE REVOLUTIONARY WAR was at hand as the Second Continental Congress opened at Philadelphia on May 10, 1775. The delegates—leaders sent by each colony—were a deeply worried group. The congress elected John Hancock of Massachusetts as president. They decided to try again to get King George III to offer some plan for peace. But all knew that the threat of war was real. Congress chose George Washington as commander-in-chief of all colonial troops. The growing but untrained militia, or state troops, around Boston were adopted as the Continental Army. Washington, born in Virginia on February 22, 1732, was a forty-three-year-old gentleman-soldier. As a young man, he had been a surveyor, looking over and making maps of land. He was a leader of the militia at twenty-two. He was a fine figure of a soldier—tall and broad-shouldered, standing straight and erect. After being named leader, Washington left for Cambridge.

THE BATTLE OF BUNKER HILL was fought before Washington arrived. The Americans had taken over the hills around Boston. On June 17, 1775, the British sent General William Howe with 3,500 troops to take Bunker Hill. The real battle was fought on nearby Breed's Hill. A force of 1,200 patriots fought under General Israel Putnam, General Joseph Warren and Colonel William Prescott. Howe led his Redcoats on their first charge. Waiting until they "saw the whites of their eyes," the colonists opened up with blazing, or red-hot, fire. The British fled down the hill, leaving many dead. A second charge met the same fate. Howe took the hill on the third charge as the patriots ran out of bullets and powder. More than 1,000 British were killed. Patriot losses were 400.

ACTUAL WAR HAD BEGUN. The British gave up Boston without a fight (1776). For eight months Washington had been training his Continental troops at Cambridge. Howe had replaced Gage as British commander at Boston. Pretending an attack from Cambridge to the northwest, Washington and 2,000 men moved to Dorchester Heights to the south of the city. Howe and his Redcoats, with several hundred colonists still loyal to England, sailed to Halifax in Nova Scotia. Washington led his army to New York early in the summer of 1776. But large British forces landed there and Washington was driven out. He then moved his army into Pennsylvania. Congress by then had formed a navy and marine corps (1775), and had voted $100,000 to fit out armed ships.

**Tall, broad-shouldered** and well respected, George Washington was named commander-in-chief of the Continental Army.

July 4, 1776 . . . the great step was taken. The Continental Congress adopted the Declaration of Independence. The members signed and the colonies broke with England.

THE TIME HAD COME! A break for independence had to be made. The fighting was spreading. England was stopping America's trade. Some colonies had formed their own governments and were seizing British property. On June 7, 1776, Richard Henry Lee of Virginia asked the Continental Congress for a Declaration of Independence. Congress named Thomas Jefferson, Benjamin Franklin, John Adams, Roger Sherman and Robert R. Livingston to write the declaration. Much of the writing of the final paper was done by Jefferson, with a few changes by Franklin and Adams. Jefferson's ringing phrases in the Declaration of Independence drove home the idea of Freedom. Jefferson was not a great speaker, but moving words flowed from his pen. The declaration said that the colonies should not have been denied their rights. It listed the unfair acts by King George III. Members of the congress listened carefully to every word as the declaration was read. Then they shouted their agreement. On July 4, 1776, the Continental Congress adopted the Declaration of Independence. The president of the congress signed it: "John Hancock." Benjamin Franklin said, "We must indeed hang together, or most assuredly we shall hang separately." News of the signing was greeted with joy in all of the colonies. In New York, a lead statue of King George was melted and made into bullets. The bell in Philadelphia's old State House rang loudly when the Declaration of Independence was adopted. The State House became famous as Independence Hall. The bell became a symbol of American patriotism, known as the Liberty Bell. It was said to have been cracked by loud ringing.

NATHAN HALE had only one life to give to his country and he proudly gave it. Before moving his army to Pennsylvania, Washington saw that his army in New York was in great danger. Washington needed to learn the British plans before deciding on his own moves. Hale offered to slip behind the British lines and learn what he could. Hale was a Yale graduate from Connecticut, twenty-one years old. He knew that to be caught spying during wartime meant death. The courageous Hale passed the British sentries by telling them he was a school teacher. He learned much about the British plans, but was caught as he tried to return and tell Washington about them. The British found notes on their plans in Hale's boots. Included were drawings of British forts. The British treated Hale roughly. They would not let him write a last letter to his family. Hale was hanged on September 22, 1776. As the hangman placed the rope around his neck, Hale said, "I only regret that I have but one life to lose for my country."

**Hale's patriotism:** "I only regret that I have but one life to lose for my country."

**The submarine** was named the *American Turtle* and it had shells like one.

THE FIRST SUBMARINE took to the water in 1776. It was invented by David Bushnell and was called the *American Turtle*. Bushnell had exploded gunpowder under water and got the idea of building an underwater ship. He built the one-man submarine from oak timber. It looked like a top made from two turtle shells joined together. Two propellers were turned by hand from inside the ship. One propeller sent the submarine up or down and the other moved it forward. A "torpedo"—a box loaded with gunpowder—was hooked to the rudder. Bushnell attempted to surprise and attack British ships in several ports, but he was not strong enough to handle the *Turtle*. Despite failure, Bushnell became known as the Father of the American submarine.

# *COLONIAL VICTORIES REDUCE SIZE OF BRITISH FORCES*

**The Hessians** were having a Christmas party at Trenton. Cakes of ice floated on the Delaware River. Washington's troops rowed across and defeated the Hessians.

WASHINGTON CROSSED the Delaware River on December 25, 1776, and handed a Christmas surprise to the enemy. The British had hired Hessian troops, called mercenaries, to serve at Trenton. It was a stormy night and ice floated down the Delaware River as Washington's men rowed silently toward Trenton. Heavy snow was falling when the colonists attacked early on December 26. The Hessians were having a big Christmas party and were caught by surprise. In only forty-five minutes of fighting, more than 900 of 1,300 Hessians were taken prisoner or were killed. Washington set up camp, but a week later moved on to Princeton, New Jersey. He caught the British garrison off guard there, too, and defeated them.

THE STARS AND STRIPES were adopted by Congress as America's flag. It first flew over patriot fighters in 1777. Brave army leaders from Europe arrived to fight under that flag. Marquis de Lafayette of France brought with him Baron DeKalb from Germany. From Poland came Casimir Pulaski and Thaddeus Kosciusko. Baron Von Steuben joined from Prussia. All five became trusted leaders of American troops under Washington. Pulaski and DeKalb lost their lives leading Continental soldiers in battle.

GENERAL JOHN BURGOYNE was sent by England to lead an army from Canada into America. Burgoyne marched in and sent 1,000 troops into Vermont to seize supplies. Green Mountain Boys under Colonel John Stark trapped these British and killed or captured 900. Burgoyne himself was trapped at Saratoga, New York, by 20,000 colonists under Horatio Gates. Burgoyne was forced to surrender. Nearly one-third of all British troops in America had been killed or captured up to that point in the war. France, which had been waiting, now openly began talks on entering the war on the side of the Americans.

THE COLONISTS WENT ON TO WIN the war, in spite of many hardships. A cruel winter at Valley Forge (1777-1778) brought much suffering to Washington and his shivering troops. Washington had followed Howe into Pennsylvania and camped on hills along the Schuylkill River, not far from the city. The soldiers lived in huts and had little clothing, food or heat. Washington was saddened as his men faced the winter's cold winds. "These are times that try men's souls," said Thomas Paine. Paine was an Englishman who had written a pamphlet, or little book, called *The Crisis*. In his first book, *Common Sense,* Paine said the colonies should break away from England. But when the winter was at its worst, America's hopes came alive with good news from France. The French had entered the war on the side of the colonists. Benjamin Franklin had won over the French to fight on America's side.

THE WAR SPREAD into the West and the South. George Rogers Clark of Kentucky raised an army and attacked the British in the Ohio River Valley. Fierce fighting took place in the Indiana Territory. Clark won victories at Kaskaskia, Cahokia and Vincennes. Clark then lost Vincennes, but won it back. His men waded through cold swamps in February of 1779 to catch the British by surprise in the second battle.

JOHN PAUL JONES won a great naval victory when he defeated England's *Serapis* in his flagship, *Bon Homme Richard*. Called on to surrender early in the battle, Jones made his famous reply: "I have not yet begun to fight." In the South, bands of colonists under such leaders as Francis (Swamp Fox) Marion hit the British as they moved in from the north. But the British, under General Lord Charles Cornwallis, took Savannah, Charleston and Camden. Returning north, Cornwallis marched to Yorktown on a peninsula, or finger of land, between the York and James Rivers in Virginia. He was trapped there. Virginia troops under Lafayette closed the peninsula's neck. Then Washington and Comte de Rochambeau moved in with a combined American-French army. A French fleet under Admiral de Grasse drove off the British fleet and sealed off Chesapeake Bay. Cornwallis surrendered on October 19, 1781, and the war's fighting ended.

**Washington** and his little army had a hard time at Valley Forge during the cruel winter of 1777-1778. But they stood up under all hardships and went on to win the war.

# *AMERICA MAKES PEACE WITH ENGLAND*

**Benjamin Franklin** led America's peace treaty delegates to Paris. He won praise for signing a good treaty with England.

"THE UNITED STATES" became the new name for the American colonies as peace treaty talks with England began. Lord Shelburne, prime minister of England, sent Richard Oswald to Paris for the talks. He told Oswald, "Treat with the Thirteen United States." Franklin led America's peace treaty group. The other members were John Adams, John Jay and Henry Laurens. The Americans faced a problem because France was still at war with England. The Americans heard about secret negotiations, talks or deals, by France and decided that this gave them the right to have separate peace talks with England.

THE PARIS TALKS began in September, 1782, and a first treaty was signed on November 30. The final treaty was signed on September 3, 1783. In the Treaty of Paris, the king of England agreed that the thirteen states were free and independent. The treaty also set the borders of the new American nation. The United States now had all of the land from the Atlantic coast to the Mississippi River. The northern border was Canada (British territory) and the southern border was Florida (Spanish territory).

AMERICANS WERE GIVEN THE RIGHT to fish in the Gulf of St. Lawrence and off Newfoundland. The United States agreed to ask each state to let lawsuits be filed to get back land taken from British Loyalists, and to collect debts. Franklin won praise for winning good treaty terms for America and for avoiding troubles with France. After the final signing of the treaty, the British sailed home for England. General Washington led his American soldiers into New York on November 25, 1783.

WASHINGTON APPEARED before congress at Annapolis, Maryland, in December and resigned as commander-in-chief. He refused all offers of pay for his services. He asked only that, when it could, the young American nation pay back the money he had spent on clothing and food for his soldiers. This was estimated at $75,000. At a farewell dinner with his key officers, Washington said with tears in his eyes, "I now take leave of you, most devoutly wishing that your latter days may be as prosperous and happy as your former ones have been glorious and honorable."

AN UNHAPPY OFFICER who was not present at Washington's dinner was Benedict Arnold. A brave and fighting patriot early in the war, Arnold had turned traitor to the American cause late in the war. He sold military secrets to the British and barely escaped capture. Arnold ended the war fighting for the British. He went to London after the war and died poor, unhappy and without respect even from the British. On his deathbed, Arnold is said to have begged to be buried in his old American uniform.

## America—land of the free

The blood of many brave men had fallen on the soil of America and out of it had grown freedom and democracy! The former British colonies now were independent—their own nation, a new nation, but one whose freedom had been well and rightfully won.

Ever since the founding of the first colony at Jamestown, the fight had been long and hard.

The first British settlers in America at Jamestown won the right to form the House of Burgesses. This was a lower house of legislature and was elected by the people.

Roger Williams granted freedom of religion and voting rights when he established Rhode Island with a colony at Providence. William Penn made his new colony in Pennsylvania a small but healthy democracy.

England and France had fought bitterly in the early colonial days. Finally, the French and Indian War had come. France had been the loser and her defeat cost her nearly all of her American lands.

The colonists' courage and fighting spirit were tested in the Revolutionary War—both were proved. America won through all hardships. And so, the new nation had grown from the very roots of freedom.

But all of America, of course, was not actually free. Some of young America's leaders already realized that no nation holding many thousands of human beings in bondage could call itself truly free. And slavery of great masses of black people existed at the time.

Many Negroes had fought alongside white comrades-at-arms to help defeat the British. Peter Salem and Salem Poor fought bravely at Bunker Hill. Other Negroes fought bravely in other battles, won official praise.

After the Revolutionary War ended, the Treaty of Paris told the world that America truly had won its freedom from England. The colonies were governed by the Articles of Confederation. The Articles had been ratified, or approved, by the colonies in 1781. They formed a union of all the colonies but said that each would keep its own freedom and independence.

The Articles of Confederation had little federal, or central, power. Congress had only one house, and the members from each state voted as one. The Articles did not provide for a president or a system of judges. The Federation could not pass laws without nine states agreeing to them. The laws were carried out by the states themselves—only if they wished to do so.

The new Congress could declare war and make treaties. It could settle affairs between the states. But it had no powers to pass or collect taxes. Money was raised by asking each state to give a share to the Confederation. The former colonists were declared to be citizens of the new nation.

What did the future hold, with its freedom so hard won? Many stormy years still lay ahead, as time was to show. But America—and democracy—were on the way. The first hard fight had already been won.

PART 3

# 13 INDEPENDENT COLONIES BECAME THE UNITED STATES OF AMERICA

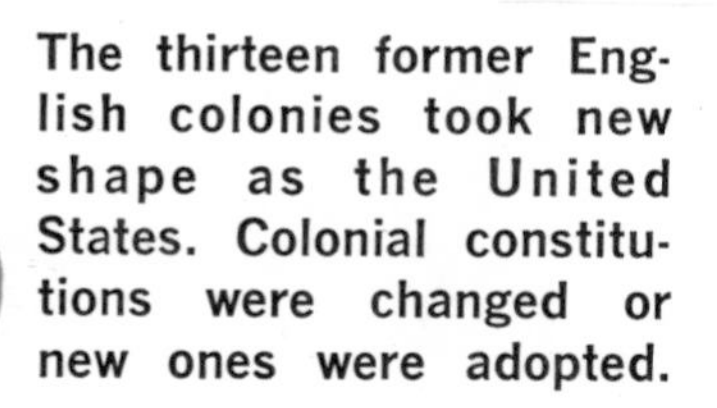

The thirteen former English colonies took new shape as the United States. Colonial constitutions were changed or new ones were adopted.

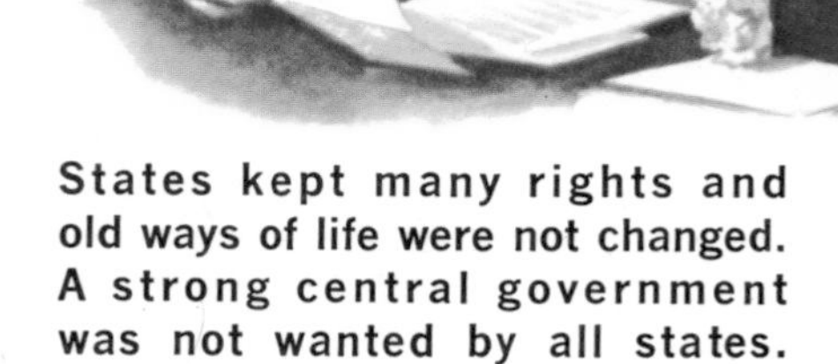

States kept many rights and old ways of life were not changed. A strong central government was not wanted by all states.

Three branches—governors, lawmakers called legislatures, and judges—made up the governments. Each checked the others.

The governors' powers were cut and legislatures were given more powers. Legislatures voted on state salaries.

Bills of rights were adopted by some states. These were laws that made sure that the personal freedoms of citizens would be guarded.

Religion no longer had a part in government. In general, the state and church had been kept apart in local and state governments.

The upper classes were given special rights in some legislatures. Only property owners could be elected to some upper houses of legislatures.

The Confederation and its congress did not have enough power to force the states to provide money. Laws still had to be accepted by individual states.

**George Washington** stood and took the oath in New York City: "I do solemnly swear that I will faithfully execute the office of the President of the United States."

## *NEW CONSTITUTION WRITTEN*

THE LEADERS OF AMERICA knew that the Articles of Confederation were too weak to rule the growing nation. Leaders from all of the states were called to a meeting which opened in Philadelphia on May 25, 1787. Fifty-five men were at the meeting. Only Rhode Island did not send its leaders. In four months a new kind of government was formed. The Constitution was written and signed. America's government today is based on this Constitution. The Constitution tells how the people should be treated and how the government should be run. It is the law of the land. When the Constitution was signed, it called for a President to be elected. The President was the highest and strongest officer in America. The Constitution also set up a Congress. There were two houses of Congress—the Senate and the House of Representatives. Members of the House were elected by the people. Senators were named by the state legislatures. After both houses passed a bill, the President had to sign it before it became a law. The third part of America's new government was the courts. The Constitution made the Supreme Court the highest court in the land. The Constitution was ratified on June 21, 1788.

GEORGE WASHINGTON was elected as the first President of the United States. The first Congress met at New York on April 6, 1789, and counted the votes for President. George Washington received all the first place votes and was elected. John Adams received the second largest number of votes and became Vice-President. Washington rode on horseback from his home at Mount Vernon in Virginia to New York to be sworn in. On April 30, 1789, Washington took the oath as President: "I do solemnly swear that I will faithfully execute the office of the President of the United States and I will, to the best of my ability, preserve, protect and defend the Constitution of the United States."

**Washington** named as his four chief advisors: Jefferson, Hamilton, Knox and Randolph.

AMERICA'S GOVERNMENT under the Constitution grew and became strong. Washington named four chief helpers after he took office as President. Thomas Jefferson of Virginia was named Secretary of State. Alexander Hamilton of New York was named Secretary of the Treasury. General Henry Knox of Massachusetts became Secretary of War. Edmund Randolph of Virginia was named Attorney General. These four men helped the President by advising him on the way he should run the government. The President's advisors became known as his cabinet. Hamilton made a plan for America to pay her debts. He formed the United States Treasury. He put a tax on goods sent by foreign countries to be sold in the United States. This tax was called a tariff. Hamilton helped form a United States Bank to print money.

UNITED STATES COURTS were set up by Congress. This was done when Congress passed a Judiciary Act on September 24, 1789. This act formed a Supreme Court, three circuit courts and thirteen district courts. John Jay was named as the first Chief Justice, or judge, of the Supreme Court. Five associate justices were named. The justices were named by the President and held their jobs for life. The United States, or federal, courts ruled in cases which had to do with the Constitution. Also the federal courts handled cases where two or more states had a part in them. In 1791, land on the Potomac River was selected as home of the nation's capital and named the District of Columbia. The capital city was named Washington.

INVENTORS, people who thought up and made new things, also were helped by the new government. Congress passed a patent law. A patent gave the inventor all of the rights for seventeen years on anything he invented. That meant that only the inventor could make and sell his invention during the period covered by the patent.

PERSONAL FREEDOMS of all Americans were listed and written into the Constitution with the passing of the Bill of Rights. The bill was the first ten amendments, or new acts, added to the Constitution. Five states ratified the Constitution only upon being promised that the Bill of Rights would be added. At first, Congress adopted twelve amendments as the Bill of Rights. But only ten were finally ratified. They were ratified, or agreed to, by the states on December 15, 1791. The Bill of Rights, telling the rights of the people, never has been changed. They have been upheld in court tests. These rights are:

FIRST Freedom of religion, speech and the press are guaranteed. People have the right to complain to the government.

SECOND A strong and trained militia being needed, people have the right to keep guns. (Laws provide limits on this.)

THIRD No soldier, in time of peace, shall be given living room in any house without consent of the particular house owner.

FOURTH Peoples' homes cannot be searched and their property cannot be taken without warrants, or legal permits.

FIFTH No person can be put on trial for a serious crime without an indictment, or legal order. He can refuse to say anything against himself.

SIXTH In all criminal cases, the person accused has the right of a quick public trial which is held before a fair jury.

SEVENTH In common-law suits, where more than $20 is at stake, the same right to a jury trial shall be observed.

EIGHTH Bail and fines that are unfair and too high are not permitted. Cruel punishments cannot be ordered by any court.

NINTH The fact that the Constitution lists some rights of the people does not mean that rights not listed are denied.

TENTH Powers not given to the federal government by the Constitution, and which are not denied by it, belong to the states.

## AMERICA'S FIRST CENSUS–1790

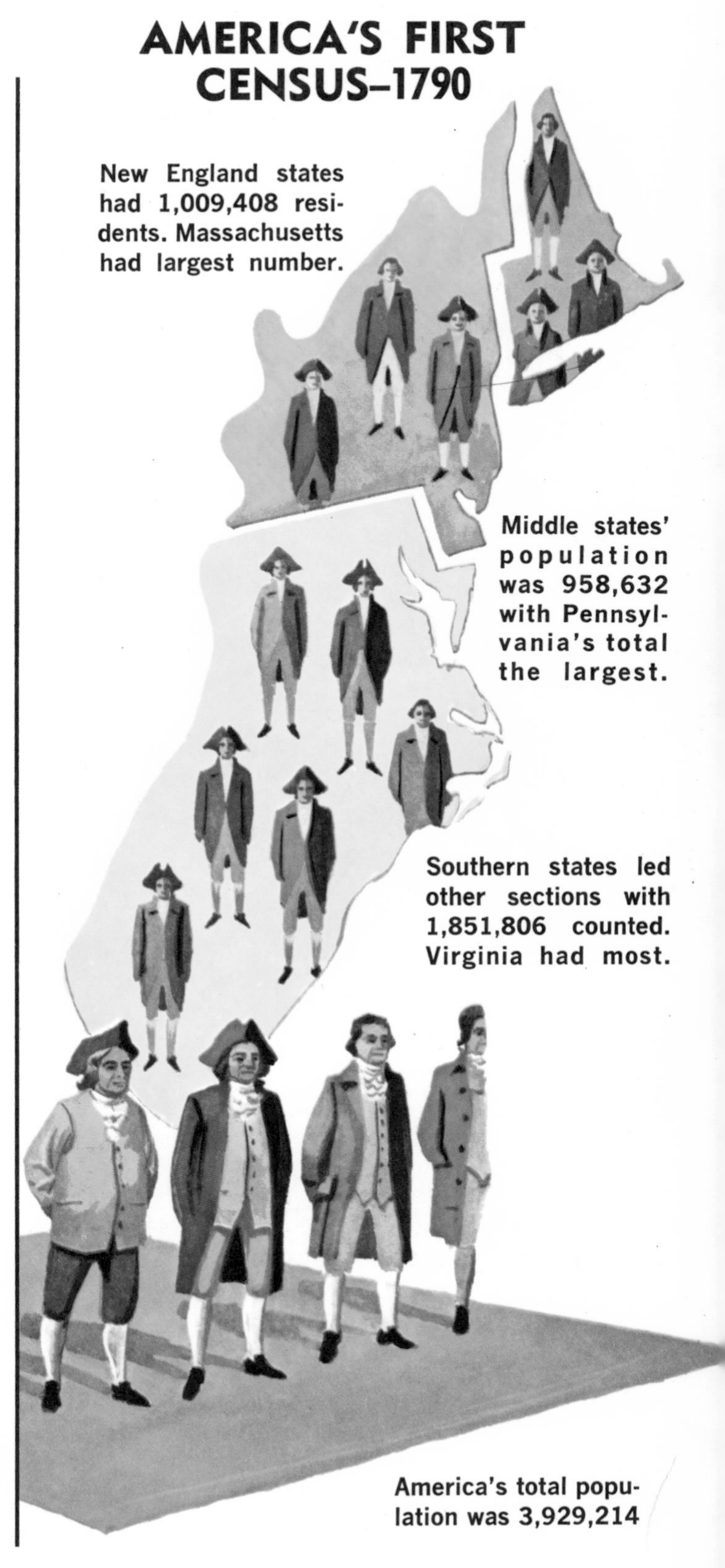

## *WHITNEY'S INVENTIONS BRING GREAT CHANGES*

**A hand crank** was turned and the cotton was pulled through a wire comb. The seeds could not pass through the screen.

ELI WHITNEY INVENTED the cotton gin in 1793, and it brought a big change in America. Whitney was a young Yale graduate who was a school teacher in Massachusetts. He visited some friends who owned a big cotton farm in the South. Whitney saw that a machine was needed to take the seeds out of cotton. One slave had to work long and hard hours to take out the seeds from only three or four pounds of cotton a day. The cotton mills were crying for more cotton as people all over the country wanted to buy cotton cloth. Eli Whitney, an amateur inventor, had a great idea. Without any trouble, and losing no time, he invented the cotton gin.

WHITNEY'S MACHINE was a box which was divided by a metal screen. It had a cylinder, or roller, with rows of saw teeth and brushes that turned with the roller. The cotton gin was turned by a hand crank. The cotton was placed in one end of the box. The saw teeth on the roller drew the cotton through the screen, but the holes in the screen were so small the seeds could not pass through it. Brushes cleaned the roller's teeth as the seeded cotton piled up in the other end of the box. The seeds had been removed by the screen.

FEW CHANGES have been made in the cotton gin which Whitney invented. It solved the problem of cotton. Whitney's first gin could seed ten times the amount of cotton that one slave could. The South said that slaves now were needed more than ever to work in the cotton fields. Textile machinery, which made cloth, already was being used in Rhode Island after being made by Samuel Slater in 1789. After the cotton gin was invented, new mills began to spring up by the hundreds in the North. Streams of water were used to run most of the mills. The name "gin" comes from "cotton engine," which was the name Eli Whitney gave to his machine.

WHITNEY HAD ANOTHER GREAT IDEA. This one gave a big lift to American manufacturing and factories after 1800. Whitney thought up a plan whereby all parts of an article being manufactured were made separately. Whitney was a maker of guns in New Haven, Connecticut. The United States government gave him a big order for guns. The order was so big that Whitney had to figure out a way to fill it. He hit upon an entirely new plan. He had each man in his plant make only one part, but make many of them. All of the parts were then put together to make the finished gun. This new plan led to mass production, or the making of things in large numbers.

# UNITED STATES STOOD UP FOR ITS RIGHTS ON SEAS

Great Britain and France went to war. Both denied American ships the right to use the seas freely.

America said that its ships could not be searched. Only a ship's papers could be seen.

The United States was aroused over seizure of its own sailors as deserters from British ships.

U. S. declared its rights. Only war goods going to a country at war were admitted to be against the law and could be seized.

A blockade, or stopping of ships, had to be enforced before it would be accepted as in force.

United States insisted that American ships had the right to trade as neutrals in any foreign port.

# *WASHINGTON RETIRES AFTER LIFE-LONG SERVICE*

GEORGE WASHINGTON refused to run for a third term as President in the election of 1796. He had served his country for forty-two years since his first mission as a young officer in the French and Indian War. Washington was tired of the worry and strain of guiding the nation as President. He was saddened by the way some people had turned against him when he would not help the French in another war against England. Other people had protested bitterly over an unfavorable trade treaty with England. Washington wanted to leave public office and spend his last years enjoying the warm life of his home at Mount Vernon. He wrote his Farewell Address to the American people. It was first printed in the *Daily Advertiser* of Philadelphia on September 19, 1796. Political quarrels had worried Washington while he was President. In his Farewell Address he warned the people against the "baneful effects of the party spirit."

STRONG ADVICE on foreign affairs was given to the young country by its retiring leader. Washington said, "Be just and act in good faith toward all. . . . The nation which indulges toward another an habitual hatred or an habitual fondness is in some degree a slave. . . . The great rule of conduct for us in regard to foreign nations is, in extending our commercial relations, to have as little political connection as possible. . . . 'Tis our true policy to steer clear of permanent alliances with any portion of the foreign world."

WASHINGTON'S FINAL PLEA to his fellow Americans was to have a "cordial, habitual and immovable attachment to the Union." At the conclusion of his term, Washington ended his public life and retired to the quiet of his Virginia home.

**Washington on retiring** told America: "Be just and act in good faith toward all." He asked his fellow-Americans to have a lasting loyalty to the Union.

# *FRENCH DEMANDS BRING ON NAVAL WAR*

**Talleyrand,** France's foreign minister, demanded $250,000 from America's peace group so he would "be friendly" toward America. A naval war was the U.S. answer.

TROUBLES WITH FRANCE faced John Adams as he became America's second President. France had overthrown its king and formed a republic. America had not joined France in a war on England. Diplomatic relations were broken off. French cruisers seized American ships. Adams sent Charles Pinckney, John Marshall and Elbridge Gerry to Paris to try to arrange peace. Talleyrand, France's foreign minister, would not see them. America's peace envoys returned home and told Adams that Talleyrand's agents had told them Talleyrand wanted $250,000 to "be friendly" toward the United States. The initials X, Y and Z were substituted for the names of Talleyrand's agents. Congress demanded that Adams release the story to the newspapers. Americans were angered by the XYZ affair. Many congressmen, editors and public leaders called for war. A two-year undeclared naval war followed. In it the United States and France each lost about ninety merchant ships. The war ended in 1800, after Napoleon Bonaparte came into power in France and made peace with America. As a result of the naval war, Congress created a Navy Department in 1798 with Benjamin Stoddert as first secretary. A Marine Corps also was formed.

THE LOUISIANA PURCHASE in 1803 brought a big and exciting change in America. President Jefferson sent James Monroe to France to try to buy New Orleans from France. Robert R. Livingston, the American minister in Paris, worked with Monroe. America wanted to buy only one city, New Orleans, and West Florida, but talks with Napoleon, the French emperor, dragged. Then Napoleon, through Talleyrand, surprised the Americans by asking, "What will you give for all of Louisiana?" . . . Not just New Orleans, but all of Louisiana! Napoleon had given up a plan for new American colonies. He feared England or the United States might take New Orleans from him. And so he sold the Louisiana Territory to the United States for 60,000,000 francs ($15,000,000). The territory covered 828,000 square miles and extended as far west as the Rocky Mountains. The size of the United States was doubled.

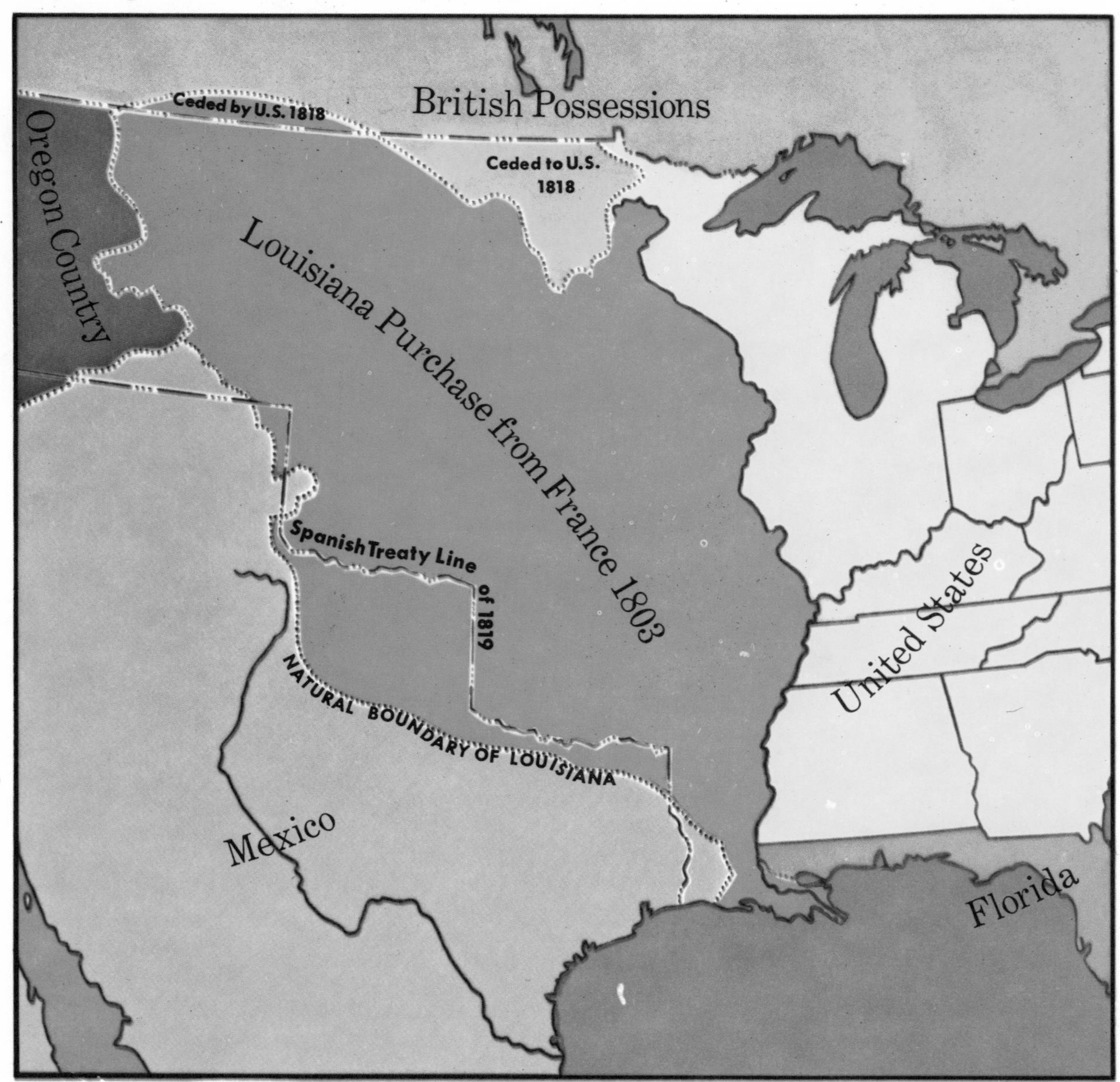

**American sailors** were seized, taken off their own ships, and forced to serve on British ships. The United States warned England that these seizures must stop.

AMERICA WAS CAUGHT in a tangle of troubles with European nations as Napoleon went to war again. The rights of United States ships to trade as neutrals, not favoring either side, were denied by England and France. Goods were taken off American ships just because the captain of the other ship, either British or French, said they were meant to be used in the war. American sailors were seized and forced to work on British ships. England, with a stronger navy than France's, gave America more trouble. Her warships stayed close to American harbors and stopped and searched American ships. In April, 1806, Congress passed a Non-Importation Act. This act kept many English goods from being shipped in and sold in America. Congress later ended the act.

ENGLAND WAS HAVING A HARD WAR with Napoleon. The British put a blockade on the European coast, stopping ships which were sailing for France. Napoleon then put a blockade on the British Isles. Both sides still denied America's neutral rights. President Jefferson sent William Pinkney of Maryland to join with James Monroe in trying to settle matters with England. America told England that the seizing of American sailors had to stop. Also, America wanted to be paid for ships and goods taken by the British. Monroe and Pinkney made a treaty with England, but it did not give America any of the things asked for. Jefferson put the treaty aside and Congress passed an embargo, which stopped all trade with foreign nations.

# *FULTON'S STEAMBOAT SHOWS GREAT POWER*

THE STEAMBOAT PUFFED, crowds along the Hudson River banks watched, and the *Clermont* moved up the river! The *Clermont* was a steamboat built by Robert Fulton. It made a non-stop trip from New York to Albany. Its paddle wheels tugged the steamboat 150 miles against the Hudson River's current at a speed of five miles an hour. This feat, in August, 1807, was the first time a steamboat had shown its real strength. A dozen other boats driven by steam had been built earlier, but the *Clermont* was the first one to pass all tests. Robert Fulton, a forty-two-year-old Pennsylvania man, was a portrait painter and inventor of machines and engines. He used the best parts of the earlier steamboats and put them together to build the *Clermont*. Within four years, other steamboats became well known sights in the East. In 1811, the first steamboat appeared on the Ohio and Mississippi Rivers. This gave thousands of pioneers, or settlers, a faster way of traveling to new lands in the West. The Louisiana Purchase had opened this door to the Golden West.

**Robert Fulton** used the best of all earlier steamboats' plans to build his *Clermont*.

JEFFERSON'S LAST YEAR as President saw America ending the bringing in of any more slaves. The Constitution said that foreign slave trade could not be ended until 1808. On the very first day after that date, January 1, 1808, a law passed by Congress went into effect. No more slaves could be brought into the United States. To be caught breaking the law meant the loss of the ship and its cargo—slaves and all. The state which seized the slave ship decided what to do with the slaves.

JEFFERSON ANNOUNCED, as his second term neared an end, that he would not run for the Presidency again. He said, "General Washington set the example of voluntary retirement after eight years. I shall follow it." Jefferson's last year was marked by new troubles over shipping. The Embargo Act had not been helpful. The British and French were not seriously hurt by America's cutting off of their trade. In the United States protests continued to mount from ship owners because their ships could not sail to other countries.

IN NEW ENGLAND, merchants suffered losses as America's trade fell off about $86,000,000 a year. The South was thrown into a bad depression (hard times with little money) because of the loss of its cotton sales in Europe. Some of the states, led by Massachusetts and Connecticut, said that their rights as states had been denied them. Jefferson realized that the Embargo Act would not work. And, so, the Embargo Act was voted out by Congress and a Non-Intercourse Act took its place. The Non-Intercourse Act opened trade with all nations except the two at war, England and France. Repeal of the Embargo Act took place on March 4, the final day of Jefferson's term. The new President, James Madison, now faced the problems.

**On January 1, 1808,** a new law banned the bringing of any more slaves into the U.S.

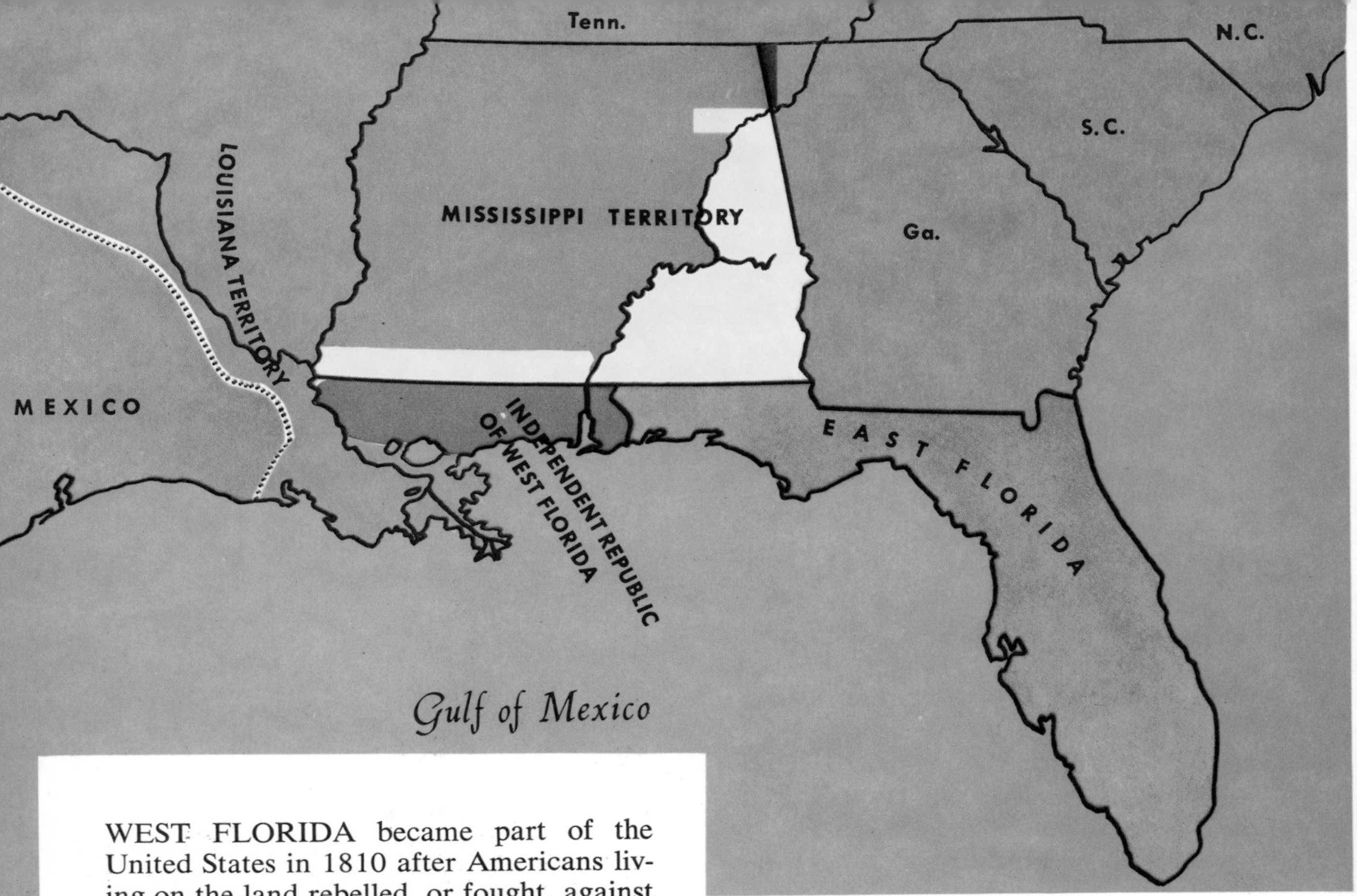


WEST FLORIDA became part of the United States in 1810 after Americans living on the land rebelled, or fought, against Spanish rule. These American settlers wanted their new homes to be part of the United States, not Spain. The United States agreed and took in West Florida. This was called annexing West Florida. West Florida spread west to the Mississippi River and went through parts of Alabama, Mississippi and Louisiana. In 1810, American settlers living in West Florida began fighting against Spain and took the Spanish fort at Baton Rouge, Louisiana.

LEADERS of the little American army said their state was now independent from Spain. They called it the Republic of West Florida. A month later, President James Madison told the people that West Florida had been made part of the United States—meaning it had been annexed. The President sent American soldiers to help hold the land. In January, 1811, Congress also agreed that United States soldiers could move into East Florida if Florida officials wanted them.

EAST FLORIDA, which occupied much of the land of the present state of Florida, was ceded, or given, to the United States by Spain in 1819. America and Spain were quarreling over East Florida at the time. Gangs of lawbreakers lived in East Florida and caused much trouble. Andrew Jackson had taken some Spanish forts during a war with Florida's Seminole Indians. All of this brought much bad feeling between America and Spain. John Quincy Adams, America's Secretary of State, told Spain she either would have to stop the lawbreaking in East Florida or give the land to the United States. Spain was angry, but finally agreed.

A TREATY WAS SIGNED in February, 1819, by Adams and Louis de Onis, Spanish minister at Washington. Spain ceded East Florida to the United States, and the United States gave up claims to Texas. The United States paid $5,000,000 to American citizens which had claims against Spain. Spain also gave up its claims to Oregon.

THE WAR OF 1812 finally came, and once again America fought against England. England had kept on denying the United States' sea rights. There were several fights between warships before the real war began. Britain's *Leopard* crippled the American ship *Chesapeake* by firing on her by surprise. The British *Guerriere* took an American sailor off the *Spitfire*. The American warship *President* pounded the *Little Belt*. A group of men in Congress called "War Hawks," led by Henry Clay and John Calhoun, loudly called for war. On June 18, 1812, Congress declared war, and America's fight for sea rights began.

PRESIDENT MADISON'S message, asking Congress to declare war, accused England of four main wrongs. One was taking American sailors off their own ships and making them serve, or work, on British ships. Another was English warships stopping American trading ships. A third wrong was the unfair laws which England passed against American ships. The fourth was England's causing the Indians in the West to make trouble for the settlers. As the War of 1812 began, America planned to invade, or move into and attack, Canada. The "War Hawks" had been asking that these attacks be made. America's plan was to send three armies into Canada. All three plans failed. General William Hull led 2,000 Americans to Detroit. But he learned that a strong force of Canadians and Indians was about to attack his men. Hull gave up without firing a shot. Hull was dropped from the Army.

AMERICA'S MILITIA, or state soldiers, would not cross from American soil into Canada. This stopped the two other plans to attack Canada. General Stephen Van Rensselaer sent 600 American regular soldiers across the Niagara River on October 13. The British defeated them while the American militiamen refused to cross the river and help their own men. The third attack, planned against Montreal, was called off. General Henry Dearborn led an American army to the Canadian border, but again the militia would not cross.

MADISON WAS REELECTED as President in November, 1812, but not without a hard fight. America was in need of money to pay for the war against England. Trading with foreign nations had fallen off during the war. In some states which had been hard hit, such as New York and the New England states, the war was called "Mr. Madison's War" by his critics.

**Henry Clay** led the "War Hawks" in Congress. They wanted America to declare war.

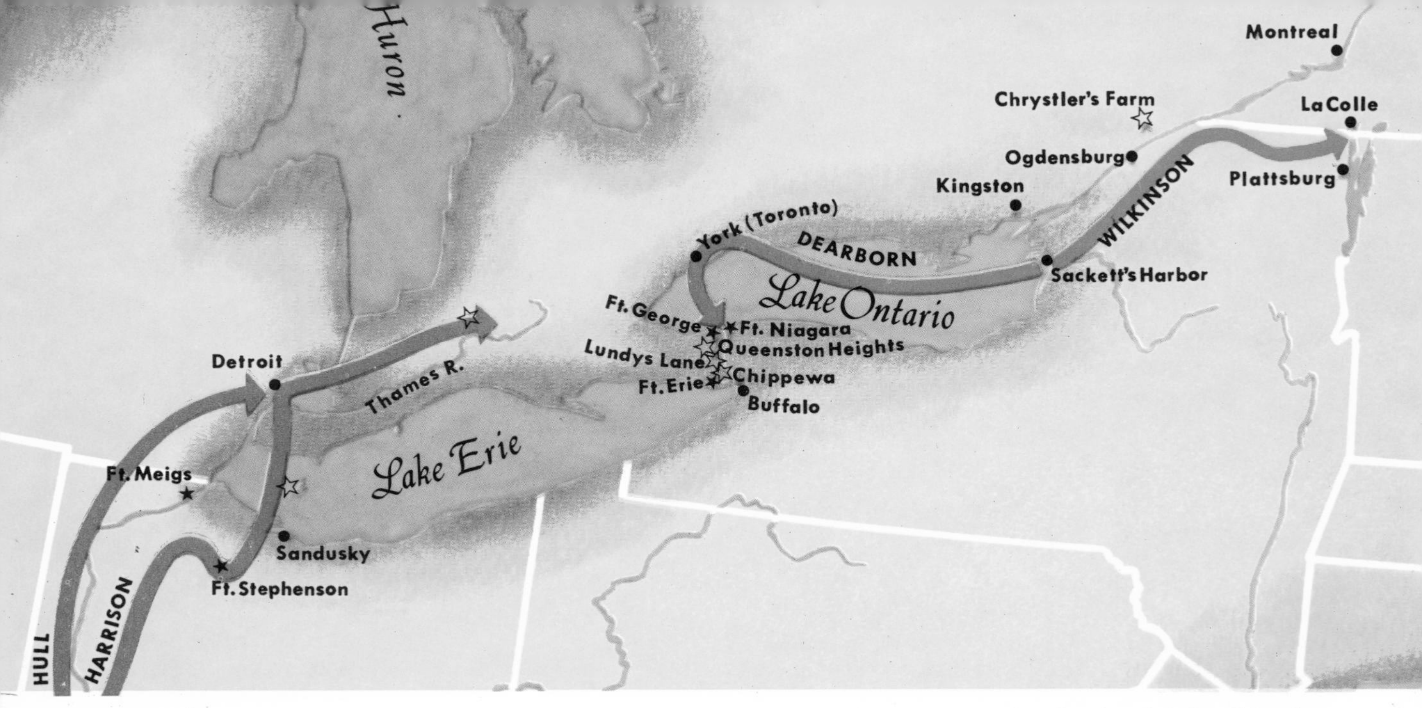


**America** won the Battle of Lake Erie, but the British kept their hold on Lake Ontario.

VICTORIES AT SEA kept America's hopes alive in the first year of the war. The land fighting was not encouraging but the sea battles were. The American warship *Constitution* had a captain named Isaac Hull, a nephew of General William Hull. Isaac Hull led the *Constitution* into a sea fight off Nova Scotia. Hull sank the British *Guerriere*. The American *Wasp,* commanded by Captain Jacob Jones, defeated the *Frolic* off the Virginia coast. The *United States,* commanded by Captain Stephen Decatur, captured the British warship *Macedonian* off Africa. The *Constitution,* with a new captain, William Bainbridge, next destroyed England's *Java* off Brazil. The *Chesapeake,* under Captain James Lawrence, was defeated by the British *Shannon* in a battle off Boston. Dying from a wound, Lawrence's last words were: "Don't give up the ship!"

WARSHIPS also fought on Lake Erie. Captain Oliver Hazard Perry sank a squadron, or small fleet, of British ships. The British ships had been blocking the way of an American army under General William Henry Harrison. Harrison was waiting to cross Lake Erie from his Sandusky River base in Ohio and march into Canada. Perry built five ships on the shore of Lake Erie. The guns and supplies were carried overland from Philadelphia. On September 10, Perry's ten ships sailed out to meet the British. After two hours, his flagship, the *Lawrence,* was sinking. Perry rowed to the *Niagara* and raked the British ships with cannonballs. The British surrendered. After the battle on the lake, Perry sent Harrison a message. It said: "We have met the enemy and they are ours." Harrison then led his army into Canada and defeated a British-Indian force at Moravian Town on the Thames River. Tecumseh, a Shawnee Indian chief who had given the Americans much trouble, was killed in the Moravian Town battle. Napoleon by now had been defeated in Europe and England sent more soldiers to America. General Winfield Scott met the British on Chippewa River Plain and his 1,300 American soldiers crushed the enemy. An American army under General Dearborn captured York (now called Toronto) and the town was burned against Dearborn's orders. An American army under General James Wilkinson was badly beaten while trying to drive against Montreal. The British took Fort Niagara and burned Buffalo on December 18, 1813.

# *WASHINGTON BURNS AS BRITISH GET REVENGE*

WASHINGTON, D.C., WAS BURNED by the British on August 24, 1814. The British burned the United States capital to get even for the burning of York. A British fleet sailed into Chesapeake Bay after raids along the New England coast. General Robert Ross landed 4,000 British veterans of the European war. American soldiers met the British army at Bladensburg, Maryland. President Madison and cabinet members were there. Mrs. Dolly Madison had the silverware, and other things which were worth much money, taken from the White House. She then left the White House, which was the President's home. The British won the battle of Bladensburg. They marched into Washington and burned the Capitol, the White House and other buildings. The British returned to their ships and Madison and his cabinet returned to their duties in Washington.

GALLANTLY STREAMING over the ramparts of Fort McHenry was the American flag, as the British fleet approached Baltimore. After the burning of Washington, an American army of 13,000 under General Samuel Smith was sent to Baltimore to defend the city. The British army landed and marched toward Baltimore. A force of 3,000 Americans met them only four miles from the city. The British lost many men, including General Ross, in a bloody battle at Godly Wood. They decided to use the fleet. The British warships opened fire on Fort McHenry and a fierce battle followed. Its glare lit the skies. A Baltimore man, Francis Scott Key, was aboard a British warship to make a prisoner trade. Throughout the night-long bombardment, Key watched anxiously. By dawn's early light, on September 14, 1814, he saw that the flag was still there. Joyously, Francis Scott Key wrote the words of the song that was to become the national anthem—*The Star Spangled Banner*.

# TREATY OF GHENT BROUGHT PEACE BETWEEN AMERICA AND ENGLAND

America and England signed the Treaty of Ghent (Belgium) on Christmas Eve, 1814. Two weeks later, not knowing of the treaty, Andrew Jackson defeated the British at New Orleans.

By terms of the treaty, each nation returned all the lands captured during the War of 1812.

A commission, provided for by the treaty, granted American ships the right to trade in all parts of the British Empire except the West Indies.

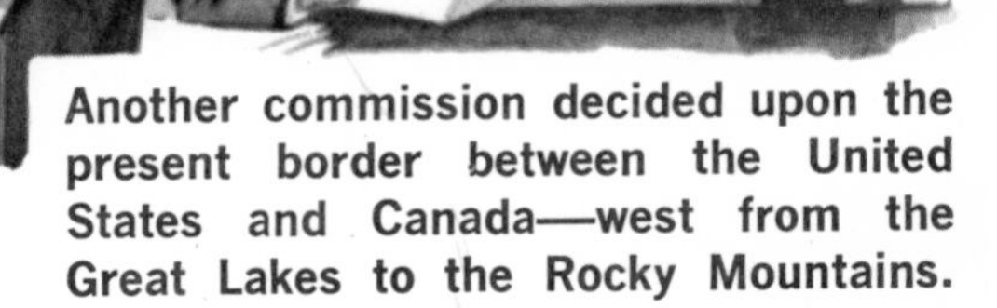

Another commission decided upon the present border between the United States and Canada—west from the Great Lakes to the Rocky Mountains.

Another commission was named to plan the disarming by both nations of the Great Lakes areas.

The rights of Americans to fish in Canadian waters were agreed upon by a fourth commission. The disarming of the Great Lakes was put into effect within four years.

## *DECATUR'S FLEET ENDS RAIDS OF BARBARY PIRATES*

A PIRATES' NEST on the Barbary Coast of Africa had been stopping and robbing American ships for many years. This nation had paid the robber countries much money to leave American ships alone. After the War of 1812 ended, America decided to do something about the pirates. Stephen Decatur, the naval leader, was sent to the Barbary Coast to clean up the pirates' nest. Decatur had been a hero in 1804. Tripoli pirates captured the American warship *Philadelphia*. Decatur led a boarding party into Tripoli harbor and burned the *Philadelphia*. During the War of 1812, the dey, or ruler, of Algiers declared war on America, trying to make this country pay more money to the pirates. On March 3, 1815, Congress ordered the Navy to take action against Algiers. Decatur was sent to the Barbary Coast with a fleet of ten warships. On June 17, Decatur's warships defeated and captured the Algerian warship *Marshouda,* which had forty-four cannon. Two days later, the twenty-two gun *Estido* was captured. Decatur's fleet then entered the harbor of Algiers and the American captain told Algiers to surrender or he would blow up the city with his big navy guns. The dey signed a treaty on June 30, promising to stop all raids on American ships and let all prisoners go free without the payment of any money. By August 5, Tunis and Tripoli were forced to take the same terms. In seven weeks, Stephen Decatur wiped out the pirates' nest which had been robbing American ships for nearly thirty years. Up to this time many thousands of dollars had been paid to the Barbary Coast's raiding pirates by America and some of the European countries. Decatur, later a Navy commissioner, was killed in 1820 in a duel with Captain James Barron.

**Stephen Decatur** forced Barbary Pirates to their knees. Raiding of U.S. ships ended.

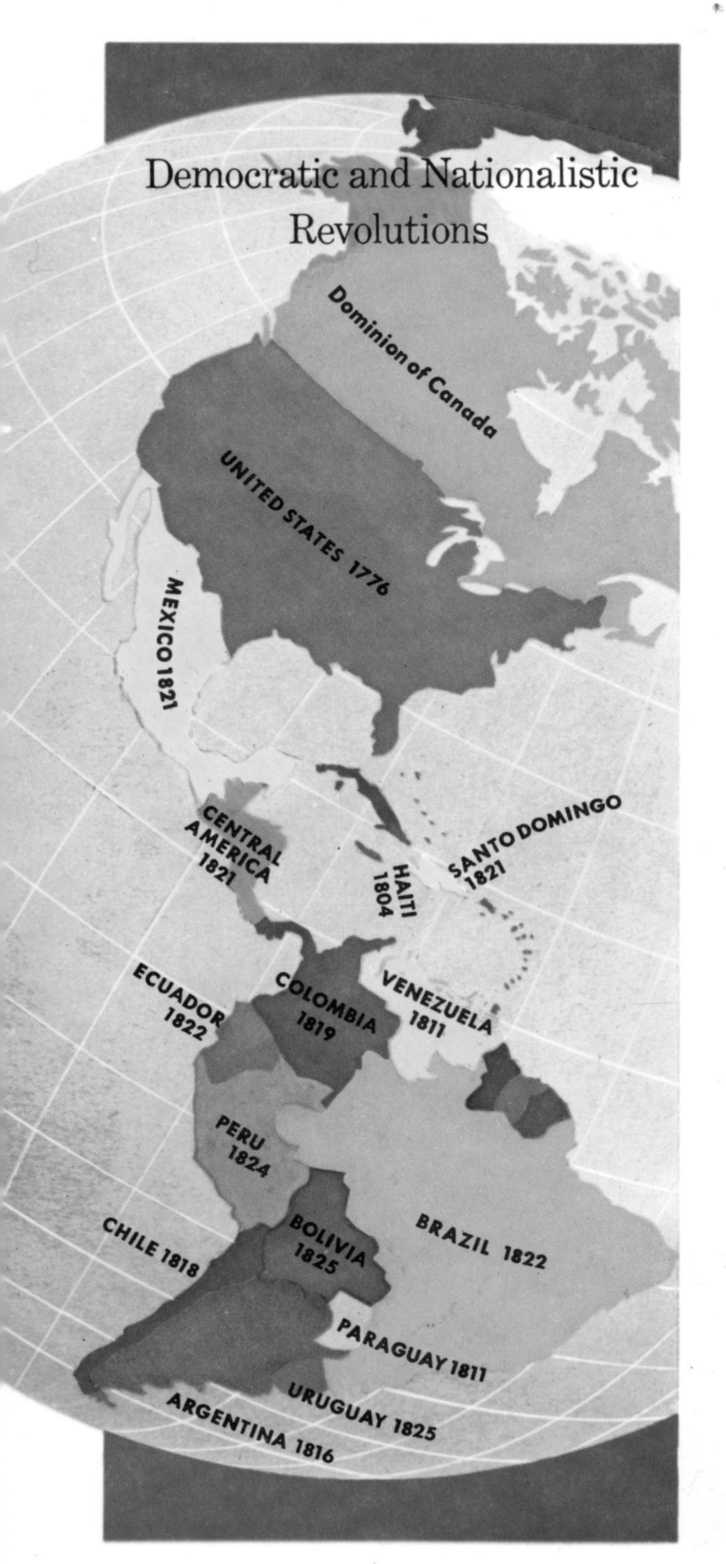


LATIN AMERICAN COUNTRIES fought against being ruled by Spain and wiped out nearly all of the once rich empire. By 1822, most of the South American colonies had thrown off Spanish rule. Simon Bolivar was the leader who first spread the feeling of freedom in South America. One by one, the countries declared their independence from Spain. Americans were very much in favor of the South Americans' fight for freedom. Some seaports in the South and on the middle Atlantic coast were used as bases for ships taking help to the Latin American countries. These ships were not helped by the American government. But, they were not stopped.

CLAY WAS ONE of the first of America's leaders to back the new republics in South America. President James Monroe and Secretary of State John Quincy Adams held back until the treaty by which Spain gave East Florida to America was signed. When the formal treaty was completed, America acted. On March 8, 1822, Monroe asked Congress to recognize the new Latin American republics, so that they would be treated as new and free nations. On May 4, Congress passed an act which called for diplomatic relations, or official government business, to begin between the new countries and the United States. By the end of January, 1823, Colombia, Mexico, Chile and Argentina were formally recognized by the United States. That meant that diplomats from each country were allowed to open offices in this country.

FRANCE OPENLY CONSIDERED joining Spain in an invasion to take back the lost Latin American colonies. George Canning, England's foreign secretary, in the spring of 1823 suggested that America join with England in warning France to stay out of South America. Adams was against the plan. He believed America should act alone.

**Latin Americans** threw off Spain's rule and the United States recognized their freedom.

## *MONROE DECLARES A NEW DOCTRINE OF PROTECTION*

THE MONROE DOCTRINE was announced by the President as a warning against any European nations trying to interfere with the government of any country in any of the Americas. Monroe took Adams' advice and talked things over with his cabinet and his friends, Jefferson and Madison. On December 2, 1823, Monroe announced his doctrine in a message to Congress. The doctrine told European nations that they could not build any new colonies in the Western Hemisphere, meaning North and South America. Monroe's doctrine said, "We should consider any attempt on their part to extend their system to any portion of this hemisphere as dangerous to our peace and safety." The doctrine said that the United States would not intervene, or take part, in Europe's wars and would not take any action against colonies of European nations which already had been built. After the Monroe Doctrine was published, France gave up its plan to join Spain in an invasion of South America. Russia gave up its claims to lands south of Alaska. In 1824, John Quincy Adams was elected sixth President.

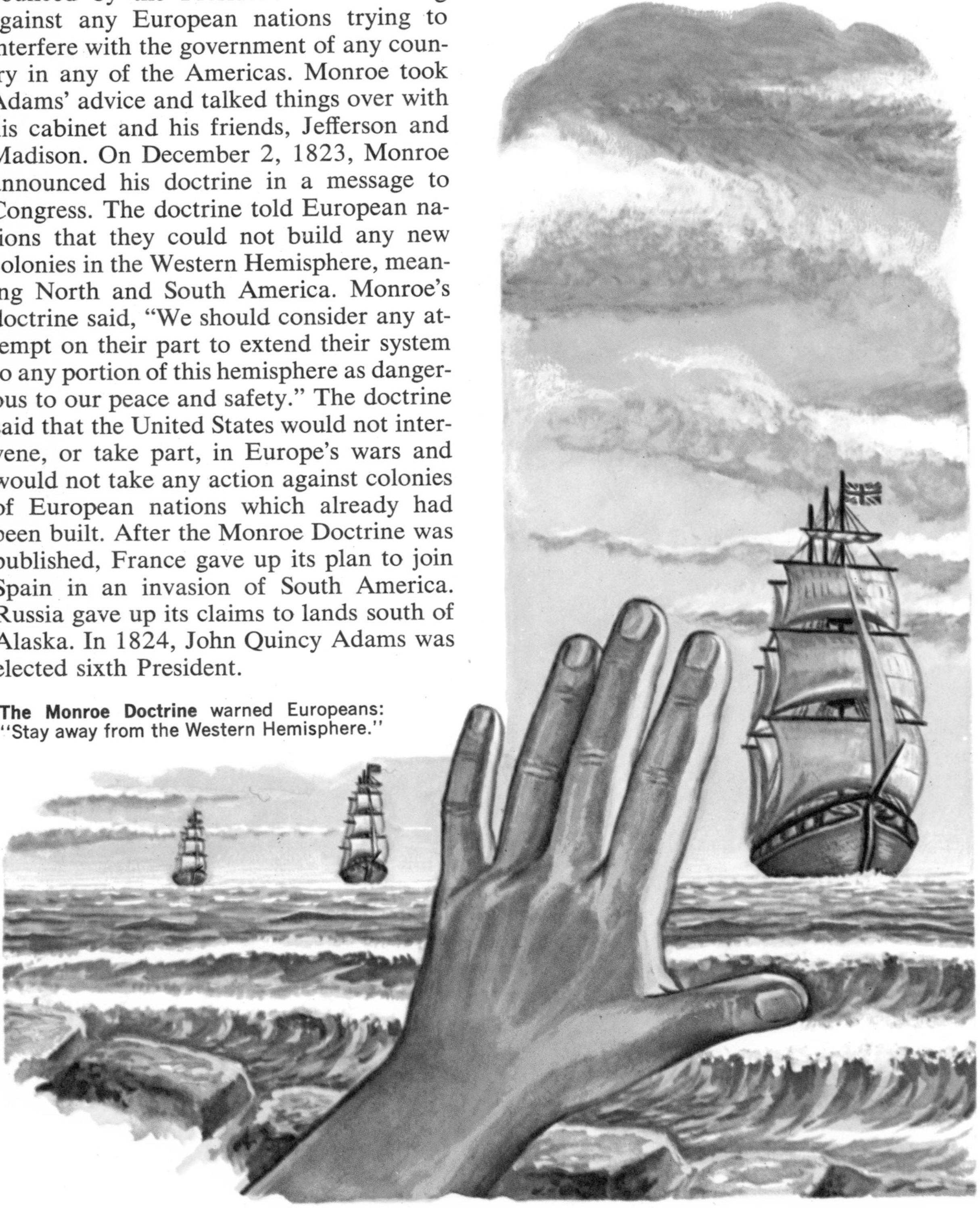

**The Monroe Doctrine** warned Europeans: "Stay away from the Western Hemisphere."

**Daniel Webster** told the Senate: "Liberty and Union, now and forever, one and inseparable." The states' rights fight grew.

AMERICA'S PEOPLE turned to fighting for national rights. One fight was for states' rights, which meant that each state had certain of its own rights and did not have to give in to the federal government. The fight for states' rights was growing, but the federal Union had many defenders. Daniel Webster had told the United States Senate: "Liberty and Union, now and forever, one and inseparable." Andrew Jackson, who had become President, said, "Our Union, it must be preserved." South Carolina was a leader in the fight for states' rights. Slavery had become a bitter subject, splitting the North and South. William Lloyd Garrison, editor of *The Liberator* of Boston, was a strong speaker against slavery. The Reverend Elijah P. Lovejoy, another editor who was against slavery, had his press burned and was killed in his shop in Alton, Illinois, by a mob of people who wanted slavery. As a result of the mob's cruelty, thousands of new members joined the anti-slavery group, called Abolitionists. Another fight had begun to win equal rights for women. The rights for women had been growing as a public issue, or subject of argument. Lucretia Mott and Elizabeth Cady Stanton were leaders in the movement. They led the first National Women's Rights Convention held at Seneca, New York, in 1848. Several other reform movements also began. Lyman Beecher headed a union backing prohibition, or the outlawing of alcoholic drinks. In 1846, prohibition was adopted by Maine, the first state to take the step. Another campaign was to help insane persons by moving them from prisons to asylums or hospitals.

## *DAVID WALKER'S APPEAL AROUSES FOES OF SLAVERY*

OPPOSITION TO THE SLAVERY of men had increased steadily since America won its freedom as a nation. In 1829, a Negro freedman named David Walker addressed a widely-read *Appeal* to the people of the United States. Walker was the Boston agent for the first Negro newspaper in America, the New York *Freedom's Journal.* His *Appeal* asked for freedom for the black people. Walker told Negro slaves they had the right to rise in bloody rebellion if they were not given freedom. He closed his *Appeal* with a warning:

"REMEMBER, AMERICANS, that we must and shall be free and enlightened (educated) as you are, will you wait until we shall, under God, obtain our liberty by the crushing arm of power? Will it not be dreadful for you? I speak, Americans, for your good. We must and shall be free, I say, in spite of you. You may do your best to keep us in wretchedness (poverty) and misery, to enrich you and your children, but God will deliver us from under you . . . Treat us like men, and there is no danger but we will all live in peace and happiness together. . . ."

NAT TURNER, A NEGRO PREACHER, led a slave uprising in Southampton, County, Virginia, in 1831. Turner's Rebellion was bloody. Fifty-seven white men, women and children were killed. An estimated 100 Negroes were killed as punishment, many of whom had not even been involved. Slaves from several plantations joined in the uprising.

THE REBELLION STRUCK on a Sunday night, when many white men were attending a meeting in another county. Entire families were attacked and slain by the slaves. A total of about 300 federal troops and militia joined in a manhunt for the rebel slaves. Nearly all of the rebels were tracked down and captured. The captured slaves were tried and twenty were sentenced to death, including Nat Turner.

**Nat Turner,** a Negro preacher, led a slave revolt in Virginia in 1831. Fifty-seven whites were killed and an estimated 100 blacks died as a result of the rebellion.

## *FRENCH WRITER PRAISES DEMOCRACY IN AMERICA*

ALEXIS DE TOCQUEVILLE, a twenty-six-year-old Frenchman, was sent by his country in 1831 to study prisons in the United States. DeTocqueville did not stop with a study of prisons. He made a trip into many parts of America. He saw the Americans' way of living. He watched them at work and play. DeTocqueville saw that Americans were hard workers and were a happy people. He was amazed at the growth of the United States and its developing democracy. On his return to France, DeTocqueville wrote a widely read book called *Democracy in America.*

"IT IS EVIDENT to all alike that a great democratic revolution is going on amongst us," DeTocqueville wrote. "It is like a deluge of men rising unabatedly, and driven daily onward. The American struggles against the wilderness and savage life. The conquests of the Americans are, therefore, gained by the plow. The principal instrument of the American is freedom." In America, DeTocqueville wrote, he saw "the image of democracy itself."

"IN AMERICAN SOCIETY, the equality of conditions is the fundamental fact from which all others seem to be derived," DeTocqueville wrote. "It may be said that no one renders obedience to man, but to justice and to law. The great advantage of the Americans consists in their being able to commit faults which they can afterward repair." DeTocqueville concluded, "The power vested in American courts of justice of pronouncing a statute to be unconstitutional forms one of the most powerful barriers which has ever been devised against the tyranny of political assemblies." DeTocqueville's report further increased the hopes of thousands of unhappy Europeans that they might find new lives in the new land of America.

**Alexis de Tocqueville** wrote: "The principal instrument of the American is freedom."

# *TEXANS WIN INDEPENDENCE FROM MEXICO*

AMERICAN SETTLERS living in Texas, a land owned by Mexico, organized an army to win independence. The Texans won independence in a short but bitter war. As the fighting began, General Santa Anna, the dictator of Mexico, marched into Texas with 6,000 troops. The Alamo, a Texas fort at San Antonio, was held by 188 Texans under Colonel William B. Travis. Santa Anna attacked the fort and captured it on March 6, 1836. All but a few of the Texans were killed in the battle and the few who lived were killed by the Mexicans after the battle. The cry rang out across the land: "Remember the Alamo!" General Sam Houston raised an army of 800 Texans and trapped 1,200 Mexicans under the command of Santa Anna on the banks of the San Jacinto River, near Galveston. The Texans sprang from a swamp and fired on the enemy. More than 600 of Santa Anna's men were killed. The Mexican general was captured and forced to sign a treaty promising his recognition of the independence of Texas. Congress in July, 1836, recognized Texas as an independent republic. The infant country was called "The Lone Star Republic."

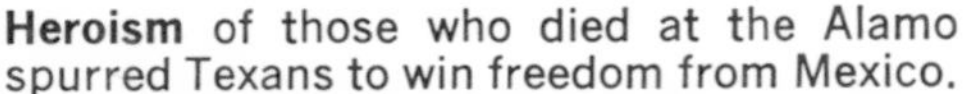

**Heroism** of those who died at the Alamo spurred Texans to win freedom from Mexico.

# PEOPLE GAINED STRONGER VOICE IN THE GOVERNMENT UNDER JACKSON

The "common man" gained a bigger voice in the running of America's government under Jackson. Democracy made many gains.

National conventions took the place of small meetings in Congress to pick candidates to run for President. The states elected men who then would choose candidates.

More and easier voting rights made the people's vote, or popular vote, more important in elections. The working people could decide elections by using their voting power.

National politics spread to reach the people of the towns and farms. City and county political groups were becoming active.

Workingmen's parties entered politics. Jackson's Democrats backed labor policies and the party had many union members.

Men who opposed Jackson were called the Whigs. The Whigs formed a new party to oppose the Jackson Democrats' policies.

## *ANNEXATION OF TEXAS BRINGS WAR WITH MEXICO*

WAR WITH MEXICO! James K. Polk was elected President in 1844 on policies which included the annexation, or the taking into the Union, of Texas. America's desire to annex Texas had grown through the administrations of Presidents Martin Van Buren, William Henry Harrison and John Tyler. But Mexico had warned that the annexation would mean war. Polk promised to annex Texas and did it. Texas was annexed in 1845, and war with Mexico began in May, 1846. The first battle came when 5,000 Mexicans commanded by General Pedro de Ampudia crossed the Rio Grande River into Texas. General Zachary Taylor drove the Mexicans back across the Rio Grande, and chased them into Mexico.

COMMODORE JOHN D. SLOAT invaded California, held by Mexico, with naval forces. San Francisco, Monterey, Santa Barbara and Los Angeles were captured by Americans under Sloat, Commodore Robert F. Stockton and Captain John Fremont. California was won. Colonel Stephen Watts Kearny marched from Kansas to Santa Fe, New Mexico, capturing that territory. Zachary Taylor invaded north Mexico, and won a victory at Monterrey. At Buena Vista, Taylor's army of only 5,000 defeated 14,000 Mexicans under Santa Anna. Northern Mexico was conquered. Taylor's army was halted, and a daring sea-land attack toward Mexico City, the capital, was launched.

GENERAL WINFIELD SCOTT led a combined Army-Navy attack on Vera Cruz to start the winning drive. Scott landed at Tampico with 9,000 troops and marched overland to meet with Navy forces under Commodore David Conner. Vera Cruz surrendered on March 27, 1848, after five days of firing by American land and sea cannons. Mexico City, the capital of Mexico, then was the only remaining target.

**Fierce fighting** gave 5,000 Americans victory over 14,000 Mexicans at Buena Vista.

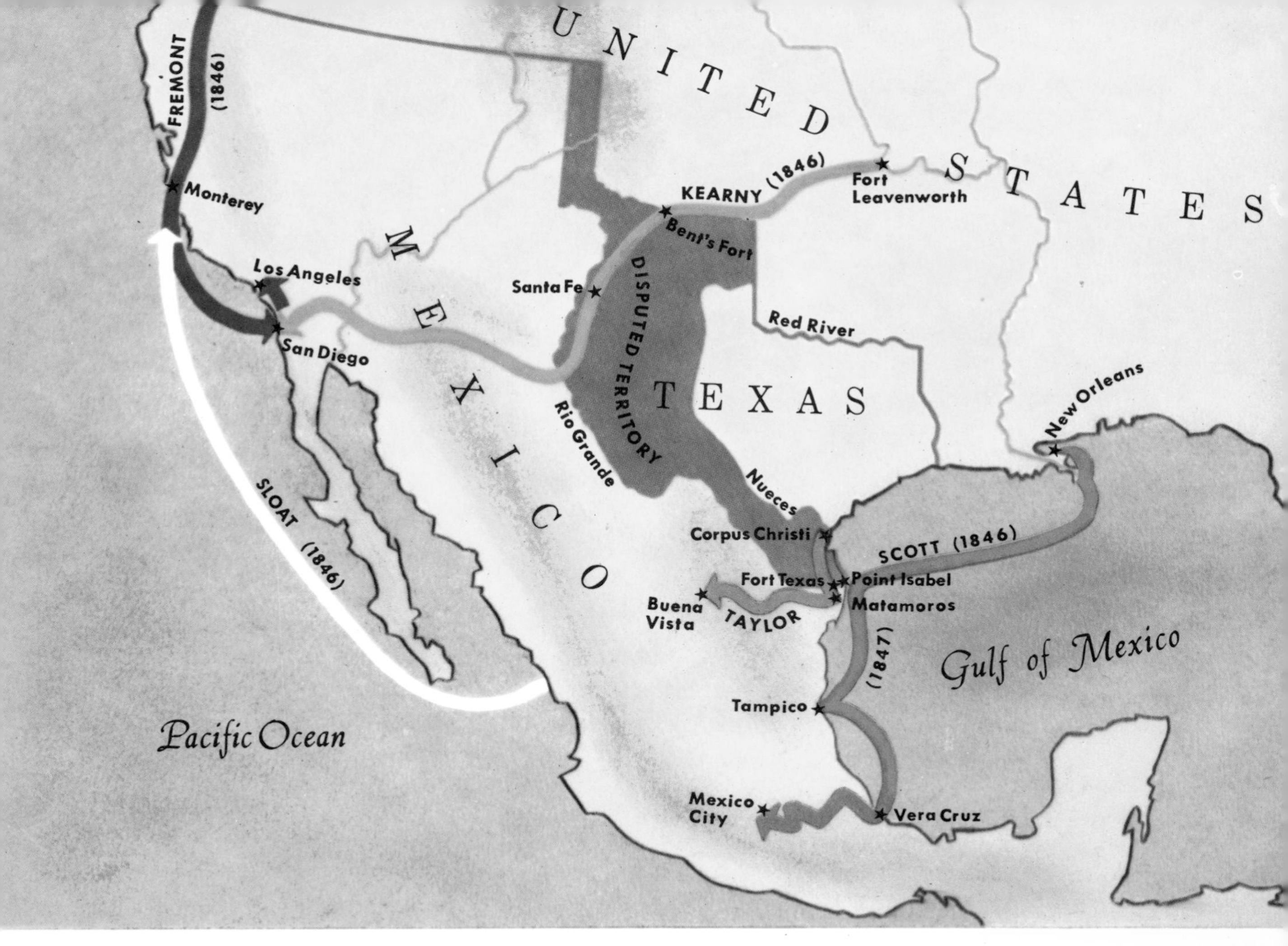


**Mexico City** was captured. America carried out its plans and won the Mexican war.

MEXICO CITY FELL before Scott's army. After the battle at Vera Cruz, Scott marched on to the capital. His soldiers climbed the rocky hillsides of Chapultepec, a walled park on top of a 200-foot high hill. Santa Anna had 5,000 men at Chapultepec. On September 12, Scott's cannon battered the walls and the next day his infantry poured into the defense positions. Chapultepec fell and Scott turned to Mexico City. Scott's 6,000 soldiers broke through Mexico City's walls by using picks and crowbars. They entered the capital during the night of September 13-14. There was little fighting and the Americans raised their flag over Mexico City's palace. United States Marines went on duty at the "halls of Montezuma." General Santa Anna fled the city and, after a short fight, fled the country. The war was over.

IN THE TREATY of Guadalupe Hidalgo, signed just outside Mexico City, Mexico gave up all claims to Texas north of the Rio Grande River. New Mexico and California were given to the United States. The Rio Grande was set as the border of New Mexico. The United States paid Mexico $15,000,000 for the territories. Including Texas, the United States had taken on 1,930,000 square miles of new land. The nation's expansion in North America was almost completed. In 1846, a treaty with England had ended the arguments over the boundaries of Oregon. The present boundary between the United States and Canada, from the Atlantic to the Pacific Oceans, was decided upon by the two countries.

MANY NEW THINGS were invented as America found a better way of life. America saw its first locomotive, or engine pulling a train, when the Tom Thumb made a good trial run in August, 1830. The Tom Thumb was a little "steam wagon" which was built for the Baltimore and Ohio railroad. It was a wagon with a boiler placed on it. The boiler had funnels, or smoke stacks, made out of rifle barrels. It was built by Peter Cooper. The Tom Thumb was America's first steam train engine and the Baltimore and Ohio became America's first railroad carrying passengers, or riders who paid fares. The Tom Thumb traveled thirteen miles from Baltimore to Ellicott's Mills, Maryland, in seventy-two minutes—fast at that time.

THE GROWING OF GRAIN, such as wheat, was given a big boost by Cyrus Hall McCormick in the early 1830's. He invented a machine called the reaper. The reaper harvested, or mowed down, the wheat crop. Grain crops before then had been cut down by hand, taking much more time. The reaper was pulled along the fields of growing grain. It pulled the grain into stacks and a knife blade cut them down.

A PISTOL which could fire several shots without stopping was invented by Samuel Colt in 1835. Colt's pistol had a cylinder, or wheel filled with bullets, which turned as the trigger was pulled. All the man with the pistol had to do was keep pulling the trigger and the pistol kept shooting. Colt's pistol was called a six-shooter.

A NEW WAY TO MAKE things out of rubber was invented by Charles Goodyear in 1844. This was called vulcanizing of rubber. By making the vulcanized rubber hard or soft, it could be used to make many things. Goodyear found the vulcanizing secret by accident. He happened to drop some raw rubber on a hot stove, and vulcanized rubber resulted.

SAMUEL F. B. MORSE invented the telegraph. This gave the world a quick way of sending messages. On May 24, 1844, Morse had his telegraph ready to be used. He sent the first message by telegraph, from Washington to Baltimore. He tapped out this message: "What hath God wrought!"

**Cyrus Hall McCormick** invented the reaper. Grain crops were quickly cut by the reaper and many big farms turned to growing wheat. Many of the farms were in the Northwest.

**Daniel Webster,** Henry Clay and John C. Calhoun were the Great Triumvirate. They made history in the United States Senate during nearly half a century as its leaders.

THE GREAT TRIUMVIRATE won fame in the United States Senate. The Triumvirate included Daniel Webster, Henry Clay and John C. Calhoun. Clay was elected to Congress in 1806, Calhoun in 1811, and Webster in 1813. The Great Triumvirate, or famous three, ended when Webster died in Marshfield, Massachusetts, on October 24, 1852. Henry Clay had died on June 28, 1852, and Calhoun died on March 30, 1850, both in Washington. Clay of Kentucky, Calhoun of South Carolina, and Webster of Massachusetts were champions of democracy. They spoke out strongly to keep alive America's way of life—with freedom and equality for all.

WHILE SPEAKING against a South Carolina act against the Union, Webster made his famous speech: "Liberty and Union, now and forever, one and inseparable!" Webster twice was Secretary of State, in addition to his many years in the Senate. Calhoun, a leader of the "War Hawks" who had shouted support of the War of 1812, was a strong defender of states' rights. He always had fought for the South's interests in matters coming before Congress. Calhoun had run for President in 1824. He twice had been Vice-President.

HENRY CLAY, also a leader of the "War Hawks," was known as the "Great Pacificator" because of the ways he kept peace in Congress. Clay helped pass the Missouri Compromise in 1820 and the Compromise of 1850, both of which tried to end the slavery argument between the North and the South. The compromises were failures, as the slavery quarrel grew, but Clay did his best to settle the argument.

# CLOUDS OF CIVIL WAR GATHERED —BREAK IN THE UNION WIDENED

The North and the South increased their argument over slavery. An act was passed making it hard for slaves to escape to the North. This was called the Fugitive Slave Act. Slaves trying to get free were given harsh punishment.

The North and South were split over slavery. California was taken into the Union as a "free" state. There was to be no slavery in California. There now were sixteen states not having slavery and fifteen allowing slaves.

Abolitionists were people who wanted to make all slaves free. They made the North angry against slavery with their speeches. They printed newspapers which said the South was cruel for having slaves. The North and the South began to quarrel bitterly.

An "Underground Railroad" was organized in the North to help slaves escape. Runaway slaves were helped to hide and move on to the next stop. Harriet Tubman, an escaped slave who was called "Moses," was a leader in forming and running the "railroad."

## *CLIPPER SHIPS AND STEAMBOATS RULE WATER TRAFFIC*

AMERICA BUILT FAST NEW SHIPS in the 1850's. These were the fastest in the world for making trips across the oceans. These ships were called clippers. They were long and slim. They carried large and wide sails which caught much wind. America's clipper ships set a new speed record for sailing ships by crossing the Atlantic Ocean in only thirteen days. The clipper ships sailed to China in about half the time it took other ships. By 1853, United States ships were leading the world in the amount of goods being carried across the seas to other countries. England, the usual leader in shipping, was in second place. The British were unhappy about losing the lead and tried to use steamboats. But Robert Fulton's steamboat was not yet ready for ocean travel. The clippers, when they had a good wind, could outrun the steamboats.

STEAMBOATS WON the right to rule the rivers of America. By 1853, more than 1,000 steamboats were using the Mississippi and the rivers flowing into it. The faster boats could make the St. Louis to New Orleans run of more than 1,000 miles in five days or less. The river boats carried many thousands of passengers and freight worth millions. The building of canals speeded other types of water travel in the West. More than 3,000 miles of canals and waterways had been dug and put into service by 1850. The State of Ohio built the Ohio and Erie Canal from Portsmouth to Cleveland, and also the Miami and Erie Canal connecting Cincinnati and Toledo. Indiana built the Wabash and Erie Canal, and Illinois built the Illinois and Michigan Canal.

**Fast and trim** sailing ships called clippers were sent across the world's seas by America. They won world leadership. A clipper crossed the Atlantic in 13 days.

# *STEEL AND OIL START TWO GIANT U.S. INDUSTRIES ON THE WAY*

**Andrew Carnegie** became the leader of America's steel industry after the blast furnace process was discovered. Under Carnegie, U.S. steel output led the world.

STEEL AND OIL ROSE AS GIANTS on America's widening industrial scene. In the 1850's, a method of making steel by a blast furnace process was developed by William Kelly, a Kentucky ironmaster, and Henry Bessemer, an industrialist in England. In August, 1859, Edwin L. Drake struck oil at Titusville, Pennsylvania. Both of these developments provided the push to start two of America's greatest industries–steel and oil–on the way. Much of America's economic advance and rising standard of living was the result of this steady industrial growth.

KELLY, THE KENTUCKIAN, discovered the blast furnace process by accident. The supply of charcoal fuel at his iron furnace ran low and the air blast blew over some uncovered melted iron. The carbon in the pig iron and the oxygen in the air acted as their own fuel. When the melted mass of metal cooled, Kelly found that it was steel. He obtained a patent for his process in 1856 and joined his patent with the Englishman Bessemer's patents. Their method of making steel, known as the Bessemer process, quickly spread.

THE RISE OF STEEL in America was largely the story of Andrew Carnegie. Born in Scotland, Carnegie came to America as a boy of twelve and started work for $1.20 a week in a cotton mill. He worked his way up through various jobs and by 1868 was in the iron business. Carnegie turned to steel and purchased the Homestead Steel works near Pittsburgh. He formed the Carnegie Steel Company and by 1900 was producing 4 million tons a year–highest in the world.

DRAKE DRILLED THE WORLD'S FIRST planned oil well to make his great strike. Oil was seen coming up from the ground at a sawmill near Titusville. A company was formed and Drake was sent to "raise oil." He did and oil quickly became one of America's biggest businesses. John D. Rockefeller from the first was a leading oil industrialist. He formed Standard Oil Company in 1867 and, step by step, gained control of most of the oil business in America. Because of this control, Rockefeller was able to obtain special low shipping rates from the railroads. In 1870, Rockefeller incorporated, or legally organized, the Standard Oil Company of Ohio, with an investment of 100 million dollars.

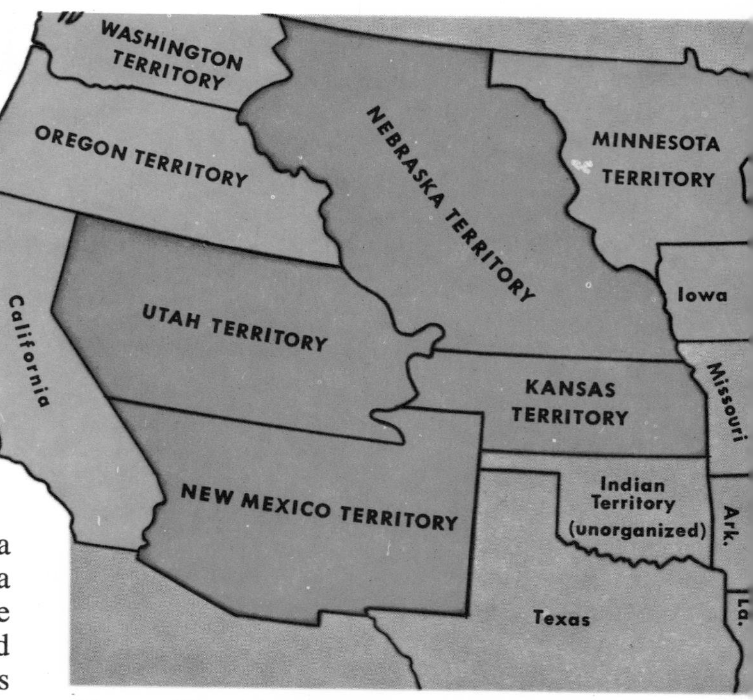


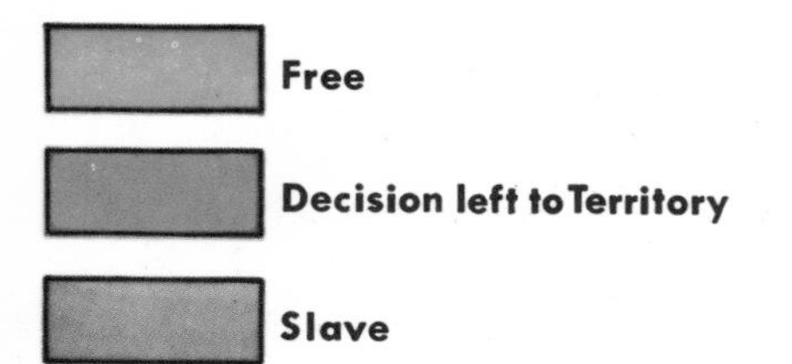


**Kansas** became a bloody battlefield over slavery. The Kansas-Nebraska Act, passed in 1854, further split the North and South.

KANSAS AND NEBRASKA became a battlefield over slavery. Congress passed a Kansas-Nebraska Act in May, 1854. The two lands were formed into territories and the slavery question was left to the wishes of those who lived in these lands. This was called "popular sovereignty," or local option. It was hoped this plan would prevent fights between the groups who were for slavery and those who were against slavery. But it did not work out that way. What happened in Kansas was many bloody fights between the two groups. Andrew H. Reeder was named governor of the new territory. Battle lines formed. Kansas had groups which were against slavery, called Free Staters. In Missouri, secret groups in favor of slavery slipped across the border and voted in Kansas. In March, 1855, about 5,000 armed Missouri men—they were called "border ruffians"—went into the polls in Kansas and helped elect a legislature in favor of slavery.

MASSACHUSETTS FORMED a group called the Emigrant Aid Society. They sent hundreds of settlers into Kansas. These settlers formed a Free State Party. Their friends in Massachusetts and other Northern states sent them rifles and bullets. Many of the guns were Sharps rifles, but were called "Beecher's Bibles." The name came from Henry Ward Beecher, a leading preacher who wanted to abolish slavery. He said the rifles could do the work of Bibles. Many fights took place and many settlers in Kansas were killed. The territory became known as "Bleeding Kansas."

BLOODY REVENGE for things which the "border ruffians" had done was taken by John Brown. On May 24-25, 1856, Brown, four of his sons, and three other men killed five pro-slavery Kansas settlers. They grabbed the victims in their homes near Dutch Henry's Crossing on Pottawatomie Creek. All five were killed at midnight in "John Brown's Massacre," or killing of many people. Pro-slavers hit back at John Brown's crime by capturing and wrecking Osawatomie, a Free State town. Gangs fought throughout the area. A new governor, John W. Geary, called in United States troops and broke up a mob of 2,500 "border ruffians." Peace came to Kansas territory for a short time, but nearly 200 people had been killed and hundreds of thousands of dollars worth of homes and goods had been wrecked, or ruined.

## *ABRAHAM LINCOLN ENTERS SLAVERY DISPUTE*

ABRAHAM LINCOLN, tall and slim, faced the 1858 Republican state convention in Springfield, Illinois. He had been picked as the party's candidate for the United States Senate. He made a famous speech in accepting the nomination. Lincoln said: "We are now far into the fifth year since a policy was initiated with the avowed object and confident promise of putting an end to slavery agitation. Under the operation of that policy, that agitation not only has not ceased, but has constantly augmented. In my opinion, it will not cease until a crisis has been reached and passed. 'A house divided against itself cannot stand.' I believe this government cannot endure permanently half slave and half free. I do not expect the Union to be dissolved—I do not expect the house to fall—but I do expect it will cease to be divided. It will become all one thing, or all the other." The speech stirred the nation.

**Abraham Lincoln** told America: "A house divided against itself cannot stand."

LINCOLN'S "HOUSE DIVIDED" speech, made on June 16, 1858, told the facts. He did not ask that slavery be done away with, and he did not criticize slave owners. But Lincoln made one thing clear. In his words, "Either the opponents of slavery will arrest the further spread of it and place it where the public mind shall rest in the belief that it is in the course of ultimate extinction; or its advocates will push it forward until it shall become alike lawful in all the states, old as well as new, North as well as South."

THE WHOLE NATION became interested in Abraham Lincoln. He had made a strong speech in October, 1854, against the Kansas-Nebraska Act. Lincoln was a fine lawyer and a good speaker. He became one of Illinois' leading citizens. Now he was running for the United States Senate. It had been a long, hard journey from the little log cabin in Hardin County, Kentucky, where Lincoln was born on February 12, 1809, the son of pioneer parents.

LINCOLN'S DISLIKE of the Kansas-Nebraska Act was shared by the new Republican Party when it was organized in 1854. Repeal of the Fugitive Slave Act was also asked. Spreading slavery into the territories was an argument that brought splits in all political party ranks. Angry Whigs, Free-Soilers and anti-slavery Democrats met at Ripon, Wisconsin, on February 28, 1854, and voted for the forming of a new party. State meetings were held in Michigan, Indiana, Ohio, Wisconsin, Vermont and Illinois. The new party was formed and was given the name of Republicans. The Republican movement spread quickly through the North. The party became strong in American politics. When the November, 1854, mid-term state and congressional elections were held, Republicans in the Northwest won nearly half of the offices. Lincoln joined the party in 1856 and was nominated for the United States Senate.

## *LINCOLN AND DOUGLAS MEET IN SEVEN DEBATES*

**Tall Abraham Lincoln** and short Stephen Douglas attracted the attention of all America as they met in Illinois debates.

STEPHEN DOUGLAS ran against Lincoln in 1858 for United States Senator from Illinois. Douglas was the Democratic candidate. He had fallen out with the national Democratic party, but the "Little Giant"—as Douglas was called—still was the best foe for Lincoln. President James Buchanan had asked that Kansas be taken into the Union as a slave state, but Senator Douglas did not agree. Lincoln dared Douglas to meet him in some debates, and Douglas agreed. Douglas was known as a powerful debater. The first debate was held at Ottawa, Illinois, on August 21, 1858. The citizens were greatly excited over this political fight. Many thousands traveled by train, wagon, horseback and even on foot to hear the rivals. There stood calm, six-foot-four-inch Lincoln and the shouting, waving Douglas, who was only five feet tall.

A THRONG OF 15,000 gathered at Freeport on August 27 to hear the second debate. Many newspaper writers crowded up front. The big crowd was rewarded with the best debate of the series. Douglas talked about his "popular sovereignty," or local option, in the territories, and said people could end slavery if they wished. All they had to do was pass local laws against the owning of slaves, Douglas said. He explained: "Slavery cannot exist a day or even an hour anywhere, unless it is supported by local police regulations."

LINCOLN SAID that he thought slavery was "a moral, social and political wrong." In between the seven debates, Lincoln made this statement: "You can fool all of the people some of the time, and some of the people all of the time, but you cannot fool all of the people all of the time."

# *LINCOLN IS ELECTED TO THE PRESIDENCY IN 1860*

LINCOLN WAS ELECTED as the sixteenth President of the United States. He and his Republican running mate, Hannibal Hamlin, won the vote of eighteen free states. In this election of 1860, Lincoln won the most popular, or peoples', votes. But he did not win a majority, or more than half. The popular vote was 1,866,352 for Lincoln, 1,375,157 for Douglas, 849,781 for John Breckinridge, and 589,581 for John Bell. Lincoln won 180 votes in the Electoral College, a majority. Breckinridge was second with seventy-two electoral votes, Bell third with thirty-nine and Douglas fourth with twelve. Breckinridge won eleven slave states. Bell won three border states, and Douglas won Missouri plus three of New Jersey's votes. The Democratic Party had split over its nominations for the 1860 election. At the regular convention at Charleston, the Southern Democrats were voted down on a demand for positive protection for slavery in the territories. The delegates from eight Southern states withdrew from the convention. A second convention was held at Baltimore and the Southern delegates seceded from the party when again voted down. The Northern Democrats then nominated Douglas. The Southern Democrats held their own convention at Baltimore and nominated Breckinridge. Had all of the Democrats voted for one candidate, instead of dividing their votes, they still would not have defeated Lincoln. Only eleven electoral votes would have been changed—in New Jersey, California and Oregon. Lincoln still would have had a majority with 169 votes, enough for election to the Presidency.

**Lincoln** was elected as the sixteenth President. The Democrats split their votes between three candidates. But Lincoln would have won even without a split vote.

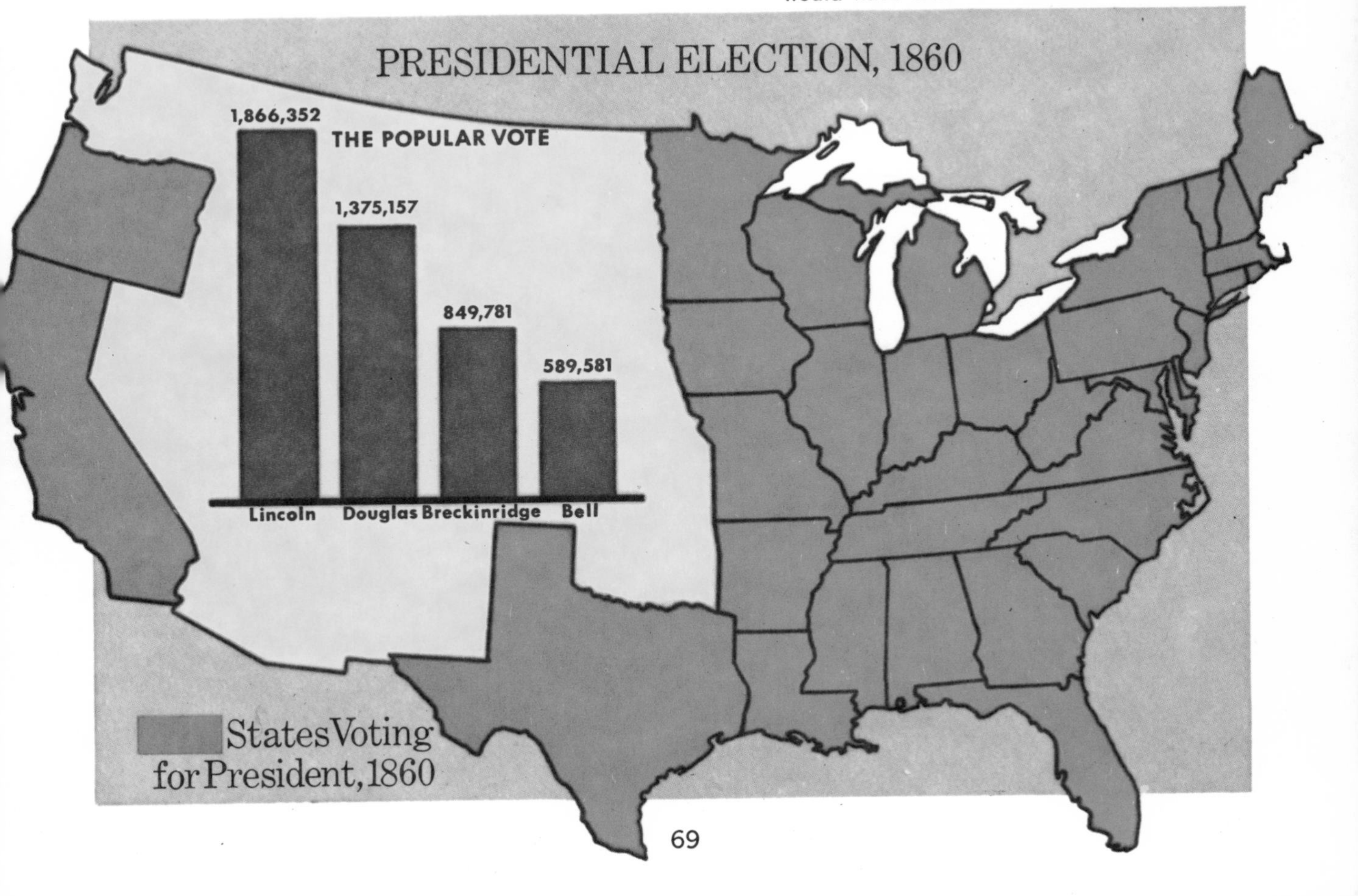

# ABRAHAM LINCOLN: RUGGED PRODUCT OF AMERICA'S HARD-WON FRONTIERS

Lincoln came from a family of western frontiersmen. He was born in a log cabin in Hardin County, Kentucky, February 12, 1809, son of Thomas and Nancy Hanks Lincoln.

Lincoln's family moved to Indiana in 1816 and to Southern Illinois in 1830. In his youth, Lincoln split fence rails, worked on a river flatboat, and clerked in a store at New Salem.

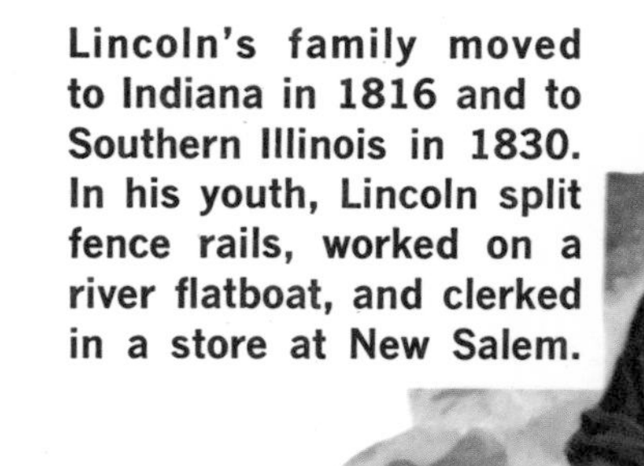

Lincoln turned to a study of law. He was admitted to the bar in 1837 and opened a law office in Springfield. Lincoln was well known as a trial lawyer in jury cases.

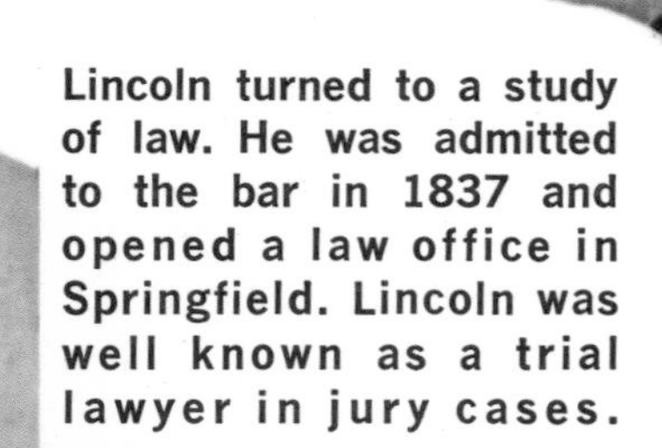

In 1842, Abraham Lincoln married Mary Todd in Springfield. They had four sons—Robert Todd, Edward, William and Thomas Lincoln.

Standing six-feet-four, thin but strong, Lincoln was a forceful public speaker. He spoke with a slight western drawl, or slowness of speech. Lincoln enjoyed telling funny stories to his many friends.

Lincoln, as a speaker, showed smartness, good sense, and a clearness in his way of talking. Lincoln served in the Illinois legislature from 1834 to 1842.

Lincoln's beliefs on slavery were mild, but he strongly opposed the spreading of slavery into the territories. He said the Constitution was a contract between the states—binding forever.

Abraham Lincoln had much sympathy for all human suffering. His sympathetic thinking and his fine manners won him great popularity with the people.

**The tragic break!** After Lincoln's election, South Carolina pulled out of the Union. Other southern states followed and the stage was set for the Civil War.

OUT OF THE UNION! South Carolina led a parade of states which seceded from the Union after the election of Lincoln. When a state seceded, it quit belonging to the United States of America. On December 18, 1860, the South Carolina legislature voted to call a special state meeting to decide what to do. This meeting began on December 20. Not one vote was cast against South Carolina's seceding from the Union. The South Carolina meeting made this statement: "The Union now subsisting between South Carolina and the other states, under the name of the 'United States of America,' is hereby dissolved." The big step had been taken. The first state, one of the original thirteen, had left the Union.

SOUTH CAROLINA EXPLAINED its reason for seceding in a "Declaration of Immediate Causes." The South Carolina leaders attending the meeting said they believed firmly in states' rights. This was the point which John C. Calhoun had defended so strongly for so many years. The South Carolina secession announcement pointed out that many attacks had been made on the state's beliefs on slavery. Lincoln's election as President was the final reason South Carolina gave for leaving the Union. South Carolina said that Lincoln was a man whose "opinions and purposes are hostile to slavery."

SOUTH CAROLINA ALSO BLAMED the power gained by the new anti-slavery Republican Party in the elections. The Republicans, who were led by Lincoln, were firmly against slavery, South Carolina said. Six other states in the lower South soon followed South Carolina into secession from the Union. These Southern states said the North had attacked slavery. The South said it must have slavery to keep its farms going. Their way of life was dependent on slaves, the South said. Mississippi voted to secede on January 9, 1861. Florida followed the next day. Alabama seceded on January 11 and Georgia on January 19. Louisiana joined the secession parade on January 26 and Texas decided on February 1 to leave the Union along with the others.

THE FOUR UPPER STATES of the South waited before seceding. They were Virginia, Tennessee, North Carolina and Arkansas. Of the seven states already out of the Union, only Texas put the decision up to the voters of its state. The six other states held elections to select men who would vote on secession. The men who were elected then made the final decisions The big break had come—the South had left the Union.

## *NEW CONFEDERATE STATES CHOOSE DAVIS FOR PRESIDENT*

THE CONFEDERATE STATES of America was formed after the Southern states left the Union. On February 4, 1861, leaders from the seven states which had seceded met at Montgomery, Alabama. They formed the Confederate States of America and adopted a government. The Confederates' government was much like the Constitution of the United States, with some changes. The states' rights of each state were recognized, the states being given standing as "sovereign and independent." However, state officers were required to swear support of the new constitution. Slavery was recognized as legal, but the Confederates' constitution said that no more slaves could be brought into the country. The need for and the protection of slavery were covered in several parts of the constitution. The rule against the bringing in of any more Negroes from Africa was adopted to please England and France. The President was given the power to rule against any appropriations, or spending of money, in any bills which he signed. It was understood that any of the slave states could leave the Confederacy whenever they wished.

JEFFERSON DAVIS of Mississippi was elected as president of the Confederacy. Alexander H. Stephens of Georgia was chosen as vice-president. Stephens in 1860 had made a last-minute effort to help avoid secession. But Stephens' effort had failed. Jefferson Davis was a Mississippi cotton grower who had fought in the Army. He was a graduate of West Point, the United States Military Academy. He was a veteran who had fought in the Mexican War. All of the actions taken at the Montgomery meeting had to be approved by a vote of the Southern citizens in November. The actions taken were approved by the voters. A last effort to make peace was made at a meeting in Washington. Former President John Tyler conducted the meeting. Twenty-one states sent their leaders to the meeting. No plan for peace could be decided upon and the Civil War was at hand. The four upper states of the South still had not seceded. Virginia, North Carolina, Tennessee and Arkansas were awaiting developments.

**The Southern states** which left the Union formed the Confederate States of America. Jefferson Davis was elected as president.

# *FORT SUMTER IS FIRED UPON—THE CIVIL WAR BEGINS*

**South Carolina** shore batteries fired on Union troops in Fort Sumter on an island in Charleston Harbor. Civil War had begun!

FIRST SHOTS OF THE CIVIL WAR were fired against Union troops holding Fort Sumter. This fort was on an island in the harbor at Charleston, South Carolina. Six days after South Carolina seceded from the Union, Major Robert Anderson had moved his Union troops from Fort Moultrie on the mainland to Fort Sumter in the harbor. President Lincoln ordered that help be sent to Fort Sumter. Earlier, President James Buchanan had sent a Union supply ship to Sumter, but Charleston shore batteries drove it back. Lincoln told South Carolina that he was sending food and supplies, but no troops to the fort.

SOUTH CAROLINA'S LEADERS at Charleston feared a trick. They ordered Fort Sumter to surrender at once. Major Anderson said he would give up when his supplies ran out, but not before. South Carolina refused the offer. At 4:30 o'clock in the morning of April 12, 1861, the South Carolina shore cannon opened fire. General Pierre G. T. Beauregard was in command of the battery, or group of guns. After thirty-four hours of bombardment, with nobody injured on either side, Major Anderson surrendered and the war's first fight ended.

ANDERSON MARCHED HIS troops from Fort Sumter "with colors flying and drums beating . . . and saluting the flag with fifty guns." The news was flashed across the nation by telegraph. Fort Sumter had been fired upon and had fallen! The North's anger rose quickly. Cities and towns held meetings and promised they would send soldiers to defend the Union. Until then, many Northerners had not believed there would be a Civil War. Some leaders had said that the Southern states should be allowed to leave the Union peacefully. But now cannon had been fired. This was it—war between the states!

SOUTHERN TROOPS already had seized federal forts and arsenals, places where guns, bullets and powder were kept. Georgia had taken over federal forts at Pulaski and Augusta. Florida had seized Apalachicola. Louisiana had taken the fort at Baton Rouge. Alabama had seized Mount Vernon, Fort Morgan and Fort Gaines. All United States forts in Texas had been surrendered. Firing of the first guns at Fort Sumter sounded the call to war and rallied the North to defense of the Union.

# *THE NORTH DECIDES ON FOUR-POINT WAR STRATEGY*

BOTH NORTH AND SOUTH made plans for war. President Lincoln met with his military leaders and approved their decisions. The North decided on four points in its strategy, or war plans. Southern ports would be blockaded, or shut off, by Union warships. This blockade would be made tighter. The Union army in the East would try to take Richmond, the permanent Confederate capital. An army in the West, backed by Union gunboats, would seek to capture the lands through which the Mississippi, Tennessee and Cumberland Rivers flowed. Another Western army would cut through Tennessee to the Atlantic coast. There the Union armies would join in a final drive to defeat the South. If it went as planned, the Confederacy would be cut both north and south and east and west.

GENERAL GEORGE B. MC CLELLAN prepared to carry out this strategy. He trained the Union's Army of the Potomac for a drive into Virginia. McClellan was to become the commander of the Potomac army. General Henry W. Halleck drilled his Union forces. The military leaders of the Confederate States army also made their battle plans. One army would be sent against Washington. If Washington were captured, this Southern army would drive into Maryland and Pennsylvania. This would divide the North's northwest and northeast sections. A big part of the Confederacy's army would be used entirely on defense. The South was mainly interested in defending its own lands and preventing invaders from coming in and wrecking towns and farms.

**Both the Union** and the Confederacy drew up plans for fighting the war. The North's navy already had blockaded the coasts of the South to stop supplies from Europe.

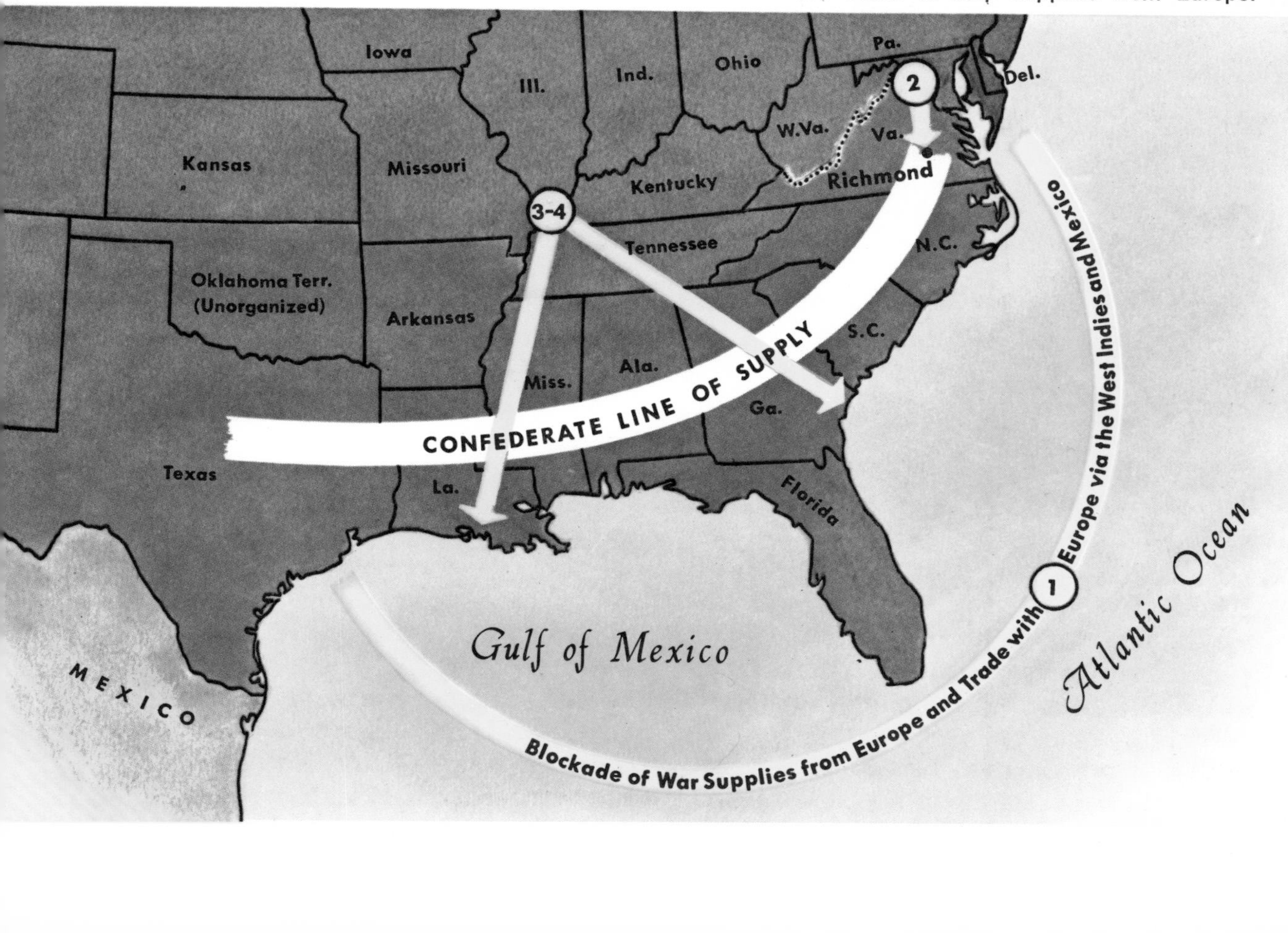

# *SOUTH WINS THE FIRST BATTLE OF BULL RUN*

**The South** won a decisive victory in the First Battle of Bull Run. "Stonewall" Jackson was a hero of the battle. Sightseers from Washington were forced to flee.

THE WAR'S FIRST BLOODSHED came in Maryland on April 19, 1861. A mob of Southern sympathizers attacked the Sixth Massachusetts Regiment as it passed through Baltimore on the way to Washington. Four soldiers were killed. A majority of Maryland's citizens were loyal to the Union and the state did not secede. Virginia, North Carolina, Tennessee and Arkansas seceded when Lincoln declared the South in rebellion. But the western section of Virginia refused to secede and later became the state of West Virginia.

THE FIRST BATTLE OF BULL RUN, fought on July 21, 1861, was a heavy defeat for the Union army. The South's General Beauregard and the North's General Irvin McDowell clashed at Bull Run Creek near Manassas Junction, Virginia. Each had about 30,000 troops. Hundreds of residents of Washington, thirty miles away, hurried to the battle scene to watch. The Union army was smashed, and the soldiers were sent running back to Washington. The holiday crowd ran back home with them. General Thomas J. Jackson, leading one Confederate army, "stood like a stone wall." He became known as "Stonewall."

U.S. RELATIONS with England were strained when Britain declared the South was not in rebellion, but was at war. Tension increased when the Union warship, *San Jacinto,* commanded by Captain John Wilkes, took two Confederate commissioners off the British mail steamer *Trent.* Lincoln feared he would "have two wars on my hands at one time," but tempers cooled. Lincoln was having troubles enough trying to find generals who could fight and win and dealing with a Congress always looking over his shoulder.

**The Battle of Shiloh** brought casualties which shocked the nation. Confederates crossed the river from Corinth, Mississippi, and attacked the Union army in Tennessee.

THE FIRST BIG STEP in the Union's plans to win the war on land was a drive to capture the Mississippi River. The first action came early in 1862 in Kentucky. Union troops under General George E. Thomas won a battle at Mills Springs. Then soldiers under Brigadier General Ulysses S. Grant and gunboats under Commodore A. H. Foote captured Fort Henry on the Tennessee River. Next the Union army attacked Fort Donelson on the Cumberland River. Fort Donelson was taken and the road to Nashville, Tennessee, was cleared. General Albert S. Johnston, the South's commander at Nashville, took his troops out of the city. The North promoted Grant to the rank of major general.

THE BLOODY BATTLE OF SHILOH followed. After Forts Henry and Donelson, Grant moved his army to Shiloh, on the Tennessee side of the Tennessee River opposite Corinth, Mississippi. General Johnston's Confederates struck the Union army at dawn April 6, 1862. In a day-long battle, Grant's army was very nearly defeated. But Union reinforcements, many more troops, arrived overnight. When the battle began again the next day, the Confederates were forced back to Corinth. The casualties, 13,000 for the Union and 11,000 for the South, brought home to both sides the full horror and sorrow of war.

MISSSISSIPPI RIVER WARFARE FLARED. On the final day of Shiloh's battle, Union troops under General John Pope and Foote's gunboats captured Island Number 10. This island, located at a bend of the Mississippi River in northwest Tennessee, was a key position in the South's river defense. To the south, Flag Officer David G. Farragut led his West Gulf Blockading Squadron past Southern forts near the mouth of the Mississippi River. Troops under General Benjamin F. Butler were taken upstream and landed. They took over New Orleans with very little fighting.

## *BATTLE OF IRONCLADS CHANGES NAVAL WARFARE*

A STRANGE MONSTER of a warship slid into Hampton Roads, Virginia, on March 8, 1862. It was the Confederate ironclad, named the *Virginia* but better known as the *Merrimac*. Union troops had sunk the former *Merrimac* on moving out of Norfolk with the outbreak of war. The Confederates raised the hull of the *Merrimac* and rebuilt it as an ironclad. The masts were chopped off and the deck was covered with two layers of sheet iron. A huge ram was put on the front end and the ironclad was armed with fifteen cannon. Renamed the *Virginia,* this was the monster that struck terror among Union ships in Hampton Roads that March morning.

HAMPTON ROADS, near Norfolk, was a favorite gathering place for Union blockade ships. The *Virginia* (or *Merrimac*) attacked the Union's wooden ships as soon as it appeared on the scene. The day was spent in dodging and fighting. Union cannon balls bounced off the South's ironclad. One federal ship, the *Cumberland,* was rammed and sunk. Another, the *Congress,* was set afire. The Union flagship, the *Minnesota,* was run aground. The Confederate ironclad then retired for the night.

THE NEXT DAY, March 9, the *Virginia* (*Merrimac*) steamed out to finish the job. A surprise was waiting. Overnight, a Union ironclad, the *Monitor,* had arrived in Hampton Roads. The *Monitor* also was covered with iron. Its decks barely cleared the water. Two cannon on a base which could be turned in a circle were in the middle of the ship. The two ironclads began fighting at once. For five hours, the fight went on, with big crowds watching from the shore. Neither of the ironclads could defeat the other. Finally, the *Virginia* was damaged running aground and lost her ram. The Confederate ironclad retired and the battle ended. Also ended was the day of wooden warships.

**The *Merrimac* and the *Monitor*** fought the first battle between ironclad warships. Neither could win, but they showed that the days of wooden warships were over.

## *PENINSULA CAMPAIGN RESULTS IN HEAVY FIGHTING*

LINCOLN ORDERED General McClellan to begin fighting in the East, after many months had been spent in training. The Peninsula Campaign followed in the spring and summer of 1862. A drive on Richmond up the Virginia peninsula, or finger of land between the James and York Rivers, was planned. McClellan started south from Washington with 105,000 men and McDowell set out with 40,000. General Robert E. Lee, leader of the South's Army of Virginia, sent "Stonewall" Jackson driving up the Shenandoah Valley to threaten Washington. Union Generals Nathaniel P. Banks and John Fremont, with 45,000 troops between them, blocked Jackson's approach to Washington.

WITH ONLY 18,000 MEN, Jackson hit his foes at Kernstown, Front Royal and twice at Winchester. Banks' army was broken and sent fleeing back across the Potomac. McClellan's army met Lee's Confederate army at the Chickahominy River and in the Seven Days' Battles. McClellan failed to gain ground and Lincoln recalled the army to Washington. The Second Battle of Bull Run was fought on August 29, 1862. It was almost as heavy a defeat for the Union as the First Battle of Bull Run. Union General Pope, who replaced McClellan as commander of the Army of the Potomac, sent many thousands of troops against Confederates led by Jackson and Longstreet. First, Jackson struck Pope's Union army in a rear attack. When Pope turned to face Jackson, Longstreet struck his army from the rear in the other direction. In two days of fighting, the Union army was defeated and sent retreating toward Washington. Two days later, McClellan replaced Pope and again became Potomac commander.

LEE LED HIS SOUTHERN ARMY on a march into Maryland. The 70,000 men of the Army of the Potomac stopped Lee's 40,000 invaders in the Battle of Antietam,

**General McClellan** led 105,000 Northern troops into Virginia. They failed to win the Peninsula Campaign and Lincoln called McClellan and his army home.

fought near Sharpsburg, Maryland, on September 17, 1862. Each side lost more than 2,000 killed. Lee returned to Virginia and set up headquarters at Fredericksburg. McClellan's failure to crush Lee's army at Antietam angered the North. Also, the Union army was kept idle in October. On November 7, President Lincoln removed McClellan from command, ending McClellan's military career. General Ambrose Burnside replaced him and, December 13, 1862, sent a strong Union army to make attacks on the front of the Confederate lines. The Union army was defeated with heavy losses. Fredericksburg was Burnside's first and last campaign as Union commander. General Joseph Hooker replaced him. After Lee's failure in Maryland, Lincoln said he would declare slaves freed on January 1, 1863. The move to free the slaves was good news to the friends of the Union in England and France.

# *LINCOLN DECLARES ALL OF THE SOUTH'S SLAVES FREE*

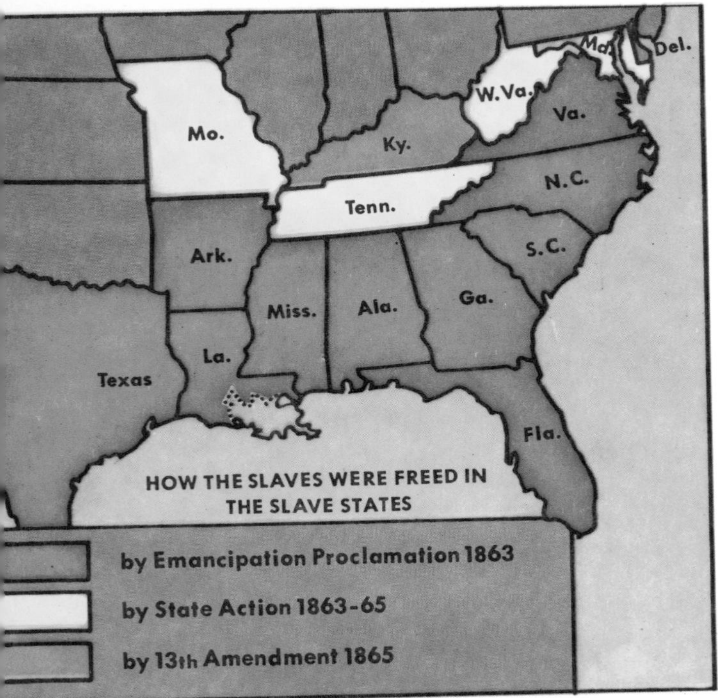


LINCOLN MADE HIS SLAVERY proclamation on January 1, 1863, as he had promised. It was the Emancipation Proclamation, declaring many slaves to be free. Lincoln said that all slaves held in rebellious areas—the South—were "then, thence-forward, and forever free." The proclamation freed few slaves at the time, but it gained its purpose in the long run. Lincoln's proclamation proved to England and other European nations that the Civil War would decide whether there would be slaves in America. Europe, which was against slavery, dropped all ideas of helping the South.

LINCOLN DECLARED the South's slaves free through an order sent under his title as commander-in-chief of America's armed forces. All Presidents of the United States have this title. By using this form, Lincoln's proclamation was a "fit and necessary—or needed—war measure." No action by Congress was needed. Congress already had ended slavery in the territories. In April, 1862, slavery in Washington, D.C., was declared illegal. One million dollars was voted to pay slave owners for their loss. For slaves wishing to leave America, $100,000 was voted for their welfare.

MOST OF THE SLAVES still remained slaves until after the Civil War ended. But as the North's troops captured new territory, all of the Negroes who had been slaves in that land became free. In the South, most of the slaves remained in their old homes with their owners' families. They did their usual tasks on the farms. Many went to battle zones to help their masters. Some former slaves, freed by Union troops, went with them on raiding parties. The Negroes who had been freed were happy about it, but they found it hard to get used to the new way of life.

**As he had promised,** Abraham Lincoln issued his Emancipation Proclamation on January 1, 1863. Lincoln declared that all slaves held by the South were freed.

**The Battle of Gettysburg** saw the Southern army under Lee stopped. Pickett's charge failed and the South's war fortunes had changed. Lee led his army back to Virginia.

THE BATTLE OF GETTYSBURG was a turning point in the war. Fierce fighting in the East had taken place during May and June, 1863. Hooker led 130,000 Union soldiers south of the Rappahannock River in Virginia. They were met by Lee and Jackson with 60,000 men. Jackson struck through the wilderness—a large thickly wooded area—to delay Hooker near Chancellorsville. Lee hit the Union's left flank. After three days of fighting, Hooker withdrew. It was a victory for the South, but its cost was high. The great fighter, "Stonewall" Jackson, was killed by his own men in an accident.

LEE WAS READY TO INVADE! A fight between cavalry fighters—soldiers mounted on horseback—took place at Brandy Station. The South's General "Jeb" Stuart beat back the Union cavalry. With Richard Ewell's cavalry leading the way, Lee marched into Pennsylvania. Hooker resigned, and George C. Meade took his place. The Battle of Gettysburg was at hand, with 75,000 Confederates facing 90,000 troops of the Union.

THE GREAT BATTLE BEGAN on July 1, 1863. Bloody fighting took place on Culp's Hill and Cemetery Ridge during the first two days. General Jubal Early was driven back in a Confederate attack on Culp's Hill. On the third day, Lee ordered Longstreet to launch a mass attack on the center of the Union line. General George E. Pickett led a charge across a mile of open land toward Cemetery Ridge. It was a hopeless and costly charge. Only a few dozen Confederates reached the top of Cemetery Ridge. Pickett's charge had lost. The Battle of Gettysburg was over.

# *LINCOLN HONORS WAR'S DEAD IN GETTYSBURG ADDRESS*

**In his Gettysburg Address,** Lincoln said: "We here highly resolve that these dead shall not have died in vain . . . that this nation shall have a new birth of freedom."

THE GETTYSBURG ADDRESS of President Lincoln was a deathless memorial to the heroic dead of both sides in that great battle. On November 19, 1863, a national military cemetery was dedicated at the Gettysburg battlefield. Edward Everett, the main speaker, talked for two hours. President Lincoln spoke for only two minutes. The night before, Lincoln had told a crowd at Gettysburg that he had no speech. He returned to his room and worked on the speech. He finished it the next morning. This was Lincoln's Gettysburg Address:

"FOUR SCORE AND SEVEN YEARS AGO our fathers brought forth on this continent a new nation, conceived in liberty and dedicated to the proposition that all men are created equal. Now we are engaged in a great civil war, testing whether that nation or any nation so conceived and so dedicated can long endure. We are met on a great battlefield of that war. We have come to dedicate a portion of that field, as a final resting place for those who here gave their lives that the nation might live. It is altogether fitting and proper that we should do this. But, in a larger sense, we cannot dedicate—we cannot consecrate—we cannot hallow—this ground. The brave men, living and dead, who struggled here, have consecrated it, far above our power to add or detract. The world will little note, nor long remember, what we say here, but it can never forget what they did here. It is for us the living, rather, to be dedicated here to the unfinished work which they who fought here have thus far so nobly advanced. It is rather for us to be here dedicated to the great task remaining before us—that from these honored dead we take increased devotion to that cause for which they gave the last full measure of devotion—that we here highly resolve that these dead shall not have died in vain—that this nation, under God, shall have a new birth of freedom—and that government of the people, by the people, for the people, shall not perish from the earth." . . . America has long remembered these words.

## *GRANT CAPTURES VICKSBURG, THE RIVER FORTRESS*

THE CAPTURE OF VICKSBURG was needed by the Union to win full control of the Mississippi River. Vicksburg held a strong position. The Confederacy also held Port Hudson, in Louisiana, to the south of Vicksburg. On this stretch of the river—from Vicksburg to Port Hudson—the South had control. Across this part of the river's banks, food and war supplies, such as guns and bullets, kept pouring in from the West. In the spring of 1863, Grant and his leading general, William Tecumseh Sherman, drove against Vicksburg. Five battles were won in Mississippi.

GRANT LAID SIEGE when he reached Vicksburg's strong position on the Mississippi River. To lay the siege, Grant surrounded the city from the land areas. Union river gunboats shelled Vicksburg from the river. General John C. Pemberton was the Southern commander in Vicksburg. He had 30,000 Confederate soldiers. For six weeks, Vicksburg was put under siege and bombardment. The food supply faded. Vicksburg was in trouble. The city either had to surrender or starve. On July 4, 1863, Pemberton surrendered with all of his troops.

A WEST-TO-EAST SLASH across the Confederacy was the next step planned in the Union's war strategy. General William S. Rosecrans, commander of the Army of the Cumberland, in Tennessee, moved east from Murfreesboro, Tennessee. He arrived near Chattanooga in September. General Braxton Bragg, the Confederate commander at Chattanooga, gave up the city without a fight. Confederate reinforcements arrived and a two-day battle took place near Chickamauga Creek. Rosecrans broke off the battle and led his Union army into Chattanooga. Bragg and his Southern army took to the hills around the city.

GRANT TOOK OVER COMMAND in the Battle of Chattanooga. Union forces under Hooker, Thomas and Sherman attacked Bragg's army on Lookout Mountain. The battle called for a rough charge up the mountain, around large rocks, through gullies, or ditches, and under heavy fire. But Bragg's army was routed. It was driven off Lookout Mountain. The Union army was ready to move into Georgia.

**Grant laid siege** to Vicksburg and forced the strong Confederate river city to surrender. The North then controlled all of the lands along the Mississippi River.

## *GRANT IS GIVEN COMMAND OF ALL UNION ARMIES*

LINCOLN HAD FOUND the general he needed to win the war—Ulysses Simpson Grant! On March 9, 1864, Grant was given full command of all Union armies. A month later, he launched a drive on Richmond. Grant led the main attack himself and for six weeks pushed south in the war's bloodiest fighting. Grant lost 18,000 men in three days in the Battle of the Wilderness. Grant lost 12,000 more in the Battle of Spottsylvania. But Lee also suffered big losses. His great cavalry general, "Jeb" Stuart, was killed. Another costly battle was fought at Cold Harbor on the Chickahominy River. By now Grant's losses in this campaign were 60,000 men and Lee's were about 25,000. Lee could not stand such big losses and took his army into Richmond. Grant attacked Petersburg, near Richmond, but lost 8,000 men. Grant then laid siege to both Richmond and Petersburg.

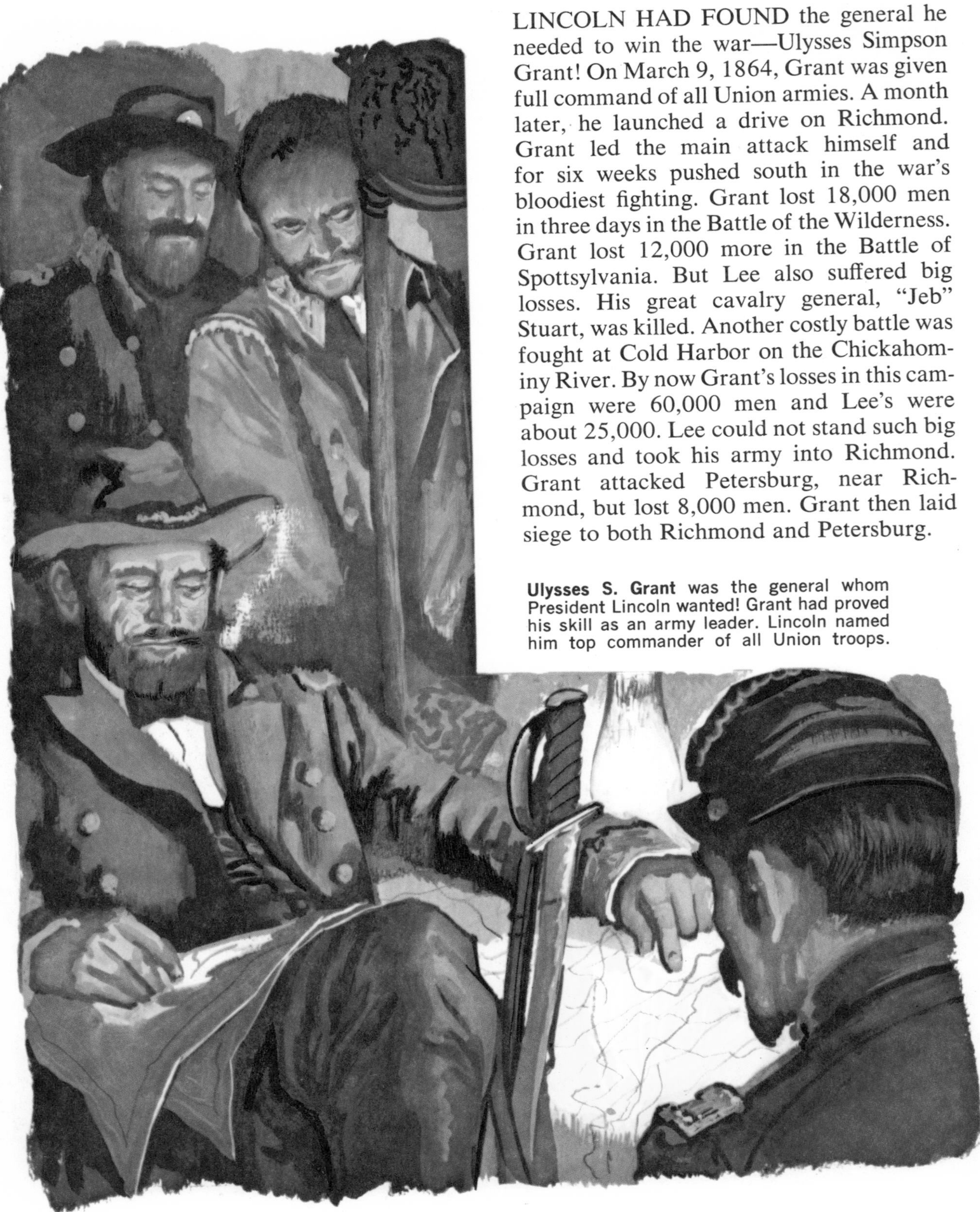

**Ulysses S. Grant** was the general whom President Lincoln wanted! Grant had proved his skill as an army leader. Lincoln named him top commander of all Union troops.

## *SHERMAN MAKES BLAZING MARCH THROUGH GEORGIA*

SHERMAN MARCHED on Atlanta as the Union began its drive across the middle of the Confederacy. Sherman had been given command of the Western armies after Grant became the commander of all Union armies. Sherman had 100,000 battle-hardened soldiers. General Joseph E. Johnston had 60,000 Confederates blocking Sherman's way. The Confederates pounded the Union army as it marched toward Atlanta, but Sherman kept on going. Jefferson Davis, president of the Confederacy, sent General John Bell Hood to take Johnston's place as Southern commander. Hood fell back into Atlanta. On September 1, 1864, he was forced to evacuate the city and Sherman's army moved in. Sherman burned or wrecked Atlanta's mills, factories and shops.

ONWARD TOWARD THE SEA marched Sherman. He left Atlanta with 60,000 cavalrymen and infantry. He started for Savannah, on the Atlantic Ocean. Only small and weak Confederate forces stood in Sherman's way. The big Union army left a long trail of burned-out and wrecked lands behind it as it marched through Georgia. The trail of ruin was 300 miles long and thirty miles on each side. Sherman wanted to destroy the land so that no Southern troops could live on it. He told his own soldiers to take whatever food they could as they marched toward the sea. Cotton gins, factories and warehouses were left in ruins.

SHERMAN DROVE close to Savannah on December 10, 1864. He captured Fort McAllister, to the south of the city. Sherman then began an attack on Savannah to end his march through Georgia. Sherman in his report to General Grant told of large amounts of food, cattle and chickens seized. He also told of freeing "countless numbers of slaves." Sherman said 100 million dollars damage was done to Georgia property.

**Sherman** began his march to the sea. He captured Atlanta on September 1, 1864, and burned or wrecked many of the city's factories. Sherman then marched to the sea.

**Robert E. Lee** took over command of all Southern forces. The outlook for the South was bleak as powerful Union armies closed in on all sides. The end was near.

THE BATTLE OF MOBILE BAY brought one of the North's biggest naval victories of the war. The North's blockading of the South's coasts was slowly choking the South as supplies were cut off. Mobile was the South's last port which was still open on the Gulf of Mexico. Confederate gunboats and ships, which slipped through the Union blockade, used the Mobile port as a safe place to stay. Rear Admiral Farragut steamed into Mobile Bay on August 5, 1864, with four Union ironclads leading his battle line of warships. Troops under General Gordon Granger captured Dauphin Island, one of four islands guarding Mobile Bay. The other forts were hammered by the Union warships' cannon. Farragut's ironclads badly damaged the Confederate warships and Admiral Franklin Buchanan, the Southern commander, surrendered his force.

FIERCE FIGHTING IN THE HILLS marked the battle for Tennessee. The finish came in the Battle of Nashville, December 15-16, 1864. The fighting spread into the hills around Nashville. General Hood and his Confederates got behind stone walls and fallen trees on the hills and fought the Union soldiers from there. The Union army finally defeated the Confederates by rushing at them in a cavalry and bayonet charge. Hood resigned, and some of his men moved on to join other Southern forces.

GENERAL ROBERT E. LEE was named commander-in-chief of all Confederate forces on February 6, 1865. He took over what was left of a once great and strong army. The South now was facing defeat and its cause was lost. Lee had only two armies left in the field, his own in Virginia and Beauregard's in the Carolinas. The *Alabama,* most famous of the Confederacy's sea raiders, had been sunk by the *Kearsarge* off France. Lee had little chance.

## *GRANT TAKES RICHMOND—THE SOUTH SURRENDERS*

THE END CAME QUICKLY in Lee's fight to keep the Civil War going. He tried to break through Grant's army surrounding Richmond and Petersburg. Lee's final attack of the war was a blow at the left side of Grant's line in the Battle of Five Forks. Lee was defeated and moved his now small army out of Richmond and Petersburg. He was soon trapped by Grant and General Philip H. Sheridan. Lee met Grant at Appomattox Courthouse on April 9, 1865, and surrendered. Grant gave Lee generous terms. All of Lee's men were given permission to return to their homes. The Confederate officers kept their pistols and swords. Grant ordered 25,000 meals served to the hungry Confederate army.

SHERMAN WON THE WAR in the Carolinas. He had marched from Georgia into these states. During an assault on Columbia, South Carolina, a fire had destroyed the heart of the city. Each side blamed the other for starting the fire. Sherman pushed into North Carolina from South Carolina. General Johnston, now back in command of the Southern troops, fought hard to stop Sherman's advance. But Sherman reached Goldsboro and then moved on to Raleigh. Johnston surrendered to him at Durham.

THE FINAL SURRENDER of other Confederate forces came quickly. At Citronella, Alabama, on May 4, General Richard Taylor surrendered to General Edward R. S. Canby all remaining Southern troops east of the Mississippi River. On May 26, General Kirby Smith surrendered Western forces to Canby at New Orleans. On May 10, Jefferson Davis, president of the Confederacy, was captured in Georgia. The war ended.

**The South** came to the sad end of a losing cause. Lee surrendered to Grant. Soon other Confederate soldiers also surrendered. The Confederates were allowed to go home.

# *PRESIDENT LINCOLN IS KILLED BY AN ASSASSIN*

**Lincoln was assassinated** only a few days before his great fight to save the Union was won. He was shot by John Wilkes Booth in Ford's Theater in Washington.

LINCOLN WAS ASSASSINATED as the war was about to end. The President was shot to death by John Wilkes Booth at Ford's Theater in Washington on the night of April 14, 1865. Lincoln was taken to a rooming house across the street. He died the next morning. He had been unconscious ever since Booth's bullet hit him. Lincoln spent his last days happy in knowing that the Civil War was about to end. On April 4, the President had visited Richmond, after General Lee left. Lincoln shook hands with 6,000 sick and wounded soldiers in Richmond hospitals. On April 9, he had received word at Washington of Lee's surrender at Appomattox Courthouse.

ON APRIL 11, Lincoln made his last public talk and held his last cabinet meeting. At both of these events the President pleaded that the South be treated generously after the war. On the evening of his assassination, President and Mrs. Lincoln attended a performance of "Our American Cousin" at Ford's Theater. Lincoln's flag-draped box seats extended over the edge of the stage. During the third act, the audience was startled by the sound of a pistol shot. A man leaped from Lincoln's box seats, tripped over the flag drapery, and ran shouting across the theater stage. Mrs. Lincoln screamed as she saw the President lean forward in his chair in the box, blood dripping on his white collar.

LINCOLN HAD BEEN SHOT at the base of his neck. He was carried to the rooming house, owned by William Peterson. The stricken President was placed on a bed in a narrow room and died there shortly before 7:30 A.M. on April 15. Within three hours, Vice-President Andrew Johnson took the oath as President. Lincoln's assassin, Booth, very deeply devoted to the Southern cause, was tracked down and cornered in a barn near Bowling Green, Virginia. The barn was set afire and a shot rang out. Booth was found dead inside the barn. Three men and one woman were hanged for plotting Lincoln's death.

SLAVERY WAS ENDED in the United States and all of its territories by the Thirteenth Amendment. The amendment was passed by Congress on January 31, 1865. It became effective on December 18, after being ratified, or approved, by twenty-seven states. The Thirteenth Amendment said: "Neither slavery nor involuntary servitude, except as punishment for crime whereof the party shall have been duly convicted, shall exist within the United States, or any place subject to its jurisdiction." The long struggle over slavery was ended—America was the land of the free.

THE CIVIL WAR'S COST in human lives was among the greatest in American history. A total of 3,200,000 men served in the armies and navies of the North and South. Some 992,500 of them were casualties, either killed or wounded. The North's losses in men were placed at 359,500 killed, 110,000 of them in battle, and 275,000 wounded. The South's casualty total was put at 258,000 killed, 94,000 of them as a result of battle wounds, and more than 100,000 wounded. The damage done to property could not even be estimated. The South had much of its land and many buildings wrecked. Farms were torn up. Big cities, with most of their factories, were badly damaged.

ALL SLAVES WERE legally freed by the Thirteenth Amendment. In March, 1865, Congress had created a Freedmen's Bureau, to help the freed slaves find new lives. The Bureau helped both the freed blacks and whites made poor by the war. After the Emancipation Proclamation, Negroes were invited to join the Union army. About 180,000 volunteered by the end of the war. Blacks fought in 499 clashes, 39 of them listed as battles. The blacks' casualty ratio was high.

**Congress passed** the Thirteenth Amendment. abolishing slavery in the United States. All former American slaves were now free.

PLANS FOR RECONSTRUCTION, or rebuilding, of the South occupied Lincoln's final days. Lincoln wanted no "revenge" on, or "getting even" with, the South. Reconstruction, he told a crowd from the White House balcony two days before his death, must be worked out by the President and the Congress. But slavery must go. The actions of the Confederate government must be disowned. And state governments must be put into the hands of citizens loyal to the Union, even if these loyal citizens were only 10 per cent of the population.

OTHER LEADERS wanted more than the end of slavery and secession. Senator Charles Sumner of Massachusetts believed that the states of the South had committed "state suicide." Congressman Thaddeus Stevens of Pennsylvania saw the South as "conquered territory." Radical Republicans led by Sumner and Stevens wanted to remake the whole Southern way of life.

ANDREW JOHNSON, the self-made man from Eastern Tennessee, had been the only Southern senator to remain in the Senate chamber in 1861. A strong Unionist and a Democrat, he joined Lincoln's ticket in 1864 to bring "War Democrats" to the Republican cause. By the end of 1865, as Lincoln's successor, he reconstructed all the former Confederate states except Texas, by Presidential order. These reconstructed state governments passed the "Black Codes" which fined Negroes for vagrancy and forced them to work out their fines in labor. To many it looked like slavery under another name.

JOHNSON LACKED LINCOLN'S SKILL in persuading Congress to follow his leadership. He vetoed, or rejected, bills to grant citizenship to all Negroes born in the United States, bills to provide equal benefits under the law, and those designed to extend the Freedman's Bureau. The "Black Codes" and these vetoes so alarmed many moderates that they supported the radical Republicans and re-passed the bills by a two-thirds vote. Relations were bitter.

**Andrew Johnson,** on becoming President, planned to carry on Lincoln's policies of fairness toward the South, but he met opposition from some Republicans in Congress.

# PRESIDENT JOHNSON'S RECONSTRUCTION PLANS BLOCKED

**Federal soldiers and Negro Militia** enrolled voters in the South. After Congress divided the South into military districts, five states had more Negro voters than white.

JOHNSON'S FIGHT with Congress grew more bitter as the months passed. The Committee of Fifteen tried to take reconstruction out of the President's hands. In the elections of 1866, Republicans won two-thirds of the seats in each house of Congress. This gave the radical Republicans control over reconstruction. Two acts were passed which cut President Johnson's power. One was a Tenure of Office Act. It forbade the President to remove certain officials from office without first obtaining the Senate's permission. The other new law was the Command of the Army Act, which said that only the general of the Army—Grant—could give military orders. The Tenure Act was passed after Johnson put several persons out of office when they tried to block his plans. The Army Command Act was aimed at giving Secretary of War Stanton power over President Johnson.

CONGRESS' NEXT MOVE was to establish military rule in the South. In March, 1867, an act was passed over Johnson's veto dividing the South into five military districts, or areas. Johnson was told to name commanders of the Southern districts and all had to have the rank, or title, of general. These commanders led 20,000 soldiers and Negro militiamen into the South. Congress ordered the military commanders to make lists of all voters, white and black. The commanders could decide whether to let former Confederate soldiers vote. A total of 703,000 Negroes and 627,000 whites were listed as voters. In five southern states, more Negro than white voters were listed.

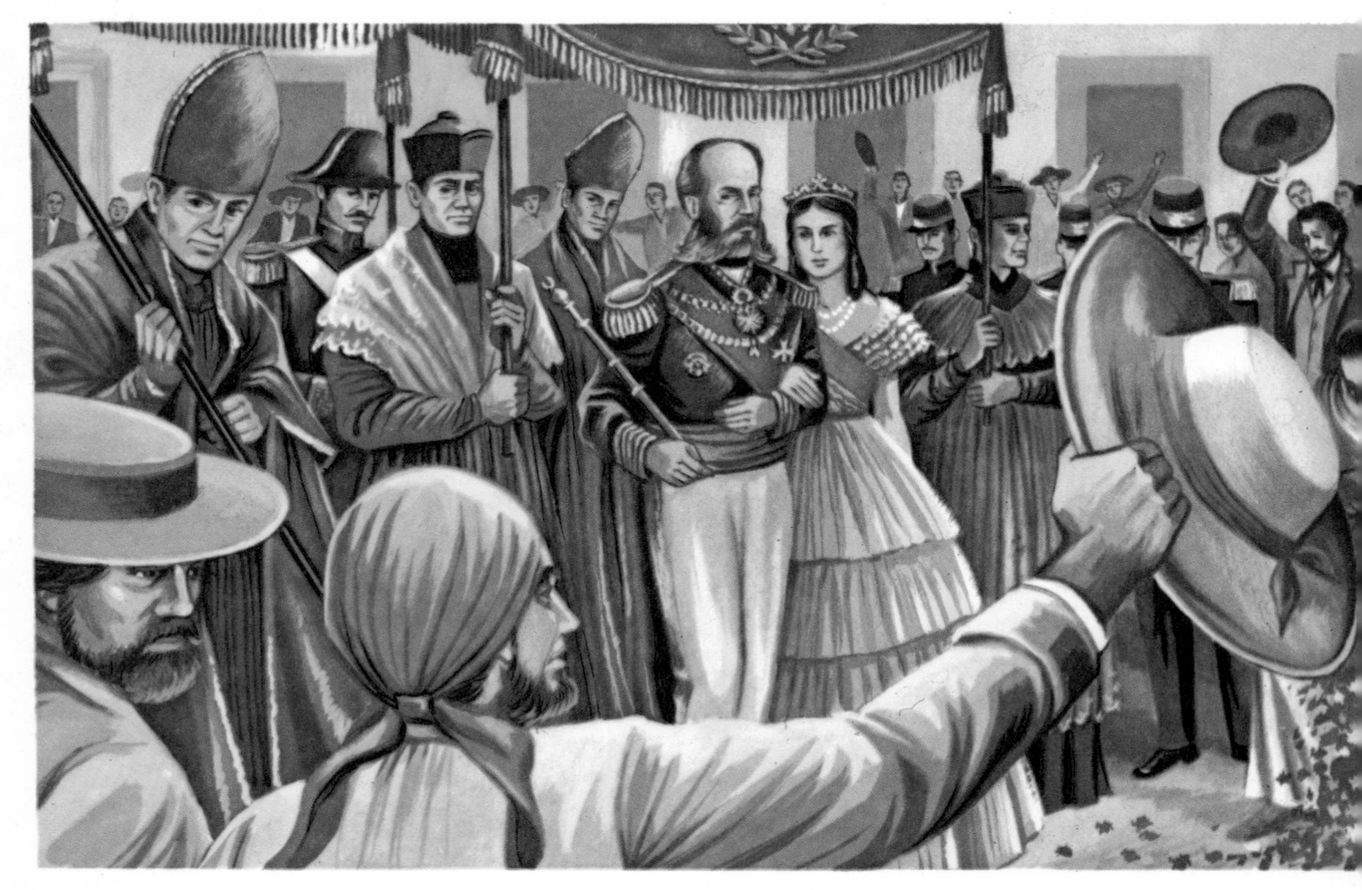

**Archduke Maximilian** of Austria paid with his life when his dream of ruling Mexico as emperor ended. Left alone by French troops, Maximilian was captured and killed.

ARCHDUKE MAXIMILIAN of Austria was put on a throne as the emperor of Mexico by Napoleon III of France in 1864. The United States said this was against the Monroe Doctrine. But the Civil War was being fought at that time and America could not force Napoleon III out of Mexico. The French ruler had many troops in Mexico to make sure that no harm came to Maximilian or his wife, Carlotta, a daughter of the king of Belgium. After the Civil War ended, the United States took steps to force Napoleon III to take his troops out of Mexico. Secretary of State Seward told the French government to call its troops home. General Grant sent 50,000 American soldiers under General Philip H. Sheridan to the Texas-Mexico border. Napoleon III called his troops home in the spring of 1867, leaving Maximilian to his fate.

MAXIMILIAN TRIED HARD to get help. His empress, Carlotta, went to France and begged Napoleon to help Maximilian, but Napoleon gave no help. Benito Juarez, a full-blooded Indian, was stirring up the Mexicans to fight against Maximilian. Juarez's Mexican guerrillas, or bandits, arrested Maximilian and ordered that he be killed. The United States and several European nations tried to save Maximilian. But he refused to leave Mexico. He said his pride would not let him leave the country which he "had made his own." Maximilian could not escape death. Juarez said he was going to "make an example" of Maximilian. On June 19, 1867, Maximilian died before a firing squad, his days of glory ended.

JOHNSON WAS IMPEACHED when he fired Stanton as Secretary of War. Congress had passed a law saying the President could not do that. The House voted to impeach, or bring charges against, the President. The vote was 126 to 47. Johnson was accused of eleven things, including "breaking the law" by firing Stanton. The biggest charge against Johnson was that he had shown no respect for Congress. The trial was held in the Senate with Chief Justice Salmon P. Chase of the Supreme Court as the judge. Members of the Senate acted as jurors, but took no part in the arguments. Johnson did not appear at the trial. The Senate voted on one charge and Johnson was acquitted by one vote. Other charges were dropped. Johnson was the only President of the United States ever impeached.

**Andrew Johnson** was impeached by the House. He faced serious charges of fighting Congress. But the Senate acquitted him.

# *EARLY UNIONS FADE BEFORE STRONG OPPOSITION*

**Philadelphia garment workers** formed the Knights of Labor with Uriah S. Stephens as leader. The Knights held secret meetings because their employers spied on them.

LABOR UNIONS FOUGHT an uphill battle to gain a foothold in America's life and economy. Early unions, both black and white, died out because of their own disunity, employer opposition and unfavorable laws. A National Labor Union was formed in 1866, led by Ira Steward, William H. Sylvis and Richard F. Trevellick.

THE NOBLE ORDER OF THE KNIGHTS of Labor was organized in 1869. The union was formed by Philadelphia garment workers, led by Uriah S. Stephens. The Knights at first were a secret order, because employers planted spies among them. The union was open to all workers, regardless of skill, sex, race or color. By 1886, the Knights had more than 600,000 members, claiming to have 60,000 black members.

BLACK WORKERS BEGAN union organizing. At the end of the Civil War, there were approximately 100,000 black mechanics in the South. The National Colored Labor Union was formed in 1869, with Isaac Myers as the president. Myers said: "The day has passed for the establishment of organizations based on color. We are organizing for the interest of the workingmen, white and colored, and to do this, let the officers be composed of both white and colored men."

IN 1867, FARMERS ORGANIZED the National Grange, or Patrons of Husbandry (agriculture). Oliver Hudson Kelly, a clerk in the Bureau of Agriculture at Washington, organized the Grangers – a secret order at first. The Grangers fought for better railroad freight rates. Congress had passed two acts in 1862 which greatly benefited farming–the Homestead Act and Morrill Land Grant Act for colleges.

**Isaac Myers** headed the National Colored Labor Union, formed in 1869. Myers urged as his union's policy: "Let the officers include white and colored men."

**Ulysses S. Grant,** the Civil War hero and winning general, was elected eighteenth President of the United States. The nation showed its liking for Grant in a huge vote.

ULYSSES S. GRANT, the North's hero of the Civil War, was elected eighteenth President of the United States. Grant was nominated on the first ballot when the 1868 Republican convention was held in Chicago. Grant defeated his Democratic opponent, Horatio Seymour, 214 electoral votes to 80. Grant began what was to be an eight-year administration. His two terms were full of dishonest acts. But none of the dishonesty was blamed on Grant. In his first year as President, a panic hit the New York Stock Exchange. It was caused by a day of large losses called " Black Friday." Grant himself stopped the plot to buy up all the gold, which had caused "Black Friday."

JAY GOULD AND JAMES FISKE tried to "corner," or buy up, the gold market. As they bought more gold, the market price of gold went higher. This meant more money for Gould and Fiske. President Grant learned about the plot and ordered the United States Treasury to sell $4,000,000 in gold on the open market. In half an hour, the price of gold dropped from 162 points to 135. Gould had sold his gold before the price dropped and he made several million dollars. Fiske had held his gold and he lost everything he had gambled.

THE TWEED RING stole some $100,000,000 from New York. It was one of the greatest thefts of public money in history. William Marcy Tweed headed the ring, or gang, which took the money from the New York treasury. Faked papers were used, claiming that New York owed money which it did not. Congress caused a scandal by voting itself a salary raise. Public protest forced Congress to cancel the raise. The public still had great confidence in Grant. He was reelected President in 1872 with 286 electoral votes to 66 won by his opponent, Horace Greeley, a New York editor.

# INDIANS WENT ON WARPATH IN THE WEST! TRIBES WERE MOVED TO RESERVATIONS

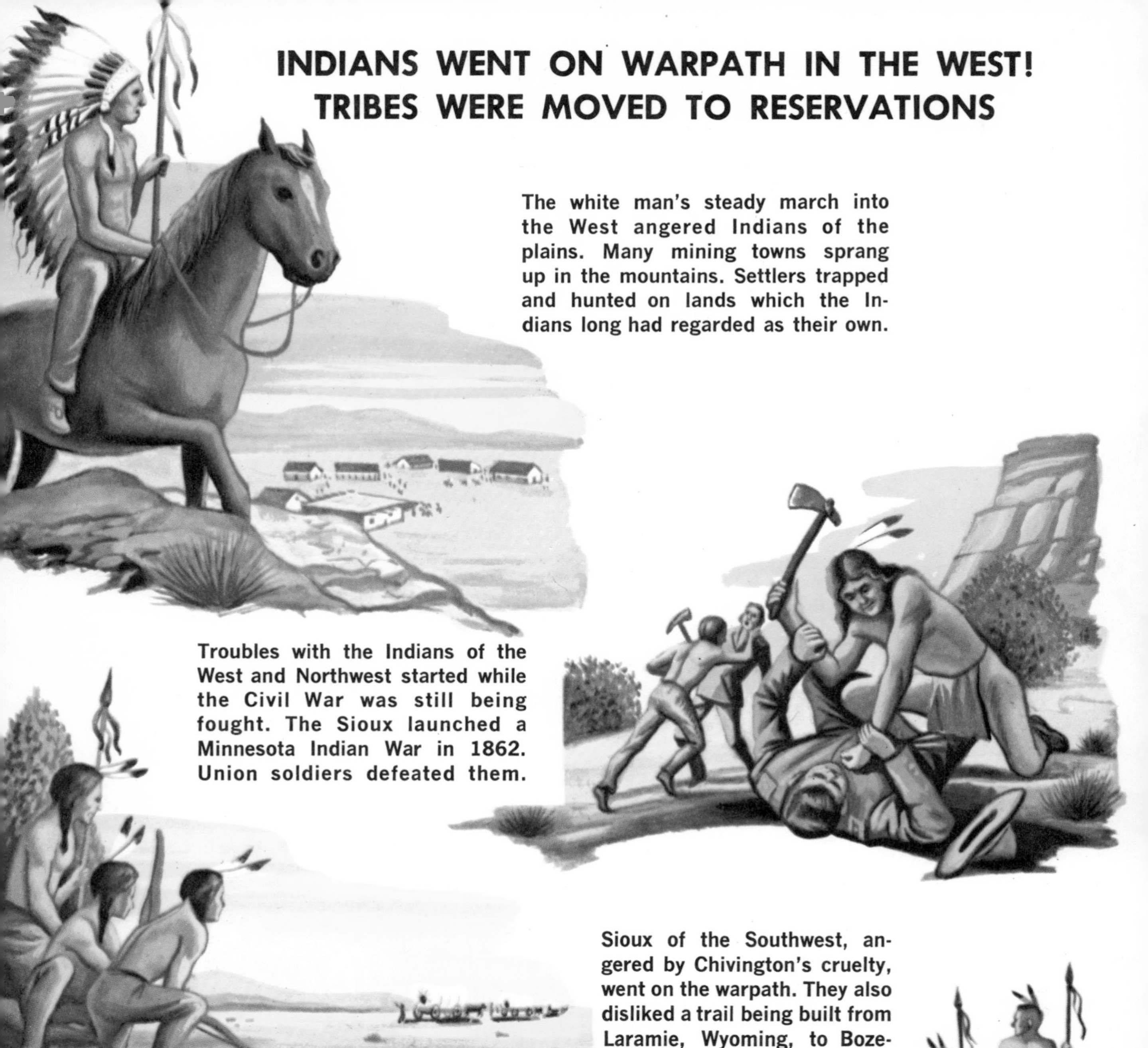

The white man's steady march into the West angered Indians of the plains. Many mining towns sprang up in the mountains. Settlers trapped and hunted on lands which the Indians long had regarded as their own.

Troubles with the Indians of the West and Northwest started while the Civil War was still being fought. The Sioux launched a Minnesota Indian War in 1862. Union soldiers defeated them.

A Cheyenne-Arapahoe War in Colorado lasted from 1861 to 1864. Mining camps were raided and wagon trains were attacked. The tribes asked for peace and returned to their camp at Sand Creek. Troops under Colonel J. M. Chivington surprised and killed several hundred.

Sioux of the Southwest, angered by Chivington's cruelty, went on the warpath. They also disliked a trail being built from Laramie, Wyoming, to Bozeman, Montana, through their favorite hunting grounds. The Sioux War lasted for three years and spread across nearly all of the western plains.

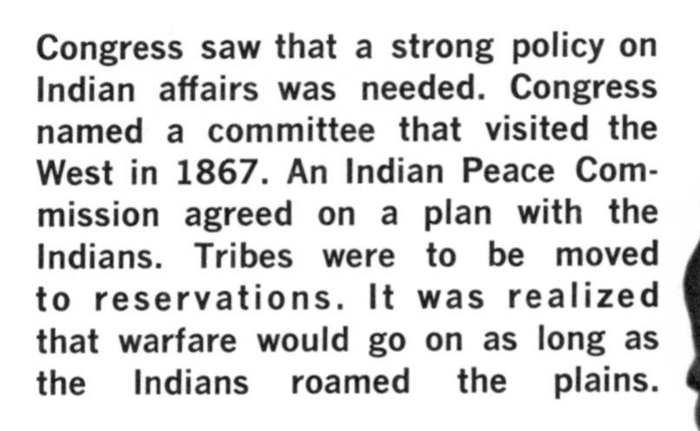

Congress saw that a strong policy on Indian affairs was needed. Congress named a committee that visited the West in 1867. An Indian Peace Commission agreed on a plan with the Indians. Tribes were to be moved to reservations. It was realized that warfare would go on as long as the Indians roamed the plains.

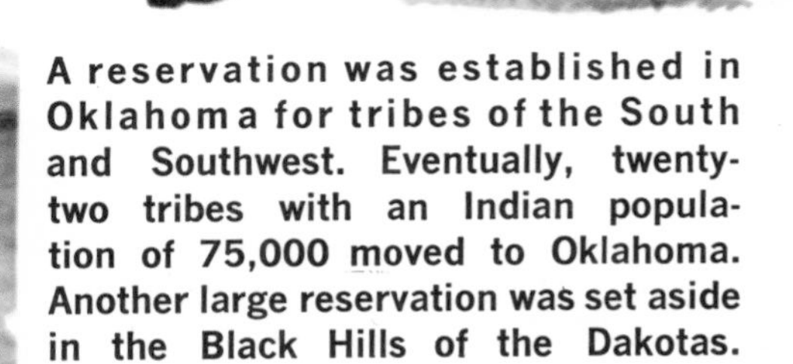

A reservation was established in Oklahoma for tribes of the South and Southwest. Eventually, twenty-two tribes with an Indian population of 75,000 moved to Oklahoma. Another large reservation was set aside in the Black Hills of the Dakotas.

Indians of the plains were angered as the once large buffalo herds were reduced in size. White hunters killed many thousands of the buffalo, the main food source for the Indians.

Tribes did not like being taken from their regular homes. Sioux Indians fought new wars in Wyoming and Nebraska. Trouble broke out in the Black Hills. George Custer and 264 of his soldiers were killed by Sioux on the Little Big Horn River.

**Negroes were granted** equal civil rights and voting privileges by the Fourteenth and Fifteenth Amendments. The fight to end many racial injustices had begun.

NEGROES WERE GUARANTEED equal civil rights and voting privileges by the Fourteenth and Fifteenth Amendments to the Constitution. The Fourteenth Amendment was passed by Congress in 1866, and was ratified by the states in 1868. It said that Negroes were American citizens and had the same rights as any other citizens. No citizen could be denied these rights without due process of law. A long uphill fight for Negroes' rights began with this amendment.

THE FOURTEENTH AMENDMENT forbade the holding of public office, civil or military, by any former Confederate who before the war had taken an oath of office under the Union. The legality of the public debt of the United States was declared. But the war debts of the Confederacy and all of its states were disowned. Claims for payment for the loss of slaves were ruled out as illegal. Ratification of the amendment was made necessary before a seceded state would be readmitted to the United States. Tennessee ratified the Fourteenth Amendment and was the first state to gain readmission to the Union.

THE FIFTEENTH AMENDMENT, ratified by the states in March, 1870, guaranteed voting rights for Negroes. The amendment said that: "The rights of citizens of the United States could not be denied or abridged by the United States or by any individual state on account of race, color or any previous condition of servitude." Reunion of the United States was completed after the Fifteenth Amendment went into effect. Mississippi, Virginia and Texas ratified the amendments and were restored to the Union. Georgia also ratified. On an order by Congress, Georgia was forced to readmit Negroes kept out of the state legislature. With the readmission of Georgia in July, 1870, all eleven of the former seceded states were back in the Union.

PUTTING THE FIFTEENTH AMENDMENT up for a vote by the states was delayed for political reasons. The voting was delayed until after the election of 1868. In the campaign before the election, the Republicans said that Negro voting rights were necessary in the South. In the North, however, the Republicans said that the Negroes' right to vote was a matter for each state to decide for itself. After Ulysses S. Grant was elected President, the Republicans in Congress announced that the people's vote was an order for Congress to write Negro voting rights into the Constitution. The Fifteenth Amendment forced some of the Northern states, as well as the South, to accept voting by Negroes. The North had not been fully in favor of this move. In the 1868 election, Negroes were not allowed to vote in Ohio, which for many years had fought to abolish slavery. Negroes also were denied voting rights in Kansas. A few other states of the Union in the past had also voted to deny Negro voting rights.

**All federal troops** were withdrawn from the South. "Black Reconstruction" had ended. The new President, Rutherford B. Hayes, made good his election promise.

RUTHERFORD B. HAYES kept an election promise and called back the last federal troops from the South in April, 1877. The 1876 Presidential election between Hayes and Samuel J. Tilden had ended in a dispute. An electoral commission ruled that Hayes was elected and Hayes promised that reconstruction in the South would be ended. When the Union troops left Louisiana and South Carolina, things happened fast. Republicans holding office in New Orleans left their posts at once, and Democratic leaders moved in. The same thing happened in Columbia, South Carolina. All nine of the other former Confederate states already had won back power in their governments. Florida had installed a Democratic governor in office.

"BLACK RECONSTRUCTION" had been a period of hardship and strife. Under "carpetbaggers"—Northern politicians who moved into the South and seized office—dishonest government was the usual thing. The Ku Klux Klan had been formed and had risen against the "carpetbaggers" and reconstruction rule. "Carpetbaggers" and Negro leaders had been mistreated. The Klansmen used such terror tactics as flogging, tarring and feathering, and even murder. Congress passed laws against the Klan.

**Laws failed to stop** the Ku Klux Klan's beatings of Negroes and other acts of terror against minority groups in the South.

"JIM CROW" LAWS were passed in the South and stirred up new racial troubles in America. The Ku Klux Klan, in spite of the laws against it, kept on mistreating Negroes for nearly 100 years. In 1881, Tennessee passed the first "Jim Crow" law. This law denied the Negroes equal rights in riding on public carriers. The first "Jim Crow" law said that Negroes had to have separate sections on trains. Later, as other Southern states passed "Jim Crow" laws, buses and streetcars were included. Negroes were given separate sections, usually in the rear of the bus, and even there Negro riders could not take seats while any white man or woman stood. Florida, Mississippi, Texas and Louisiana soon followed Tennessee's lead by adopting "Jim Crow" laws. It was the beginning of segregation. This was to become one of America's most bitter issues —the segregation of many public services.

THE CIVIL RIGHTS ACT of 1875 was declared unconstitutional by the Supreme Court in 1883. The 1875 law had given Negroes equal rights and service in such public places as restaurants, hotels and theaters. The Supreme Court ruled that the act protected social rather than civil or political rights. In 1890, Mississippi barred Negroes from politics by adopting hard tests for Negroes to pass before they could get voting rights.

A "SEPARATE BUT EQUAL" policy in services for Negroes was upheld by the Supreme Court in 1896. This set an example for more segregation of Negroes. It was not until fifty-eight years later that the Supreme Court reversed the ruling and ordered white and Negro children admitted to the same schools.

# AMERICA BECAME A WORLD POWER

TWO GREAT INVENTORS gave to America and the world new inventions which were called miracles at the time. Today, they are just part of everyday living in most homes. Alexander Graham Bell invented the telephone, and Thomas Alva Edison made the first home light bulb that really gave out light. On March 10, 1876, Bell showed, at Boston, the first telephone over which talking could be heard and understood. He organized the Bell Telephone Company in 1877.

BELL, BORN IN SCOTLAND, was a professor in the school of speech at Boston University. His father had invented a system for the deaf and dumb to "talk" with finger signals. Young Bell became a teacher of the deaf. He invented a "speaking telegraph." Operated by electricity, the "telegraph" recorded and repeated sounds of the voice. The telephone was developed from this invention. In 1880, Bell invented a photophone, carrying sounds by light.

THOMAS ALVA EDISON's new light bulb was described as incandescent. In October, 1879, Edison closed a switch in his research laboratory at Menlo Park, New Jersey, and showed how it worked. Electricity flowed into a glass bulb and a wire thread inside became white hot. It was this blazing little thread that gave off the light.

HOMES AND OFFICES now could be lighted by the pressing of a button or pulling of a switch. Arc lamps already had been invented to provide street lighting. But Edison's bulb was the first to provide lighting inside buildings. Edison, who was called the Wizard of Electricity, was a tireless worker. It was said that he could "cat nap" for half an hour and then wake up fresh and ready for more work. Edison did not work alone. He had a large staff of experts to help in his Menlo Park laboratory.

**Edison** gave to America and the world the electric light bulb. The Wizard of Electricity was a tireless worker. He could take a half hour's nap and wake up refreshed.

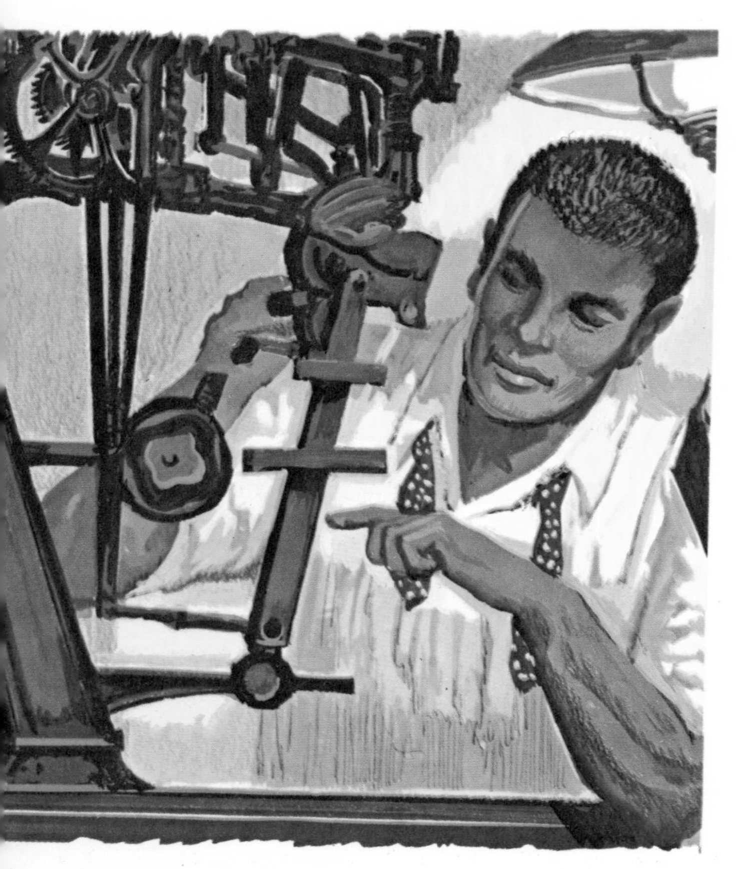

**Jan Matzeliger,** a black inventor, perfected a shoe-lasting machine making shoe manufacturing faster and easier. He sold his patent and others profited from his idea.

THE GENIUS OF AMERICA'S inventors steadily improved the machinery which built up the nation's industry. In the twenty years from 1870 to 1890 important inventions stepped up the pace. Jan Matzeliger, a black from Dutch Guiana, in 1883, invented a shoe-lasting machine that in time helped make Lynn, Massachusetts, one of America's leading shoe manufacturing centers. When perfected, Matzeliger's machine could gather a shoe's materials—sole and upper—fasten them together, and turn out the finished shoe in minutes. Matzeliger came to the United States when eighteen years old and worked in a shoe factory at Philadelphia. He moved to Lynn, Massachusetts, where he perfected his shoe-lasting machine.

BIG CITY MASS TRANSPORTATION for the public had its beginning in the 1870's. Andrew S. Hallidie invented a cable streetcar in 1871 and two years later San Francisco tried it out on one of the city's steep hills. The cable cars became familiar tourist sights in San Francisco far into the Twentieth Century. Stephen Dudley Field invented the first electrically powered streetcar. Field's streetcar, often called a "trolley" because of the long pole which connected with overhead electric wires, had its first successful run in New York City in 1874. America's fast-growing business also received boosts. William S. Burroughs perfected the adding machine in 1888. Door E. Felt introduced the comptometer, or calculating machine, in 1884.

ELIJAH MC COY, black inventor, patented nearly sixty inventions, starting in 1872. McCoy's inventions were devices for lubricating, or oiling, heavy-duty machinery's parts. One of his inventions was a "drip cup," a cup filled with oil which flowed to the moving parts. The "drip cup" system of lubrication was used in many large industrial machines. McCoy, born in Canada, moved to Ypsilanti, Michigan, after the Civil War and did much of his work there. Lewis Howard Latimer was another black inventor, who worked with Bell and Edison. Still another was Granville T. Woods, who, in 1887, patented a railroad telegraphic system which kept each train warned of movements of the trains immediately behind and ahead of it.

OTHER INVENTIONS of the period covered a wide field. In 1875, William A. Anthony built the first dynamo to generate, or produce, electricity for lighting systems. In 1890, Charles B. King patented a pneumatic (air pressure) hammer, which was a great aid in construction and street repair work. In 1888, George Eastman invented and patented the "Kodak" hand camera—a big boost to photography.

**President Garfield** was shot in the back by Guiteau, a crazed lawyer who had been refused a political job in Washington. Chester A. Arthur became the new President.

JAMES A. GARFIELD was America's second President to be killed by an assassin, or murdered. Lincoln was the first. Garfield was shot only a few months after becoming President. On July 2, 1881 Garfield walked into the Washington railroad station to take a train to attend a meeting a Elberon, New Jersey. In those days, Presidents had little personal protection when they appeared in public. As Garfield walked through the crowd in the station, a man stepped out of the crowd behind him, and shot the President in the back. The gunman was Charles J. Guiteau, a crazed Chicago lawyer who had been refused a job by Washington politicians.

GARFIELD DID NOT DIE IMMEDIATELY. He clung to life throughout the summer, but finally died on September 19, at Elberon. Chester A. Arthur, the Vice-President, took office as the new President. Garfield had been an Ohio Civil War hero. He was one of many national leaders who came from Ohio, and the state mourned the death of its native son. On November 14, Guiteau, who was a French-Canadian by birth, was found guilty of Garfield's murder and was hanged on June 30, 1882.

PRESIDENT GARFIELD'S MURDER brought on a cry for reform, or change, in politicians giving their friends government jobs. The public demand resulted in civil service reform. The new Civil Service Act, passed on January 16, 1883, was a blow to political job hunters, but a relief to those who were willing to work hard at their jobs. The Civil Service program offered a fair and equal plan for hiring government workers. A three-man board was created to conduct tests for federal job seekers. The tests were given to all. The persons with the highest grades were hired for the jobs. Once he was hired under Civil Service, the worker was protected. He could be discharged only if he failed in his duties or was found to be dishonest. He could not be forced to give money to political campaigns, as he had to do in the past.

**A public demand for reform** in hiring of federal workers brought on Civil Service. Job seekers were given tests and those making the highest grades won the jobs.

**America built** a "steel navy." The new warships had steel armor plate. Their guns fired larger shells that could reach their targets at a distance of many miles.

GROVER CLEVELAND was elected in 1884 as the first Democratic President in twenty-three years. The last Democratic President had been James Buchanan, who left office early in 1861 following the election of Lincoln. Cleveland was the only President to serve in two different terms, four years apart. He was defeated by Benjamin Harrison in 1888, but then was elected President again in 1892. As a result, Cleveland's name appears twice on the list of Presidents—first as the twenty-second and then as the twenty-fourth.

A NEW "STEEL NAVY" which raised America's standing among world sea powers was a great gain during Cleveland's terms. By 1884, America had sunk to twelfth place among the world's navies. The building of three steel cruisers was the beginning of the modern new navy which America had decided to build. On August 3, 1886, further shipbuilding and strengthening of the Navy Department were decided upon. William C. Whitney of New York, Secretary of the Navy, began a rebuilding program. He rushed the laying of keels for additional steel warships. He dealt with American steel producers to manufacture heavy steel plates as armor for ships' hulls and decks. Within three year's Whitney's program built twenty-two modern warships. America's "steel navy" was well under way!

A NAVAL WAR COLLEGE was established at Newport, Rhode Island. The college was created to give selected officers advanced training in modern naval methods and to instruct them in international laws of the seas. Captain Alfred Thayer Mahan, naval historian and leader, became an instructor. Mahan taught the lessons of how sea power had influenced world history.

AMERICA BEGAN TO LOOK outward and began to display a new interest in world affairs. With many of its post-Civil War problems settled, America turned its thinking toward winning a place in world leadership. Alfred Mahan, then a lecturer at the Naval War College, had much influence on U.S. national policy at the time. In 1890, Mahan published a book, *The Influence of Seapower Upon History, 1600-1783.* England's rise to a great empire was traced by Mahan to its seapower. Mahan concluded that a nation's greatness and strength depended on its trade and commerce, which had to be protected by a strong navy. At the time, America already was building a new steel navy and Mahan's urging for a further buildup found many listeners.

OVERSEAS BASES were needed, Mahan said, for refueling and repairs to keep the navy prepared to guard the sea lanes. These bases would be strung along the shipping routes. According to Mahan, England's overseas bases kept the British navy always able to support any part of the far-stretched empire. Also, England's navy was able to blockade enemies and cut off supplies in time of war. Mahan believed in America's Manifest Destiny, or obvious certainty, to become a world power. Manifest Destiny was an inspirational belief expressed by many of America's leaders in the middle and late 1800's. Mahan believed that a nation could never stand still —it had to expand, or decline. As America expanded its trade, Mahan said, a strong navy would be needed to protect the trade and back up America's policy.

A CANAL ACROSS THE ISTHMUS of Central America was a necessity, in Mahan's view. A canal between the Atlantic and Pacific Oceans would provide a short cut which would speed America's domestic east-west sea trade, and would permit warships to move quickly from one ocean area to the other. America would need a strong navy, Mahan believed, and also bases to protect such a canal's sea routes. He said that Cuba in the Caribbean and the Hawaiian Islands in the Pacific would be perfect main bases. Mahan's blueprint called for the U.S. to take complete control of the American sea frontier stretching from the Atlantic Coast to the Caribbean to the Pacific Coast. He believed that the European powers should be removed from the canal area as soon as possible.

**Alfred Mahan** believed that America's future strength depended upon a build-up of world trade, defended by a strong navy. He said supply bases would be needed.

ALFRED MAHAN STRONGLY influenced Americans to think in terms of world power. His books and other writings were widely read, both in America and Europe. Theodore Roosevelt, a close friend, believed in Mahan's ideas. In England, Mahan was awarded honorary degrees and dined with the queen. The kaiser made Mahan's writings required reading for Germany's naval officers.

# *FRANCE GIVES U.S. A STATUE OF HOPE FOR THE WORLD*

A GUIDING LIGHT OF LIBERTY rose from a tiny island in New York Harbor and was dedicated by President Cleveland on October 28, 1886. It was the Statue of Liberty, a gift of friendship to America from the people of France. Frederic August Bartholdi, an Alsatian sculptor, came to America after France's defeat by Prussia in 1871. He had an idea of building a monument to freedom, to stand in New York's harbor. Backed by the Franco-American Union, Bartholdi campaigned for donations by citizens of France. Individuals in 180 French cities gave $250,000. Bartholdi sculptured the Statue of Liberty in sections. The statue's sections were shipped to the United States in 214 packing cases. The people of the United States, meanwhile, contributed $250,000 in a campaign to construct a handsome base for the statue. Gustave Eiffel, of Eiffel Tower fame, designed a huge steel supporting framework. New Yorkers watched the day-to-day progress as the cases were unloaded and the statue's parts were fitted together. Finally, the statue was completed and stood high on Bedloe's Island. On the dedication day, thousands of Americans saw the thrilling event. A majestic woman, 151 feet tall, stood on a huge base. In her upraised hand she held a torch, to be lighted every night—the Statue of Liberty, hope for the world.

**The Statue of Liberty,** hope for the world, rose on a small island in New York Harbor.

# *LABOR STRIFE SWEEPS ACROSS U.S. IN LATE 1800'S*

**The bloody Haymarket Riot** at Chicago on May 4, 1886, cost eleven lives. The riot began when a bomb was thrown among police during a meeting held by workers.

CONTROVERSIES AND STRIKES deeply troubled America's labor scene in the final quarter of the Nineteenth Century. The rising trend toward labor unionism and employer opposition led to several major strikes and disorders. In 1877, a railroad strike hit many parts of the country. It began as the result of a rate war between the East's "big four" railroads—the New York Central, Erie, Pennsylvania, and the Baltimore and Ohio. To recover rate losses, the railroads cut workers' pay.

THE STRIKE BEGAN at Martinsburg, West Virginia, and disorders spread into New York, New Jersey, Illinois, Ohio, Michigan, Indiana, Kentucky, Missouri and as far west as California. The Great Railway Strike of 1877 finally was ended—at the point of army guns. Chinese labor troubles reached a climax in California when Chinese "coolies", who worked for low pay, took the jobs of thousands of American workers. Congress in 1882 passed a Chinese Exclusion Act, stopping for ten years the immigration of Chinese laborers. The act was extended in 1892 and 1902.

ONE OF THE MOST VIOLENT labor disorders was the bloody Haymarket Riot in Chicago on May 4, 1886. A national eight-hour campaign was begun and, as part of it, a general strike was called for May Day, 1886. Rioting began on May 3 at the McCormick Harvester plant in Chicago. Four were killed as police moved in. The following evening (May 4), an estimated 2,000 workingmen attended a protest meeting at Chicago's Haymarket Square. A bomb was thrown among police, who then opened fire. Seven police and four workers were killed. Eight anarchists were convicted of causing the riot and four were hanged. Illinois Governor John Peter Altgeld later freed those still in prison.

A STRIKE AT THE HOMESTEAD PLANT of the Carnegie Steel Company, near Pittsburgh, lasted nearly five months—from June 30 to November 12, 1892. Violence began when detectives, hired as plant guards, were fired upon as they rode a barge on the Monongahela River. Seven persons were killed then and others later. In 1894, workers at the Pullman Palace Parlor Car Company plant at Pullman, Illinois, struck when wages were cut. Railroad workers in many areas refused to work on trains which hauled Pullman cars. A new American Railway Union, headed by Eugene V. Debs, joined the strike. Train service was affected in twenty-seven states before federal troops and a court injunction ended the strike.

**Samuel Gompers,** president of the Cigarmakers Union, was chosen as first president of the A.F. of L. With the exception of one year, he was president until 1924.

IN THE MIDST OF LABOR'S unrest, America's workingmen organized a national body of great strength and influence —the American Federation of Labor. It was America's first permanent labor federation and brought together craft, or skilled, unions. The American Federation of Labor was organized at the sixth annual convention of the Federation of Organized Trades and Labor Unions. Held at Columbus, Ohio, the convention was attended by leaders of twenty-five labor groups with 150,000 members. On December 8, 1886, they organized the American Federation of Labor. Samuel Gompers, president of the Cigarmakers Union, was elected first president of the federation.

THE AMERICAN FEDERATION of Labor differed from previous national unions. Under Gompers, who had begun his career as a cigarmaker's apprentice in London, the A.F. of L. permitted self-rule by individual trade unions. Each union of organized craftsmen was permitted to do its own bargaining for contracts. It could call strikes and control its own affairs. The federation offered general leadership and assistance. This differed from the policies of the previous Knights of Labor, which acted as one union for all crafts.

MANY INDIVIDUAL, OR SINGLE, GROUPS and members of the Knights of Labor were taken in by the American Federation of Labor. The Knights soon were broken up. The A.F. of L. fought for rules that were popular with workingmen. These included an eight-hour day, six-day week, higher wages, and payments for workers injured on the job. The federation was against labor political parties and tried to get rid of radicals in the labor movement. Frank K. Foster, secretary of the trades federation which had joined in organizing the A.F. of L., said: "Federation is the motto of the future." The A.F. of L. pursued "pure and simple trade unionism" which meant getting better wages, better conditions, and shorter hours rather than seeking large-scale changes in society.

## *A.F. OF L. FACES PROBLEMS ON BLACK MEMBERSHIP*

THE AMERICAN FEDERATION of Labor faced questions of racial policy from its beginning. There were two main questions: (1) Should blacks be admitted to membership? (2) Should black workers be organized in separate unions? Samuel Gompers, the A.F. of L. president, gave these answers to the racial questions: (1) Efforts should be made to eliminate objections to permitting blacks in the unions; (2) if all else fails, black workers should be organized into their own locals, but with full connection and all rights in their unions' national organizations.

GOMPERS EXPLAINED HIS STAND: "If we fail to organize and recognize the colored wage-workers, we cannot blame them if they accept our challenge of enmity (ill-will) and do all they can to frustrate (block) our purposes . . . The employing class won't be so short-sighted and will play them against us. Thus, if common humanity (decency) will not prompt us to have their cooperation, an enlightened self-interest should." The A.F. of L. at its 1890 convention went on record with a statement that it "looks with disfavor upon trade unions having provisions which exclude from membership persons on account of race or color."

THINGS DID NOT WORK OUT the way these declarations said they should. The federation had little control over the actual policies of the member unions. But in two major cases, the federation tried to get its member unions to follow non-racial policies. In one of these cases, the A.F. of L. in 1891 denied a charter to the National Association of Machinists because its membership was limited to white workers. The federation sponsored and chartered a new International Machinists' Union, whose charter admitted all races to membership. In the second case, in 1893, the Brotherhood of Boiler Makers and the Iron Ship Builders of America merged, or combined, with blacks barred from membership. The A.F. of L. refused to give the merged union a charter, and helped organize a new Boiler Makers' Union without rules against blacks. This union was given a charter. Although the machinists and boiler makers were open to black members, most local unions remained closed.

**Black workers** faced difficulties in joining unions. The A.F. of L. said it "looks with disfavor" upon barring blacks from membership, but many locals still did so.

GOMPERS APPOINTED several black labor leaders as A.F. of L. organizers. They included George L. Norton, secretary of the Marine Firemen's Union in St. Louis; James F. Porter, financial secretary of the Longshoremen's Association of New Orleans; and J. Madison Vance, a black lawyer. The A.F. of L. supported a general strike in New Orleans in 1892 asking all affiliated, or local, New Orleans unions to join the strike. As a result, 25,000 black and white workers from 49 unions stayed off their jobs for four days. The strike was settled with the workers winning their demands for a ten-hour day and more pay.

# *INDIANS OFFERED A CHANCE TO OWN THEIR OWN FARMS*

AMERICAN INDIANS' PROBLEM of finding new lives was made more difficult by new wars and loss of their lands to white men. A ray of hope came in 1887 when Congress passed the Dawes Severalty (separation) Act, offering individual Indians the chance to own their own farms. After becoming President in 1829, Andrew Jackson had started the policy of sending Indian tribes to territories, or special lands set aside for them by the government. After the Civil War, the bitter Indian fighting in the West led to the sending of other tribes to reservations, or other special lands reserved for them.

PRESIDENT CHESTER A. ARTHUR in 1881 sent a message to Congress on the Indian problem. He said that the United States policy of treating the tribes as separate nations and sending them to reservations was "encouraging them to live a savage life, undisturbed by an earnest and well directed efforts to bring them under the influences of civilization". Arthur pointed out: "We have to deal with the appalling (alarming) fact that thousands of lives have been sacrificed and hundreds of millions of dollars expended (spent) in the attempt to solve the Indian problem, and it has until the past few years seemed scarcely nearer a solution than it was half a century ago." Arthur proposed a law giving individual Indians, if they chose, the right to leave their tribes and obtain farm lands of their own. Six years later, Congress passed the Dawes Act, which was a move to break up the tribes.

**The Dawes Act** offered each head of an Indian family 160 acres, as his own farm, if he would give up tribal connections. The land would be held in trust for 25 years.

THE SEVERALTY ACT provided for lands on reservations to be divided into farms and offered to individual male Indians living on the reservations. Each head of an Indian family was offered 160 acres. Each single Indian over 18 was offered 80 acres. Each orphan child under 18 was to be given 80 acres, and all other single Indians under 18 were to receive 40 acres. The Indians who received the farm lands under the Severalty Act could not sell or get rid of the lands for 25 years. The lands would be held in trust by the U.S. government for use and the benefit of the Indians living on them. The Indians who renounced, or gave up, their tribal connections for Severalty Act lands were granted U.S. citizenship.

# AMERICA NO LONGER HAD A FRONTIER
# DAYS OF INDIAN WARFARE CAME TO AN END

America no longer had a frontier. The director of the 1890 census announced that remaining open lands of the West were so thickly settled that occupied and unoccupied areas could not be separated.

The capture of Chief Geronimo in 1886 ended the long Apache War in Arizona and New Mexico. Geronimo was exiled from the West to Florida.

The 1890 census showed 62,622,250 population in the United States. This was a gain of 12,466,467 in ten years, during which 5,246,613 immigrants came over from Europe.

A "Ghost Dance War" in the Black Hills ended warfare with Indians. The Indians staged strange dances, alarming settlers. Federal troops ended the war, killing 200 Sioux in Battle of the Wounded Knee (1890).

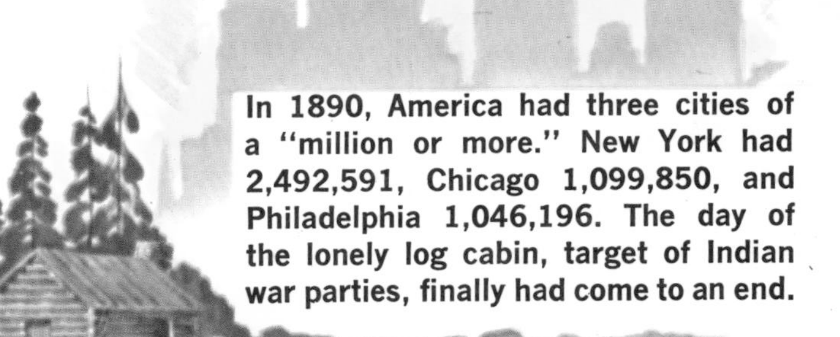

In 1890, America had three cities of a "million or more." New York had 2,492,591, Chicago 1,099,850, and Philadelphia 1,046,196. The day of the lonely log cabin, target of Indian war parties, finally had come to an end.

# *SHERMAN ANTI-TRUST ACT ENDS STANDARD OIL TRUST*

**Standard Oil Trust's** hold on the oil business was broken by the Ohio Supreme Court.

JOHN D. ROCKEFELLER built up a Standard Oil Trust that squeezed almost all rivals out of business. The trust was a monopoly which gave Standard Oil almost all of America's oil business. Similar monopolies developed in other business fields, such as whiskey, sugar and lead. Several Western and Southern states passed laws making trusts illegal. The first state to fight the trusts was Kansas, in 1889. But the Supreme Court ruled that states could not make laws covering goods and services that were sold in more than one state. Then Congress took a hand.

A SHERMAN ANTI-TRUST ACT was passed on July 2, 1890. It put the federal government on record against monopolies, or trusts. The act declared any trust, or combination of companies which "restrained trade," to be illegal. But even the federal law could not be used at once. It had to wait for court rulings describing clearly the meaning of such legal terms as "trust," "combination," and "restraint of trade."

STANDARD OIL'S TRUST came under the Sherman Anti-Trust Act rulings. Standard Oil was named in a law suit, which reached the Supreme Court of Ohio. On March 1, 1892, the court ruled that the Standard Oil Company of Ohio—main company of the trust—was guilty of "attempting to establish a virtual monopoly." The court ordered the Standard Oil Trust broken up. Rockefeller next formed Standard Oil of New Jersey, a "holding" company through which he retained control. In 1911, the Supreme Court banned the company.

## *BATTLESHIP MAINE IS SUNK IN HAVANA HARBOR*

**"Remember the *Maine!*"** The cry rang out as the battleship was sunk in Havana Harbor by an underwater mine. 260 Americans were killed. The nation long remembered.

THE U.S. BATTLESHIP *MAINE* was sent to Havana to protect Americans during a revolution in Cuba. On the night of February 15, 1898, a terrific explosion hit the *Maine* while the battleship was in the harbor. The *Maine* sank with a loss of 260 American officers and men. The New York Journal issued a "war extra" with the headline, "The warship *Maine* was split in two by an enemy's secret infernal machine." Later, a naval court decided the *Maine* had been sunk by an underwater mine. No evidence could be found to place the blame.

CUBA'S REVOLT AGAINST SPAIN had broken out in 1895. The Cuban rebels wrecked many sugar mills, including some owned by Americans. But Americans sympathized with the Cubans. Some U.S. newspapers, which made a specialty of horror stories, reported shocking treatment of Cuban patriots who were sent to concentration, or cruel, camps by General Valeriano Weyler, the Spanish commander in Cuba. After the sinking of the *Maine,* the cry for war against Spain rang out in America. But President William McKinley hoped to avoid war. He instructed Stewart Woodford, U.S. minister at Madrid, to inform the Spanish government that the U.S. had no desire to take over Cuba. The only demands on Spain were that an armistice, or "cease-fire", be declared with the Cuban rebels and that Weyler's concentration camps be closed. The Spanish government agreed on April 9, but it was too late.

WAR FEELINGS HAD BUILT UP in America. On April 11, McKinley asked Congress for authority to "forcibly intervene" to restore "peace in Cuba." On April 20, Congress recognized Cuba's independence. A demand was made that Spain withdraw her armed forces from Cuba. McKinley was authorized to use armed forces, if necessary. When Cuba's independence was established Congress promised that the government of Cuba would be left to the Cuban people. An ultimatum, or final warning, was sent to Spain. On April 24, 1898, Spain declared war on the U.S. and the next day the U.S. declared war.

## *DEWEY DESTROYS SPANISH FLEET IN MANILA BAY*

AMERICA'S NEW "STEEL NAVY" was ready for the war. An Asiatic Squadron was based at Hong Kong under Commodore George Dewey. Theodore Roosevelt, young Assistant Secretary of the Navy, had given Dewey secret orders to move against the Spanish fleet in Manila Bay in the Philippines if war broke out. Two days after America declared war, Dewey sailed from Chinese waters and entered Manila Bay on the night of April 30, 1898. The next morning the U.S. squadron attacked ten old Spanish cruisers and gunboats under the command of Admiral Montojo. The American shells hit the Spanish fleet from end to end. Forts and shore batteries around the harbor were silenced. In seven hours, the Spanish fleet was destroyed, with not one of Dewey's ships damaged.

THE BATTLE OF SAN JUAN HILL, on the other side of the world, was the heaviest land fight of the Spanish-American War. Powerful U.S. naval forces, commanded by Admiral William T. Sampson, had the Spanish Atlantic fleet bottled up in Santiago Harbor in Cuba. A U.S. invasion force under General William Shafter sailed from Tampa, Florida, and landed east of Santiago on June 22, 1898. Spain's land troops were attacked and day-long fighting took place on July 1. First, El Caney village, with 600 defenders, was taken by 7,000 U.S. troops under General H. W. Lawton.

10,000 OTHER AMERICAN FORCES under General J. F. Kent moved toward San Juan Hill. The Americans broke through jungles and finally charged up the hill. Theodore Roosevelt's Rough Riders helped win the fight. Roosevelt had resigned his Navy post to organize the Rough Riders. Also helping take San Juan Hill was the Third Negro Cavalry, commanded by Captain John J. Pershing. Heights over Santiago were occupied.

**Spain's fleet** in Manila Bay was destroyed by America's steel warships under Dewey.

# *VICTORY AT SANTIAGO AND MANILA! WAR WITH SPAIN IS WON*

**Admiral Pascual Cervera** led the Spanish fleet out of Santiago Harbor and U.S. battleships opened fire. Enemy warships were set afire and the fleet was destroyed.

SPAIN'S FLEET WAS TRAPPED in the harbor at Santiago. Outside, a powerful American fleet waited, under the command of Admiral Sampson and Commodore Winfield S. Schley. On July 3, 1898, Spanish Admiral Cervera made an attempt to escape to the open sea. The blazing guns of five American battleships met the Spanish warships as they steamed out. The wooden decks of the Spanish ships were set afire. Those ships not sunk were run onto the beaches. Spanish casualties were 474 killed or wounded and 1,750 taken prisoners. American losses: one killed and one wounded. After this second Spanish fleet was destroyed, General Shafter's American land troops shelled and starved Santiago's 24,000 Spanish troops into surrender on July 17. Four days earlier, the French embassy at Washington, acting at Spain's request, had opened armistice talks with the U.S. On July 25, General Nelson A.

MANILA WAS CAPTURED two days after an armistice halting the war was signed in Washington. Dewey blockaded Manila Harbor three months after destroying Spain's fleet there. The U.S. sent General Wesley Merritt and 11,000 American troops to Manila. The U.S. troops were joined in an attack on Manila by General Emilio Aguinaldo, a Filipino rebel who had been exiled by the Spaniards but was brought back by Dewey. The drive to capture Manila took two days. Parts of the city's walls were battered down and American troops entered the city. Manila surrendered on August 14, and the war with Spain was over.

Miles and American troops occupied Puerto Rico with little opposition.

THE FILIPINO REVOLT did not end with America's defeat of Spain. Many Filipinos were disappointed when they were not declared free and Aguinaldo carried on the revolt, this time against the U.S. Aguinaldo was captured in 1901, but 100,000 Filipinos kept up the fight for another year. The U.S. used 70,000 troops and spent 175 million dollars to end the revolt. More Americans were killed than were lost in actual fighting with Spain.

**The United States** changed its mind and decided it wanted all of the Philippines. Businessmen saw new trade markets and bases from which to trade in the Far East.

THE PEACE TREATY WITH SPAIN after the war of 1898 aroused heated debate in America. The main argument was between those who wanted America to build an empire by taking over Spanish possessions such as the Philippine Islands and those who opposed expansion. The U.S. entered the war with Spain mainly to free Cuba, but by the end of the war had occupied faraway islands. As the peace talks began at Paris, President McKinley told Spain that all the U.S. wanted in the Philippines was the island of Luzon on which Manila was located. Spain's main point in the talks was that Manila was the only Philippine land taken by the U.S.

OTHER EVENTS CHANGED America's attitude, however. While Admiral Dewey's fleet was anchored in Manila Harbor, waiting for U.S. troops to invade and take Manila, German warships had arrived. The Germans so interfered with Dewey's maneuvers that he threatened to fire on them. Many Americans were sure that if the U.S. gave freedom to the Philippines, Germany would try to seize them.

AMERICAN BUSINESSMEN and missionaries saw opportunities in the Philippines. The islands would give U.S. trade new markets and bases within easy reach of the Orient. The missionaries wanted to send Protestant workers to convert the natives. McKinley changed his mind. He informed Spain that the U.S. wanted the entire Philippine Island chain. Spain hesitated but, when the U.S. offered 20 million dollars as payment, the treaty was signed on December 10, 1898. Spain also gave the United States Puerto Rico and Guam.

THE SENATE APPROVED THE TREATY in February, 1899, but only after bitter debate. William Jennings Bryan at first opposed the American expansion as imperialistic. Others disputed America's right to take over territory that might not become states. They said that America's tradition had been not to become involved overseas. But Bryan finally changed his mind and supported the treaty, as the best and quickest way of securing peace. Bryan's influence helped win enough votes for Senate approval, 57 to 27. The war had been costly in human lives for America. A total of 5,462 had died during the fighting or in camps, but only 379 men were battle casualties. Others died of disease.

# AMERICA DEVELOPED ITS OWN CULTURE —NEWSPAPERS, MAGAZINES, ART, SPORTS

The story of the American people was told by noted writers. Among them were O. Henry (William Sidney Porter), Mark Twain (Samuel L. Clemens) and William Dean Howells. Stirring Western tales were written by Bret Harte.

Daily newspapers kept Americans informed of the news. In New York, leading dailies were the *Tribune, Sun, World,* and *Journal*. Joseph Medill's *Chicago Tribune* was a leader in the Middle West. Leading magazines included *Harper's Weekly, Nation,* and *Ladies Home Journal.*

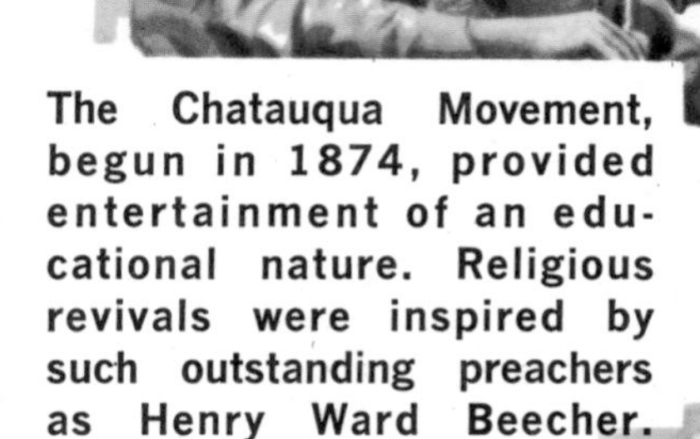

The Chatauqua Movement, begun in 1874, provided entertainment of an educational nature. Religious revivals were inspired by such outstanding preachers as Henry Ward Beecher.

Native American painters won international fame — Albert Ryder, Mary Cassatt, Thomas Eakins, George Inness and Winslow Homer. American architects such as Frank Lloyd Wright designed new purposeful skyscraper styles.

Baseball became the national sport. The National League was formed in 1876 and the American in 1900. John L. Sullivan, James J. Corbett and Robert Fitzsimmons, in that order, held heavyweight boxing title.

## America—miracle of the nineteenth century

America's growth and gains in the Nineteenth Century won the world's praise. In these 100 years, the United States won full rights to freedom of the seas. The present areas of the United States on the North American continent were established.

A chain of islands was won. Four wars were fought, all having to do with the freedom of lands and people. In the War of 1812, the rights of seamen and shippers to sail the seas and trade freely were upheld. In the war with Mexico, the freedom of Texas and its entry into the Union were defended.

In the Civil War, America's Union was saved and several million Negro slaves were freed. And in the Spanish-American War, the people of Cuba were rescued from Spain's cruel rule. America's growth in land area was largely the result of settlers' wishes, buying, and victory in war.

Thomas Jefferson in 1803 bought the Louisiana Territory from Napoleon of France for $15,000,000. Secretary of State William Seward in 1867 arranged for the United States to buy Alaska from Russia for $7,200,000.

The island chain was obtained near the century's close. American settlers in Hawaii wanted the islands to become part of the United States, and in 1898 America annexed, or took over, Hawaii. In 1899, the Samoan Islands were divided between the United States and Germany.

By the Spanish-American peace treaty, Puerto Rico, Guam and the Philippines became United States islands. Wake Island was taken because it lay on the ocean cable line to Manila. A force of troops on the way to the Philippines stopped at Wake and, in 1900, the island was formally occupied.

Many inventions and new and better ways of living were given to the world by Americans. Included were Eli Whitney's cotton gin, Robert Fulton's steamboat *Clermont,* Samuel Morse's telegraph, Alexander Graham Bell's telephone, Thomas Edison's incandescent light bulb, Isaac Singer's sewing machine and Jan Matzeliger's shoe-lasting machine.

America's standing among other nations of the world had grown and reached such faraway nations as China. In 1899, Secretary of State John Hay arranged an "Open Door" trading policy in China. This gave China the right to trade with any or all nations.

As the century closed, the Boxers of China, in 1900, revolted against the "foreign devils," as they called the people from other nations who were living in China. The Boxers killed 300 foreigners before the other nations sent in an army and put down the revolt. The United States Marines and Army troops from the Philippines took part in the fighting.

America's population grew from 5,308,483 in 1800 to 75,944,575 in 1900. The thirteen miles of railroad track over which the little Tom Thumb rode in 1830 had spread into nearly 200,000 miles of track reaching from coast to coast. America: Truly the Miracle of the Nineteenth Century!

# UNITED STATES BECAME A WORLD POWER —STOOD HIGH AMONG OTHER NATIONS

Entering the Twentieth Century, the United States had won its place as a leader among other great nations of the world.

In the war with Spain, America's "steel navy" proved its strength and showed it could carry large land forces to distant fighting zones.

A chain of island possessions in two oceans was won. Included were the Philippines, Puerto Rico, Hawaii and Guam.

America's strong handling of Great Britain's dispute with Venezuela over the Venezuelan-British Guiana borders brought about peaceful border talks.

The United States led in establishing an "Open Door" policy in China. American fighting forces helped put down the Boxer revolt in China.

# AMERICA IN NEW WORLD ROLE

CUBA WAS GIVEN SELF-RULE by the United States, but with certain strings attached. After the war with Spain, the island remained under American Army control, headed by General Leonard Wood. The Cubans were told to draw up a constitution for self-government. When drawn up, the constitution had no plans for relations with the United States. Secretary of War Elihu Root ordered General Wood to tell Cuban leaders that their constitution must include American relations. Only then would the United States take it troops from Cuba.

CONGRESS OUTLINED what the Cubans would have to write into their constitution. Cuba was to agree never to sign a treaty with a foreign nation which might endanger Cuba's freedom. The public debt could not exceed revenues. The United States would have the right to step in and stop any riots or other troubles which might break out in Cuba, including interference by a foreign nation. Land must be sold to the United States for naval bases and supply stations where American ships could take on fuel. When these pledges were added to the constitution, America kept some control over Cuba. On June 12, 1901, the Cubans rewrote their constitution on the lines asked by Congress. The Cuban leaders then formed their government, and American troops were withdrawn from the island in March, 1902.

**Cuba rewrote its constitution** to keep ties with the United States and was given self-rule. American troops left the island in 1902. In 1901 the U.S. had cleared yellow fever from Havana, the capital. Swamps were drained and sprayed and disease carrying mosquitoes destroyed.

# *DEBS LEADS SOCIALISTS—RUNS FOR PRESIDENT 5 TIMES*

THE SOCIALIST MOVEMENT came to America at the start of the Twentieth Century. It went into politics and its most prominent leader, Eugene Debs, once received almost one million votes for President of the United States. From 1900 to 1920, Debs ran five times for the U.S. Presidency on Socialist tickets. After serving a jail sentence for his part in the Pullman strike, Debs had become a full-fledged Socialist and, with Victor Berger, helped form the Socialist Party of America in 1901. Debs had been an official of the locomotive firemen's union at his hometown of Terre Haute, Indiana. His own union background and socialism's concern for the working man explained the Socialist Party's strong support of trade unionism. The party engaged in independent political action and won many supporters of government ownership of industry.

DEB'S PERSONAL CHARACTER and happy family life appealed to the public. His speeches drew large crowds. Tall and slim, Debs would lean over the platform and point at targets in the crowd as he shouted his messages. Debs ran for the Presidency in 1900, 1904, 1908, 1912 and 1920. He made a speaking tour of the nation in 1908, traveling in a "Red Special" train. Debs' final Presidential campaign in 1920 came while he was in prison serving a term for violation of a World War I Sedition Act. Debs, while still in prison, received 919,799 votes for President.

INDUSTRIAL WORKERS OF THE WORLD, known as IWW, was another group which Debs and Berger helped form. The IWW was organized at Chicago in June, 1905, with Debs and Berger attending. The IWW had issued a Union Manifesto, or statement of policies. The manifesto was against the mechanization of labor, or using machines instead of men, and it attacked "capitalist power." Unlike Debs and Berger, the IWW was opposed to political action and preferred to organize everyone into one big union which would take over power through a general strike. Many Americans also associated the IWW with violence because of its aggressiveness.

**Large crowds gathered** to hear Debs speak. Tall and slender, Debs would lean over the platform, point at persons in the crowd, and shout his messages at them.

**The IWW was accused** of using violent means to accomplish some of its goals.

# *McKINLEY ASSASSINATED, ROOSEVELT BECOMES PRESIDENT*

**Theodore Roosevelt** became America's twenty-sixth President. He took office after the assassination of President McKinley.

PRESIDENT McKINLEY was assassinated while attending a Pan-American Exposition, or fair, at Buffalo, New York. He was shot on September 6, 1901, by a crazed anarchist, a man who hated all government. McKinley died eight days later, the third American President to be killed by an assassin's bullet. The day before he was shot, McKinley made a speech at the exposition. He talked about America's new role as the owner of island lands. McKinley said that America wanted to trade with all nations of the world and that fair dealing on both sides would be the rule.

MC KINLEY'S SPEECH was cheered by the large crowd which heard him. The next day the President attended a public reception, or party, in one of the exposition halls. Another large crowd was present. A man stepped forward and pointed his right hand, covered with a handkerchief, at the President. A pistol was concealed beneath the handkerchief, and the stranger fired two shots. He did not say a word as the shots struck McKinley. The President fell with deadly wounds. Vice-President Theodore Roosevelt was sworn in as the twenty-fifth President on September 14, a few hours after McKinley's death.

THE ASSASSIN was captured and identified as Leon Czolgosz, a young factory worker. Czolgosz admitted that he was an anarchist and gave no reason for his act except that he hated all government. He was tried and convicted by the Supreme Court of New York and was electrocuted on October 29, 1901. Two other Presidents who had been assassinated were Abraham Lincoln and James Garfield. Robert Todd Lincoln, oldest son of the Civil War President, was at the scene of the assassinations of all three Presidents.

ROOSEVELT WAS THE YOUNGEST man to become President of the United States. He was only forty-two years old. "I will continue unbroken the policies of President McKinley," he said at his inaugural. Roosevelt was a well educated man and came from a wealthy family. As a young boy he was weak and in poor health. But he built himself up by going West and becoming a cowboy. He loved hunting, camping and the rugged life. Roosevelt read and wrote many books on history. He believed in a strong foreign policy.

# *LEADERS FIGHT TO IMPROVE LIVES OF THE BLACK PEOPLE*

**Frederick Douglass,** William E. B. DuBois and Booker T. Washington were leaders in the fight to win blacks' rights. They had differing methods, but the same goals.

THE FIGHT FOR BLACKS' RIGHTS moved into the Twentieth Century with leaders taking strong positions. The blacks' lack of education and basic skills was pointed out by Booker T. Washington, important black educator. Washington was less concerned with voting and more concerned with education and jobs. William E. B. DuBois, on the other hand, took a forceful view of his people's struggle for civil and political rights. Earlier, Frederick Douglass, a leading fighter for the black people's rights, had fought for full integration and against all forms of segregation. Douglass held many government posts and reached a high point in 1889 when President Benjamin Harrison appointed him Minister Resident and Consul General to the Republic of Haiti.

BOOKER T. WASHINGTON in 1895 made a speech known as the Atlanta Compromise (agreement for peace), which troubled some black leaders. Washington said: "Our greatest danger is that in the great leap from slavery to freedom we may overlook the fact that the masses of us are to live by the production of our hands, and fail to keep in mind that we shall prosper (make gains) in proportion (the same rate) as we learn to dignify and glorify common labour and put brains and skill into the common occupations (work) of life."

WILLIAM E. B. DU BOIS was a scholar and author. In 1903, DuBois wrote a book, *The Souls of the Black Folks,* in which he said: "In the history of nearly all other races and peoples the doctrine preached . . . has been that manly self-respect is worth more than lands and houses, and that a people who voluntarily surrender (willingly give up) such respect, or cease striving (trying) for it, are not worth civilizing . . . Blacks do not expect that the free right to vote, enjoy civic rights, and to be educated, will come in a moment . . . but . . . the way for a people to gain their reasonable rights is not by voluntarily throwing them away and insisting that they do not want them . . . Negroes must insist (on their rights)."

DU BOIS AND OTHER BLACK LEADERS met on the Canadian side of Niagara Falls in 1905 and began the Niagara Movement. This movement did not agree with the Atlanta Compromise policies of Booker T. Washington. DuBois said of the Niagara Movement: "We are men! We will be treated as men. And we shall win!"

**The U.S. chose a route** across the Isthmus of Panama for the building of a canal connecting the Atlantic and Pacific. The canal speeded travel to rich new trade markets.

AMERICA HAD LONG DESIRED a canal across Central America to shorten the sea route to California and for U.S. defense. When Theodore Roosevelt became President in 1901, the canal had become a major issue. In 1879, a French company had spent 260 million dollars trying to dig a canal through Panama. The company failed and its rights were taken over by a Panama Canal Company. In 1850, the U.S. and Britain had signed the Clayton-Bulwer Treaty. The treaty said that any Central American canal would be built by both countries and would not be armed. But now the U.S. wanted to build and control the canal alone. On November 18, 1901, a new pact was signed with Britain—the Hay-Pauncefote Treaty. This pact canceled the Clayton-Bulwer Treaty, giving the U.S. full canal rights.

CONGRESS PASSED the Panama Canal (Spooner) Act on June 28, 1902, authorizing building of the canal. The act provided 40 million dollars to purchase the French company's Panama rights and property. But Panama was then a province of Colombia and the Spooner Act said that permission must be obtained from Colombia before the U.S. could build the canal. In 1903, a U.S. treaty offered 10 million dollars in cash and $250,000 a year rental for a six-mile-wide canal right-of-way. The Colombian senate rejected the offer and treaty in August, 1903.

THE PANAMA CANAL COMPANY stood to lose 40 million dollars unless its canal rights could be sold before 1904 when they were scheduled to end. Philippe Bunau-Varilla, a company official, toured the U.S. lecturing on the importance of a canal to America. Bunau-Varilla met with President Roosevelt and congressional leaders to discuss the Colombia canal situation. Bunau-Varilla also talked of stirring up a revolt in Panama. On November 3, 1903, a revolution did break out in Panama. President Roosevelt, aware of revolt plans, had sent U.S. naval forces to the area to keep the isthmus railroad operating and to prevent disorder. On November 4, Panama declared itself independent from Colombia and the U.S. recognized the new republic.

PHILLIPPE BUNAU-VARILLA was named Panama's first ambassador to Washington. On November 18, he signed a treaty giving the U.S. canal rights through Panama. Panama was paid the 10 million dollars cash and $250,000 a year. Building of the Panama Canal finally got fully under way in 1907, with Lieutenant Colonel George Washington Goethals as the chief engineer. Roosevelt defended his handling of the canal problem. He called it his most important action in foreign affairs. Colombia bitterly protested the U.S. part in the Panama revolt. Finally, in 1921, the U.S. paid Colombia 25 million dollars in settlement.

## *THE WRIGHTS' FLYING MACHINE ACTUALLY FLIES!*

A NEW MACHINE called an airplane actually took off from the ground and went flying through the air! This flying machine was invented by Orville and Wilbur Wright, brothers who owned a bicycle shop at Dayton, Ohio. They built and flew the first successful airplane. On December 17, 1903, they made four flights in their airplane at Kitty Hawk, North Carolina. Orville Wright made the first flight, keeping the crude craft in the air for twelve seconds and traveling 120 feet. Wilbur made the longest flight of the day—remaining in the air for fifty-nine seconds and covering 852 feet. The Wright brothers' airplane was the first heavier-than-air craft powered by an engine to fly successfully. Men had been working on the idea for years.

THE WRIGHTS' AIRPLANE looked like a box kite. It weighed 750 pounds and was driven by a twelve-horsepower gasoline engine weighing 170 pounds. The pilot lay on the front edge of the lower wing, looking straight down at the ground. Flying through the air was not new to the Wright brothers. Since 1900, they had been flying in a two-man glider—a soaring plane without an engine—at Kitty Hawk. They built a wind tunnel and tested the air currents' actions on various types of wing surfaces and controls. They decided on a scientific plan for flying—and now they proved that it worked.

RETURNING TO DAYTON, the Wrights made many improvements in their plane. After making a flight of thirty-eight minutes, they obtained a patent in May, 1906. In August, 1909, the United States Army accepted the Wrights' airplane after making tests at Fort Myer, Virginia. Few newspapers had even mentioned that eventful December day's feat at Kitty Hawk!

**Orville Wright** lay on the wing of the Wright brothers' new flying machine. He saw the ground passing below him. He was in flight! The airplane was a success.

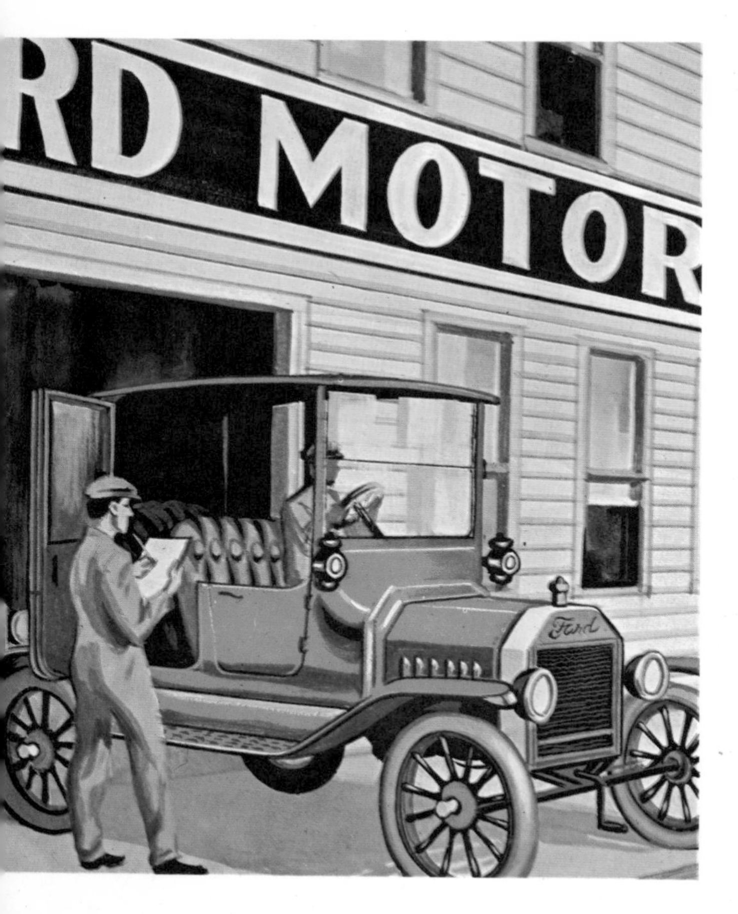


**Henry Ford** introduced the "flivver" auto in 1908. By 1927, 15 million had been sold. Ford's assembly line methods were the start of mass production of autos.

STRANGE "HORSELESS CARRIAGES" came sputtering into the American picture as the Nineteenth Century turned into the Twentieth. They were crude and awkward machines, with small gasoline engines at the rear or under the drivers' seats. But they were America's first automobiles and the beginning of a giant automotive industry. J. Frank Duryea and his brother Charles drove the first auto in Springfield, Massachusetts, in 1892-1893. Henry Ford in 1896 made a little car with bicycle tires. Other engineering and manufacturing leaders soon joined with Ford in pushing the auto out front in American industry. Such leaders as Ransom E. Olds, William C. Durant, Alexander Winton, David Buick, Louis Chevrolet and Walter Chrysler were among auto pioneers.

FORD BUILT HIS FIRST AUTOS in a little shop beside his Detroit home. In 1901, he built a shaky little racer which sped at 44 miles an hour to defeat a trim car entered by Winton in a big race at Grosse Pointe, Michigan. The next year, Ford entered another racer, the "999", which Barney Oldfield drove to victory over Winton and his "Bullet." In 1908, Ford put his Model T "flivver" on the market. The "flivver" was not built for style, but it was cheap. At first it sold for $950, but the price was reduced by stages to as little as $360. By 1927, Henry Ford had sold fifteen million Model T "flivvers" and put Americans on the road. Meanwhile, a huge General Motors Corporation had been built up under the early leadership of Durant.

MECHANIZATION WAS WELL ADVANCED in industry by then, meaning the use of machines to increase production. Ford introduced another method of speeding up production—the moving assembly line. The assembly line carried all the separate parts of the Ford engines and bodies down long lines of workmen, who put the whole car together part by part. This was the beginning of modern mass production and soon other auto manufacturers were using the moving assembly line.

**William C. Durant** was another early leader in the automotive industry. Durant introduced his own cars, purchased others, and finally put together a big corporation.

## *ROOSEVELT DECLARES POLICE POWERS OVER LATIN AMERICA*

AMERICA'S TAKING a strong hand in Caribbean and Latin American affairs was decided upon by Roosevelt as the best way to keep Europeans out. The President announced a policy known as the Roosevelt Corollary to the Monroe Doctrine. Its main point was that, if any Latin American nation got out of line, the United States should take whatever action was needed—and no other nation should. The Corollary said: "Chronic wrongdoing, or an impotence which results in a general loosening of the ties of civilized society, may in America, as elsewhere, ultimately require intervention by some civilized nation, and in the Western Hemisphere the adherence of the United States to the Monroe Doctrine may force the United States, however reluctantly, in such cases of wrongdoing or impotence, to the exercise of an international police power."

A TEST SOON CAME in the Dominican Republic, whose treasury had become bankrupt. In January, 1905, the Dominican Republic signed an agreement for the United States to put an American financial expert in charge of its treasury. Santo Domingo named a director of money suggested by Roosevelt. Forty-five per cent of the customs receipts, taxes on goods being shipped, were used to pay the island's governmental expenses. Fifty-five per cent was paid on debts. Stealing from the customs houses was ended, income rose and debts fell. Santo Domingo's problems were settled.

**An American expert** was sent to Santo Domingo to handle the Dominican Republic's money problems. Roosevelt's new policy was to "police" Latin American republics.

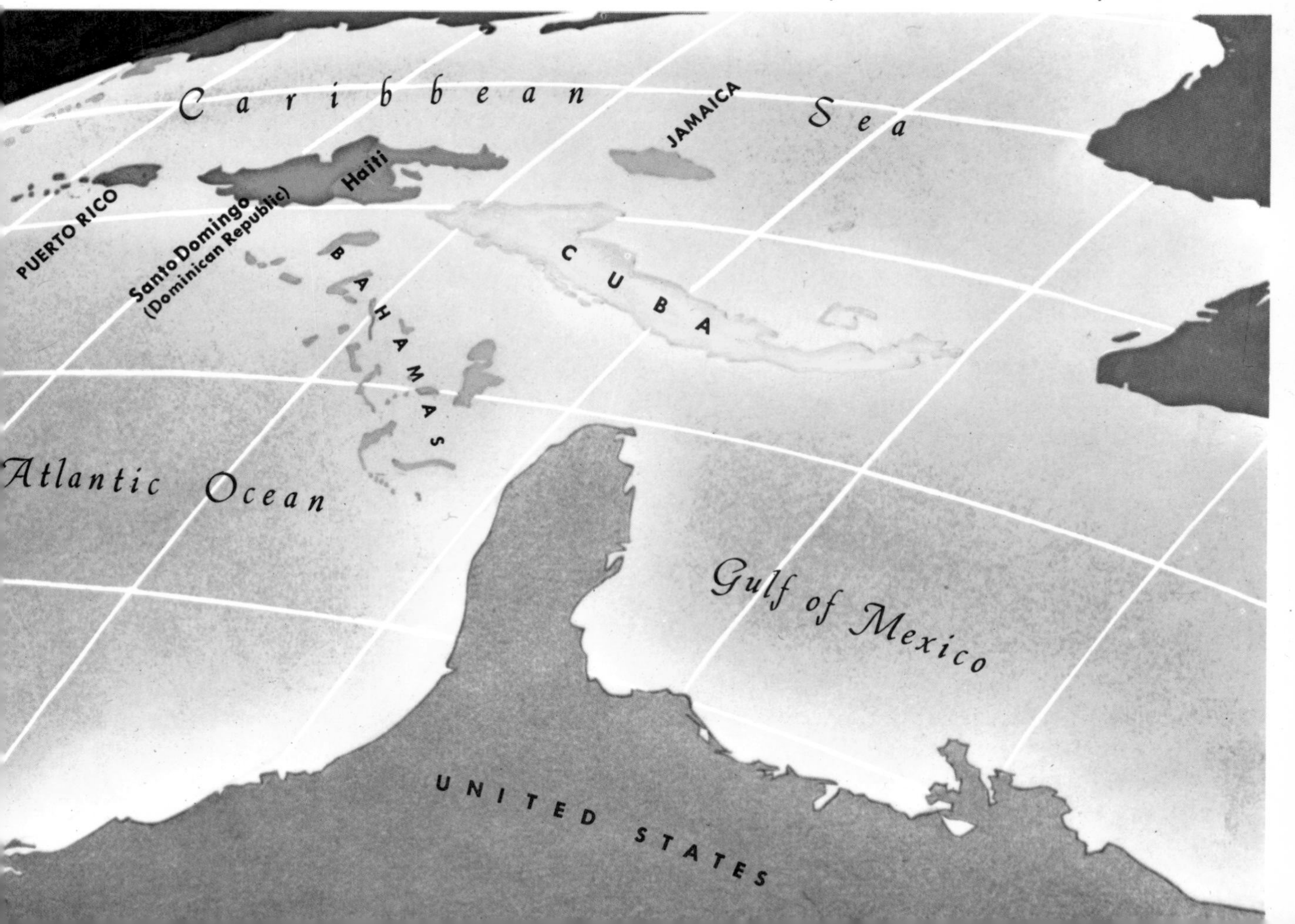

# *MOROCCO IS SAVED FROM BEING SEIZED BY FRANCE*

**Morocco's freedom** was saved with America's help. Roosevelt helped set up a meeting of European nations to discuss an effort by France to take over Morocco.

EUROPEAN RIVALS BECAME OPEN enemies as the race for empires and world power gained speed. In 1904, England and France signed an Entente Cordiale, or friendly agreement, recognizing each other's interests in Egypt and Morocco. France wanted to take over Morocco, an independent North African state ruled by a sultan. France tried to get Spain and Italy to agree to the "takeover." In return, England, Spain and Italy were to be given support for their own plans elsewhere in North Africa. Kaiser Wilhelm II of Germany was opposed to the entire deal. He wanted Morocco to remain free from French rule.

KAISER WILHELM II of Germany was against any French gain. In March, 1905, the kaiser made a strong speech at Tangier in which he declared Germany's support of Morocco's independence. Roosevelt's help was asked by the kaiser as the European nations involved studied the problem. The kaiser wanted the President to help get France, England, Italy, Spain and Germany together for talks. Roosevelt wanted to keep hands off the dispute, but he feared that Europe's rivalries could blaze into a world war which might spread to the United States. Roosevelt helped arrange the meeting. France and England agreed to meet with Germany. The talks began at Algeciras, Spain, in January, 1906. Henry White was America's senior delegate, or member, of the conference group. An act of Algeciras was signed on April 7. It upheld the independence of Morocco and gave equal trading rights to all nations. An international bank was formed to help Morocco solve its money problems. The French and Spanish were given control of Moroccan police. The Senate ratified the decisions, but repeated, "America must keep hands off European policies."

# *WORLD BATTLESHIP TOUR SHOWS AMERICA'S STRENGTH*

**Sixteen American battleships** steamed into Tokyo Harbor. They were met by Japanese children singing *The Star Spangled Banner*.

AMERICA'S NAVAL POWER was shown in a cruise around the world by the entire battleship fleet. Roosevelt ordered the cruise to show other nations, mainly Japan, how strong America's navy was. Roosevelt said, "The United States will no more submit to bullying than it will bully." Sixteen battleships under the command of Admiral Robley D. Evans sailed from Hampton Roads, Virginia, in December, 1907. They steamed around South America, stopping on short good will visits. When the fleet reached San Francisco after sailing up America's west coast, Roosevelt ordered it to continue around the world. Admiral Charles S. Sperry took over command.

ROOSEVELT had been angry with Japan since 1906, when they had taken seals in American waters off Alaska. Japan also was aroused over treatment given to Japanese in California. Roosevelt wanted Japan to see the might that lay behind America's soft words. His chance came when the fleet was invited by the Japanese to visit Yokohama. When the battleships steamed into Yokohama and Tokyo Harbors, they were met by hundreds of Japanese schoolchildren singing *The Star Spangled Banner* in English. The Japanese cheered the fleet and gave it a warm welcome. In Australia, the Middle East and Europe, thousands of people turned out to see America's powerful battleship fleet.

CRITICS HAD SAID the Navy could not do it. Most experts said no fleet could sail around the world. Ship breakdowns, fuel shortages and bad weather would end the voyage, they said. Congress also was against the cruise. Many feared it would anger Japan. Others thought it too expensive. No money was voted for the long voyage. But Roosevelt was not stopped. He knew that the sight of sixteen long, gray battleships would impress upon many nations America's ability to defend her interests, both at home and in foreign lands. And he knew the good-will, ceremonies and celebrations provided by the fleet would show America's peaceful intentions. With only enough money to send the fleet part way around the world, he sent them off. When asked about how they were to get back home, he said, "If Congress wants them back, they will have to put up the money to bring them back!" The battleships steamed back to Hampton Roads in 1909, as Roosevelt's administration ended.

**Well known American leaders** joined in organizing the National Association for the Advancement of Colored People. Negroes began a national crusade for their rights.

BLACKS ORGANIZED in their fight to gain equal rights and full standing as American citizens. In 1909, the National Association for the Advancement of Colored People (N.A.A.C.P.) was formed in New York. The action was taken on the anniversary of Abraham Lincoln's birth. Among the black leaders of the N.A.A.C.P. were William E. B. DuBois, Archibald H. Grimke, Alexander Walters, Ida Wells Barnett, Mary McLeod Bethune and Mary Church Terrell. White supporters included John Dewey, Jane Addams and Lincoln Steffens. Dedicated to the achievement of full equality, the N.A.A.C.P. took cases to the courts, lobbied in the state legislatures and in Congress, and conducted a massive educational program against discrimination. The N.A.A.C.P. also used the prominence of some of its members to alarm the newspapers of the lynchings and other violations of personal right. Organization of the N.A.A.C.P. grew out of the Niagara Movement. By 1914, the association had established fifty branches in the U.S.

A "GREAT MIGRATION," or movement of blacks from the South to big cities in the North, was well under way by 1915. World War I had begun in Europe, and America's plants and factories were working day and night to fill European orders for war supplies. Many new workers were needed, and blacks hurried to leave the farms of the South and get jobs in the factories. In a few years, about 2,000,000 Southern blacks joined the "Great Migration" from Dixie's fields.

BLACKS BEGAN PARADING to attract America's attention to their fight against wrongs. In 1917, some 10,000 blacks marched down Fifth Avenue in New York City to protest lynchings, or killings, of blacks by mobs in the South. N.A.A.C.P. leaders DuBois and James Weldon Johnson were among the march leaders. In 1921, the N.A.A.C.P. sponsored 200 meetings protesting lynchings. But no U.S. law was passed.

## *UNITED STATES MARINES ARE SENT TO NICARAGUA*

DOLLARS INSTEAD OF BULLETS were used by President William Howard Taft to end new troubles in Latin America. Nicaragua needed help to pay off a large national debt. The republic elected a president who was friendly to the United States, Adolfo Diaz. In June, 1911, an agreement was signed giving the United States the right to stop any foreign nation from trying to build a canal across Nicaragua. Such a canal would link the Atlantic and Pacific Oceans. In return, the United States was to pay Nicaragua's debts and take over control of the republic's customs houses.

PHILANDER C. KNOX, Taft's Secretary of State, made the agreement, but the Senate refused to ratify, or approve, it. In July, Nicaragua failed to pay its debt to a British group because it did not have the money. Taft used "dollar diplomacy." The President dealt personally with a group of New York bankers to lend the $1,500,000 which Nicaragua needed. The American bankers were given control of the National Bank of Nicaragua and the government owned railroad. In effect, Taft established a financial protectorate over Nicaragua. A protectorate protected a country against foreign nations.

THE NICARAGUAN PUBLIC accused the United States of taking over their treasury. A revolt broke out in 1912. United States Marines were sent to Nicaragua to protect American interests. The revolt ended but Marines remained in Nicaragua for many years. Taft used the same "dollar diplomacy" to help Honduras when that republic had debt troubles. Again, American bankers put up the money to pay European debts of Honduras. Earlier, American bankers had turned down a plea for help in building a railroad in Manchuria. Both Japan and Russia were against the plan and America's bankers withdrew. Japan and Russia then signed a treaty giving each of them a share in the control of Manchuria.

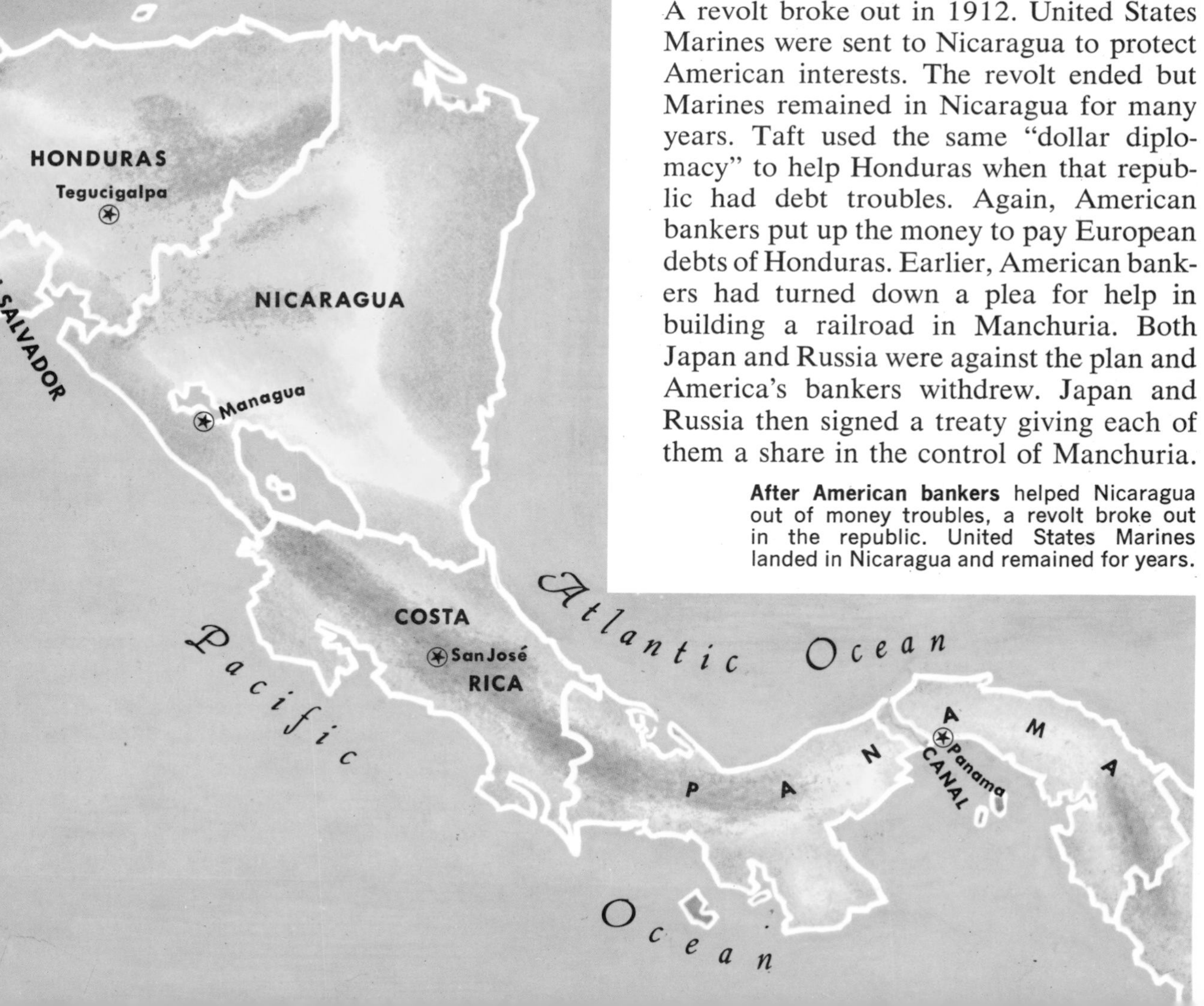


**After American bankers** helped Nicaragua out of money troubles, a revolt broke out in the republic. United States Marines landed in Nicaragua and remained for years.

# MEXICO OVERTHREW DIAZ, RULER FOR 33 YEARS —UNITED STATES MARINES LANDED IN VERA CRUZ

Porfirio Diaz for thirty-three years was the dictator, or one-man ruler, of Mexico. He was overthrown in 1910 by a revolt in Mexico. A period of fighting followed and the United States finally stepped in. Some 50,000 Americans lived in Mexico and owned businesses and property worth about a billion dollars.

Francisco Madero led the revolt which drove Diaz out of the country. Madero tried to establish a democracy and President Taft supported Madero's government. The Mexican government's treasury was in good condition. But Mexico's 15,000,000 people were poor and unhappy.

Madero was taken prisoner and murdered during another revolt. Victoriano Huerta, the new rebel chief, was suspected of being the murderer. President Woodrow Wilson refused to back Huerta. Wilson said he would not "force Huerta on Mexico's poor people."

Twenty-six other nations, including Great Britain, joined Wilson in withholding support of Huerta. The American fleet blockaded Vera Cruz to stop shipments of guns to Huerta. But guns were sent to Venustiano Carranza and "Pancho" Villa, Huerta's rivals.

A fight between American and Mexican forces finally came on April 9, 1914. American sailors loading supplies at Tampico were arrested. Although the Americans were freed with an apology, the dispute with Huerta grew and Wilson ordered fourteen battleships to Vera Cruz. United States Marines landed in the city on April 21. Nineteen Americans were killed in the fight. War with Mexico appeared close at hand.

Wilson accepted an offer of peace talks by Argentina, Brazil and Chile. Huerta fled to Spain and a new government was established under Carranza. Political and farming reforms were promised by Carranza. Although he would not back Carranza's government at the time, Wilson withdrew property damage claims and the Marines were called back from Vera Cruz in November.

**For the first time,** airplanes were used in war. "Dog fights," or battles between airplanes, soon covered the skies as many European nations entered World War I.

WORLD WAR I BROKE OUT in Europe and the United States declared its neutrality. Nations which had been rivals and enemies for many years finally went to war. Most of Europe's big nations were drawn into it. The event which started the war was a Serbian patriot's assassination, in Bosnia, of Archduke Franz Ferdinand, heir to the Austrian throne. Austria declared war on Serbia on July 28, 1914. Russia called up all of its army troops to help Serbia, and on August 1 Germany declared war on Russia. Two days later, Germany also declared war on France, which was Russia's ally. The German army then invaded Belgium. On August 4, England went to Belgium's rescue and declared war on Germany. The five largest and strongest nations of Europe were now at war.

THE WAR DECLARATIONS joined into a general fight between the Allies—England, France and Russia—and the Central Powers—Germany and Austria. On August 4-5, President Wilson declared America's neutrality. America's policy of neutrality, or taking no sides, had lasted for more than a century. In 1793, George Washington refused to take part in a war between England and France. In 1794, Congress passed an act against United States citizens joining the armies of any foreign nations at war. After declaring neutrality, Wilson offered to help halt the war and open peace talks under Hague Conference rules.

KAISER WILHELM II sent a note to Wilson defending Germany's war moves and invasion of Belgium. The President in a special message to this country asked Americans to "be neutral in fact as well as name . . . impartial in thought as well as action." Secretary of State William Jennings Bryan asked American banks not to lend money to any of the nations at war.

# *PANAMA CANAL OPENS—SHORT CUT BETWEEN TWO OCEANS*

**Steam engines** pulled steamships through the Panama Canal. It was a short journey between the Atlantic and Pacific. It took a long trip around South America before.

THE PANAMA CANAL WAS OPENED and the first ocean steamship passed through on August 15, 1914. Seven years had passed since Colonel George W. Goethals was named chief engineer and began the actual building of the canal in April, 1907. The cost of building the canal was $275,000,000 and the United States spent an additional $113,000,000 on canal defense works. The canal provided a water passage across the Isthmus of Panama from the Caribbean Sea to the Pacific Ocean.

A SYSTEM OF LOCKS AND LAKES let the largest ships use the Panama Canal. Previously a long voyage around the tip of South America was the only way ships could travel from the Atlantic Ocean to the Pacific, or from the Pacific to the Atlantic. A dam was built near the mouth, or ocean entrance, of the Chagres River on the Caribbean side, creating an inland Gatun Lake at a height of eighty-five feet above sea level. Locks at each end of the canal let in ocean waters which raised ships to the level of the lake. The ships then entered the lake and crossed to the other side. Locks at that end of the canal let out water and lowered the ships back to sea level as they left Lake Gatun. The ships were drawn through the locks by locomotives, or train engines, running on tracks along the canal.

DIPLOMATIC TROUBLES with England arose over Panama Canal tolls. The Hay-Pauncefote Treaty of 1901, in which Britain gave up all isthmian canal rights, had guaranteed that all nations would pay equal canal tolls. In 1912, Congress exempted, or excused, American coastwise shipping from paying the tolls. Britain protested this act as a violation of the Hay-Pauncefote Treaty. President Wilson, after a bitter fight with Congress, had the exemption repealed and U.S. ships paid the tolls.

## *GERMAN SUBMARINE SINKS THE LUSITANIA WITHOUT WARNING*

**A German submarine commander** broke an order not to torpedo a ship without warning.

AMERICANS WERE WARNED by the German government that the waters around the British Isles had been declared a war zone. Americans who traveled there did so at their own risk. The German embassy issued the warning in an advertisement in New York newspapers on May 1, 1915. Just at that time, the liner *Lusitania* was about to sail from New York for England, and many Americans were passengers. The *Lusitania* was torpedoed without warning by a German submarine off Ireland on May 7. The British Cunard liner sank with a loss of 1,198 lives—128 of them Americans. President Woodrow Wilson sent notes of strong protest to the German government.

A SECRET ORDER was issued by Berlin to its submarine commanders. No more passenger ships were to be torpedoed without a warning first being given. The safety of the passengers had to be kept in mind. On August 19, 1915, a U-boat, or submarine, commander broke the rule and sank the British liner *Arabic*. Two Americans were among those who lost their lives. Meanwhile, public feeling in America had turned against Germany. This was because of sabotage, or property damage, and espionage, or spying, by German agents in this country. Setting of fires and bombings in the U.S. were blamed on the Germans.

WILSON WAS REELECTED in 1916 with the campaign cry of "He kept us out of war!" But America's entry into World War I was drawing closer. On January 31, 1917, Germany announced that unrestricted submarine warfare (without any limits) would be carried on in the future. Then British intelligence agents turned over to America a message from Berlin to the German minister in Mexico. The minister was told to invite Mexico to join Germany in the war. If the war were won, Mexico was to get Texas, New Mexico and Arizona.

THE UNITED STATES finally opened relations with troubled Mexico. Venustiano Carranza had kept peace in Mexico since United States Marines were withdrawn from Vera Cruz in November, 1914. The United States and several Latin American countries backed Carranza's government. The State Department on October 19, 1915, opened full relations with Mexico. Carranza was given the right to order guns and ammunition in the United States. But the American public was not too sure about Carranza. He had kept peace, but he had not fully kept his promises of political and farming reforms, or changes for the better, for Mexico's millions of farmers.

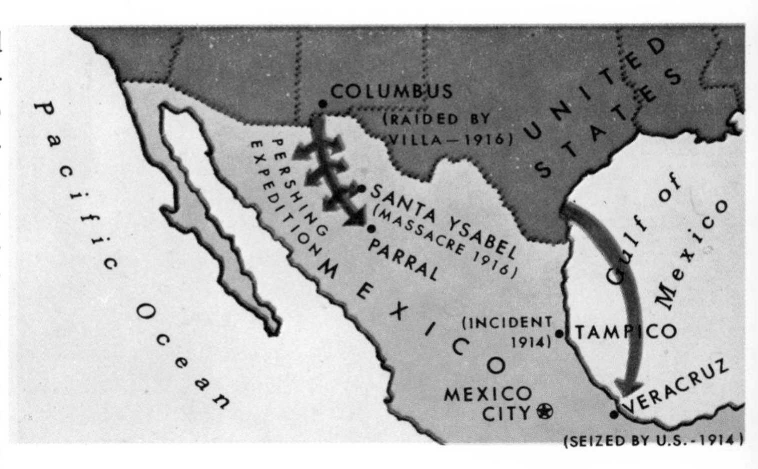


**America's troubles in Mexico** continued as "Pancho" Villa raided Santa Ysabel and Columbus, New Mexico. In 1914, U.S. Marines landed in Vera Cruz.

FRANCISCO (PANCHO) VILLA, Carranza's bitter political rival in Mexico, was angered. Villa was cruel to his enemies, but Mexico's poor and unhappy people believed he was their friend. They stood loyally behind him. Villa led raids on government offices and warehouses. Many persons were killed, including some Americans.

GENERAL JOHN J. PERSHING was sent into Mexico at the head of a United States army with orders to capture "Pancho" Villa. At Santa Ysabel in January, 1916, Villa and his bandits had murdered eighteen American engineers who had been brought in by Carranza to operate Mexican mines. In March, Villa had crossed the border and raided Columbus, New Mexico. Seventeen Americans were killed. President Wilson obtained Carranza's consent to send American troops after Villa. Carranza's troops had not been able to capture the slippery "Pancho."

WILSON CALLED OUT 150,000 militia and stationed them along the Mexican border under the command of General Frederick Funston and General Pershing. On March 15, Pershing led a force of 6,000 into Mexico with 6,000 others joining them later. Villa and his bandits were met at San Geronimo and were scattered by Pershing's troops. But Villa escaped and fled to the mountains. Pershing's cavalry dashed 300 miles into Mexico in a hot chase after Villa. Several fights took place, but in each fight "Pancho" galloped off to safety just in time to escape capture.

CARRANZA AND THE MEXICAN people did not like American troops being in their country. A plan to organize a double border patrol, with each side working on its own, was turned down by Carranza. On Carranza's demand, Pershing's forces were withdrawn from Mexico. Mexico adopted a new constitution and Carranza was elected President. The United States supported the new Mexican government.

AFTER MEXICO ADOPTED its new constitution in 1917, the United States campaigned for Americans' oil rights in that nation. The constitution put limits on foreign ownership of lands, mines and oil fields. These troubles with Mexico eased during Calvin Coolidge's administration. Dwight D. Morrow was sent to Mexico City as ambassador and, through his efforts, Mexico changed its oil laws. The land laws also were changed to remove some of the limits on foreigners, who owned huge estates in Mexico.

# AMERICA DREW NEAR TO WORLD WAR I —PREPARED FOR THE COMING STRUGGLE

Congress began to prepare as war drew near. In June, 1916, the regular Army was increased to 175,000. National Guard strength of 450,000 was approved. Officer training camps were built.

The Federal Farm Loan Act provided loans to farmers on easy terms. Increased production of food was desired for possible wartime needs.

The Naval Appropriations Act provided $300,000,000 for the building of 156 new warships. A shipping board was created.

A Council of National Defense was established. The President was given the authority to take over the transportation system should war make it necessary.

The Adamson Act granted an eight-hour day to railroad workers employed in interstate commerce. This was to help avoid strikes.

# MAKING THE WORLD SAFE FOR DEMOCRACY

PART 7

**"The world must be made safe** for Democracy!" Wilson called for war on Germany.

WAR WITH GERMANY! World War I finally had been "thrust upon America," President Wilson decided. As Germany's submarines attacked American ships, Secretary of State Robert Lansing wanted to declare war at once. Wilson's other cabinet members agreed. A March revolution in Russia had overthrown Czar Nicholas and set up a people's government. Lansing and the cabinet told the President that America's entry into the war would lead the Russian people to adopt democracy. Also, they said, it might stir up the Prussian-ruled German people. On March 21, 1917, Wilson called for a special session of Congress to meet on April 2. All of America waited for the results.

WILSON ASKED CONGRESS for a declaration of war, as everybody expected he would. The President listed the wrongs that the Germans had done to America. He called the unrestricted, or unlimited, submarine attacks "warfare against mankind." Wilson said he was not asking for war against the German people, but against their government. Congress heard the President declare that the United States should fight "for the ultimate peace of the world and for the liberation of its people, the German people included; for the rights of nations great and small and the privilege of men everywhere to choose their way of life and of obedience. The world must be made safe for democracy." The halls of the Capitol echoed with Congress' cheers.

THE SENATE PASSED the war declaration on April 4. Only six votes against war were cast by what Wilson called a "little group of willful men." The House passed the war declaration on April 6, 1917, by a vote of 373 to 50. President Wilson signed the declaration that same day . . . The United States was at war with Germany! During World War I the United States was not a formal member of the Allies. To the end of the war, the United States was called an "Associated Power" of the "Allied and Associated Powers."

# AMERICA'S MIGHT JOINED FOR UNITED WAR EFFORT

Less than a week after the declaration of war on Germany, America began gathering her resources. Congress, government heads, industry, public and private groups all acted to provide the nation's military needs. The American people united in a mighty war effort.

The moving of millions of men and huge stores of supplies were needed. On April 11, 1917, the American Railroad Association named a board of five men to head operation of the railroads during the struggle. This board kept the big trains rolling.

The United States Shipping Board and the Emergency Fleet Corporation were organized on April 16. Charles M. Schwab was named director. The shipping board's job was to buy, lease, build and operate ships. Many cargo vessels and warships soon were being built.

A Committee on Public Information was formed with George Creel as director. Creel chose a staff of other newspapermen and historians. By May 10, an *Official Bulletin* was being published daily, keeping the public informed on progress of the war. The Committee on Public Information also had the duty of encouraging newspapers to adopt their own censorship rules.

The First Liberty Loan drive for two billion dollars began on May 14. War Savings Stamps also were sold. The public reacted quickly and generously. Americans bought the bonds in large numbers and gave funds to private groups serving the armed forces. Leading citizens offered to make short speeches boosting the war effort. They became well known as America's "Four-Minute Men."

The Selective Service Act, or draft, became law on May 18. This provided for a draft to supply the manpower needed by the armed services. All men twenty-one to thirty years of age were registered for military service. The age limits later were changed to eighteen to forty-five. At the start of the war, the Army had 200,000 men and the Navy and Marine Corps had 90,000. In a short time, Admiral William S. Sims led a fleet of United States destroyers to Europe.

Food also "went to war." America's new allies needed much food. Herbert Hoover was named to organize a Food Administration to assist the Allies in Europe and increase farm production at home. "Food will win the war!" became the rallying cry as Americans began "Hoover programs."

A War Industries Board was created on July 28. This board was charged with increasing the production of guns, ammunition, war machinery and other articles needed for victory. Bernard M. Baruch was head of the board.

# *PERSHING LEADS AMERICAN EXPEDITIONARY FORCE TO FRANCE*

GENERAL PERSHING WAS GIVEN command of the American Expeditionary Force which was sent to France. He was appointed on May 10, 1917, and arrived in Paris with his staff on June 17. Pershing was instructed to work closely with the Allies in warring on the enemy. But the American Expeditionary Force (A.E.F.) was to be "a distinct and separate component of the combined forces, the identity of which must be preserved." The purpose of this was to make sure that the American Army would remain the American Army and not become just another part of a general force. Pershing, who was warmly welcomed by the Allied command, made this point clear after reaching Paris. He asked that the A.E.F. be given its own sector, or battle area, on the Western Front. Pershing was given the right by President Wilson to use his own judgment in the use of American troops in Allied drives.

**Pershing** kept America's Expeditionary Force as a separate army. It gave the Allies great fighting help, but never became just another part of a general force.

THE FIRST AMERICAN troops reached France on June 26, 1917. The young American soldiers, who stepped off troop ships and marched along the docks, were greeted with cheers by the French. The American Expeditionary Force's first group was not large, but it carried the promise of a great army to come, and of America's badly needed support.

THE ALLIES WERE in trouble when the Americans arrived. The French army had failed to make gains in Aisne and Champagne offensives, or drives, during April. In July, the Germans had broken a Russian offensive and forced Russia to quit the war. Czar Nicholas had been overthrown, and in 1917, Nicolai Lenin led a Bolshevik revolt to set up a Communist government. Czarist Russia had become the Soviet Union.

WAR ON THE HOME FRONT reached high speed in America. The government took over control of the railroads on December 26, 1917. William G. McAdoo, Secretary of the Treasury, was put in charge. Actual running of the railroads remained in the hands of the usual work forces, but under McAdoo's command and with wartime rules. Railroad services which could be spared were shut off. Shipment of war goods was speeded. The government's control of the railroads during World War I was marked by good results and the loss of little time in speeding war deliveries.

ALL OF AMERICA joined in the war effort. The War Industries Board took over materials needed for the making of war supplies—guns, ammunition, trucks and warship parts. Waste was wiped out and the making of goods not needed for war use was cut back. Telegraph, telephone and cable control was put under Postmaster General Albert S. Burleson. A Fuel Administration stocked coal and oil for use by the war plants and the armed services. The National War Labor Board, under former President Taft and Frank P. Walsh, and the War Labor Policies Board held down labor strikes.

THE AMERICAN Expeditionary Force's needs in France were taken care of as preparations overseas were rushed. Ten thousand tons of wheat had been sent ahead of the first American troops. Harbors were dredged, or made deeper, and docks were built to receive new troop ship arrivals. Landing centers were set up for the troops. A communications system was installed. Supply bases and hospitals were built. Meanwhile, the United States Navy—first on actual combat duty—sailed back and forth across the Atlantic Ocean convoying, or protecting, the troop and supply ships. Before the war ended, 2,084,000 American troops were landed in France. In the U.S. a huge training camp program began.

**America's ports** became scenes of busy wartime activity. Huge amounts of supplies were shipped to meet the needs of thousands of U.S. soldiers overseas.

**President Wilson** asked Lloyd George of Britain and Georges Clemenceau of France to outline their peace goals. Not satisfied, Wilson then listed America's peace goals.

A PLAN FOR WORLD PEACE was outlined by President Wilson in his Fourteen Points of World War I. In January, 1917, before America entered the war, Wilson had urged a "peace without victory." But Allied leaders refused. As 1917 drew to a close, a demand arose for the warring nations to tell their war goals. The Bolsheviks had published secret treaties made by the Allies. The Russians called this proof of a desire for imperialism. Pope Benedict XV wanted the war halted and peace talks begun. Wilson said that the United States also wanted a just peace, but could not depend upon German promises. The Allies held a conference in Paris during November and December, but could not agree on an announcement of their peace terms. Prime Minister Lloyd George then outlined Great Britain's goals, and Wilson decided the time had come to speak up for America. He talked it over with Colonel Edward M. House, his private advisor, and a council called the Inquiry. On January 8, 1918, President Wilson listed his Fourteen Points before Congress. The League of Nations was contained in Point No. 14. Wilson's Fourteen Points were:

1. Open treaties for peace, openly arrived at, and with no later private agreements of any kind between nations.
2. Absolute freedom of the seas, outside of a nation's own waters, except when closed in order to enforce general rules.
3. The removal, so far as possible, of all economic, or means of making a living, handicaps; equal trading chances to be offered to all nations.

4. Guarantees by all that armaments, or war materials, would be reduced as low as possible without risking a nation's safety.
5. Free and fair settlement of all colonial claims, based on the principle that the interests of the peoples concerned must be given equal treatment with those of the government in control.
6. Withdrawal of troops from all Russian territory and Russia having the right to decide her own political future and policies.
7. Withdrawal of all troops from Belgium, with no effort being made to limit the independence which Belgium would win back.

8. Withdrawal of troops from France with all captured territory freed; Alsace-Lorraine to be returned to France by Germany.
9. New frontiers, or borders, for Italy; these borders to be decided along clear lines of the nationalities involved.
10. The people of Austria-Hungary to be given the freest chance to decide upon and establish their own self-government.
11. Withdrawal of troops from Rumania, Serbia and Montenegro; the release of all captured lands, and free access, or passage, to the sea for Serbia.
12. Independence for Turkish parts of the Ottoman Empire; autonomy, or self-government, for other nationalities under Turkish rule; and free passage, or travel for all ships of all nations through the Dardanelles.
13. An independent Polish state, to include sections which had Polish populations; an outlet to the sea for Poland.

14. A general union, or league of nations, formed under rules guaranteeing the territories of large and small states alike. The league would be formed under strict treaties for mutual guarantees.

**Those who tried to block** America's war effort faced prison terms and large fines.

AMERICA STRENGTHENED the laws against those who tried to block the war effort, with passage of the Sedition Act on May 16, 1918. This law made the Espionage Act of 1917 wider and stronger. The Espionage Act provided for $10,000 fines and twenty years in prison for disloyalty and treason. The two laws—the Sedition and Espionage Acts—were aimed at all who attempted to slow down America's efforts to win the war. It was ruled against the law to stir up insubordination, or refusal to obey orders, in the armed services. Those who plotted to lower America's morale, or fighting spirit, with untrue, disloyal or critical statements about the government, Constitution, flag, or Army and Navy could be arrested and tried under the two acts. The Postmaster General was given the power to keep out of the mails papers or writings which made seditious, or disloyal, statements. The Attorney General could decide on how far civil liberties should be permitted to go before he stepped in and enforced the laws. Eugene V. Debs and Victor L. Berger, socialist leaders, were convicted of breaking the Sedition Act and served prison terms.

**Troops of the Big Red One,** the First Division, were the first Americans to see action. Much of the fighting was from trenches.

AMERICA'S FIRST FIGHTING in World War I came when Pershing sent troops to the front on October 21, 1917. The first Americans to see action were units of the First Division, known as the Big Red One. American troops joined in heavy fighting in March, 1918, to help meet a German drive. France's Ferdinand Foch became supreme commander of the Western Front. Pershing put American units under Foch's command. These American fighting men helped stop the German drive at Amiens. The first American victory of the war was won by the Big Red One as it captured and held Cantigny, an important point on the road from Amiens to Paris.

THE GERMAN ARMY struck another blow, this time to the south of the Aisne River sector, or area, held by the French. The Germans established a forty-mile line only fifty miles from Paris. As the enemy moved in for an attack, Pershing rushed 85,000 American troops into the fight. Three Army divisions and United States Marines were included. A battle was fought at Chateau-Thierry on June 3-4 and the Germans were stopped. The Americans provided the strength needed to halt the threat to Paris.

MORE HEAVY FIGHTING by the Americans at Belleau Wood helped put new blocks in the path of the Germans' advance. It was the largest action thus far for the Second Division. The Fourth United States Marine Brigade was joined with them. The Americans recaptured Vaux, Bouresches and Belleau Wood, which had been taken by the Germans when they broke through at Soissons. The Marines attacked across tall fields through heavy German fire to provide a thrilling chapter in Corps' history. Another German attack was stopped after a gain of six miles. The First Division held an Allied flank, or one end of a line, during the six-day battle.

## *PERSHING'S ARMY WINS AT ST. MIHIEL*

A MILLION FIGHTING AMERICANS had been convoyed to France by the Navy by the middle of July. America's fighting weight was ready to be thrown against the Germans. On July 15, German General Erich Von Ludendorff launched a drive to seal off Rheims. A second drive to the west took German troops across the Marne River. The Allies made a stand, with 85,000 American troops taking part in the battle. The Allies took the initiative and, on July 18, Foch began a counter-offensive against the Germans' Chateau-Thierry salient, or advanced battle area bulging out from the main line. About 270,000 Americans fought in this offensive. One American force drove a German force back across the Marne. This threw the Germans into retreat, and the Allies drove forward.

GENERAL PERSHING recalled a large number of his troops from the Allied armies which they had joined. The war had reached a turning point and Pershing was ready to strike in the first entirely American campaign. St. Mihiel, which had been held by the Germans since 1914, was Pershing's target. St. Mihiel was southeast of French-held Verdun. With Metz to the northeast, St. Mihiel formed a triangular salient of the Toul sector threatening Verdun. Pershing's Americans struck on September 12, 1918, with French colonial troops and British and French warplanes helping. Heavy fighting drove the Germans back in twenty-four hours. In three days, the Americans turned the battle into a rout. More than 500,000 American troops were engaged in the action. The A.E.F. was now in full stride, ready to strike a decisive blow.

**Americans,** now fighting on their own, drove through enemy defenses and wiped out the salient threatening Verdun. The A.E.F. was now ready for a decisive blow.

THE A.E.F. HAD BECOME a mighty fighting force, able to handle any task given it. Pershing led this army of more than 1,000,000 battle-hardened men into its greatest battle of World War I. They won the battle, called the Meuse-Argonne, and helped bring the Central Powers to their knees. The main supply line for the German army on the Western Front was the Sedan-Mezieres railroad. Pershing was assigned to cut the railroad at Sedan. The way to Sedan led along the Meuse River and through the Argonne forest. Pershing used every available American division in this, the largest action any United States army ever had undertaken.

THREE ATTACKS WERE MADE on the German line as the Americans fought through the Meuse-Argonne. The first two attacks, with heavy losses on both sides, wore down the Germans. The final drive, begun on November 1, 1918, completed the mission. Sedan was won and the railroad was cut. The action cost America 100,000 casualties, but it was one of the death blows to Germany. It was during the Meuse-Argonne campaign that Sergeant Alvin C. York of Tennessee won the Allied command's praise as the "greatest citizen soldier of World War I." When his patrol was trapped by German machine guns, York killed twenty-five Germans and with a few men captured 132 others.

ALLIED ARMIES were successful on all fronts in delivering the death blows to Germany and her allies. The British battered the Germans in the Somme campaign, driving back the enemy closer and closer to his own land. French forces drove near the Belgian border in the Oise-Aisne offensive. Bulgaria was knocked out of the war after big losses. Turkey quit after a defeat in Palestine. The Austrian army was crushed on the Italian front. Surrender or disaster—Germany had no other choice.

**A mighty American army** of a million men fought through the Argonne forest to cut off Germany's main railroad supply line at Sedan. The end of the war drew near.

## GERMANS ADMIT DEFEAT—ARMISTICE ENDS THE FIGHTING

ARMISTICE! World War I came to an end with a "cease-fire" on November 11, 1918. The war had moved swiftly toward its ending with the blows struck by the Allies in October. General Ludendorff, the German field commander, admitted defeat as early as September 29. On that date he asked the German government to seek an armistice. On October 2, a new German government was formed with Prince Max of Baden as the head. On October 6, through the Swiss, Germany asked President Wilson for an armistice. The Germans also asked that Wilson's Fourteen Points be used in the writing of a peace treaty.

A MONTH'S DELAY followed while Wilson sought agreement of the other Allied nations. England and France were against the Fourteen Point plan. They finally agreed when a threat developed that the United States might make peace with Germany on its own. Meanwhile, Germany's navy mutinied, or revolted, against its commanders. A revolt broke out in Bavaria and Austria surrendered. Kaiser Wilhelm II abdicated, or gave up his throne, and fled to Holland. A republic was formed in Germany.

Marshal Foch, meanwhile, had begun talks with a German armistice commission in the Forest of Compiegne. Armistice terms were agreed upon. Germany's surrender was complete. The German army was to withdraw to the left bank of the Rhine. Allied prisoners were to be returned. The remaining German submarines were to be surrendered and the fleet was to be tied up in port. A large amount of military supplies and many railroad engines and cars were to be turned over to the Allies. At 5 A.M. on November 11, Foch and the Germans signed the armistice in a railroad car at Compiegne. Fighting ended at 11 A.M. and wild rejoicing resulted in the United States. All other celebrations faded before America's great joy in this one.

**Ludendorff admitted** defeat. Max took over Germany's government. The kaiser fled to Holland. An armistice came on November 11, 1918, ending the war's fighting.

MANY LANDS TORN BY THE WAR were filled with hungry and homeless people. The hearts of the victors went out to the victims. A European Relief Council was formed on January 3, 1919, with Herbert Hoover as its chairman. Hunger and poverty held in their grasp not only the defeated enemy countries, but also other nations which had been overrun and seized. The Allied victory freed the captured peoples, but they still faced a fight to live. They needed food, clothing, fuel and medical supplies and the relief council under Hoover rushed help.

HERBERT HOOVER was the natural choice to head the relief council. When the war broke out in 1914, Hoover was in Europe. He became head of the American Relief Committee in London. Americans gave money generously. Hoover was National Food Administrator in America during the war and helped conserve food.

**Secretary of War Newton D. Baker** appointed Emmett J. Scott as his special assistant to help solve blacks' problems.

DURING AND AFTER WORLD WAR I, blacks faced military and economic struggles. When America declared war on Germany in April, 1917, many blacks rushed to volunteer, most of whom were not accepted. But 700,000 reported on the first day of registration for the draft, and 2,290,525 in all registered before the end. About 367,000 of them were called into service, many with combat units. Blacks were kept within all-black units, under both white and black officers. Many racial problems arose and, to help solve them, Secretary of War Newton D. Baker appointed Emmett J. Scott as his special assistant. Scott had been Booker T. Washington's secretary for eighteen years. He helped black soldiers on problems of the draft, war risk insurance, army allowances and pay, and discrimination.

A GREAT MIGRATION of blacks from the South to the North took place during the war. With northern industry in massive wartime production, the need for more workers increased. Hundreds of thousands of blacks migrated from the South. They helped produce guns, ammunition and other war goods. More than 25,000 worked in shipyards, building warships and merchant vessels. Many black women also worked in war plants. The National Urban League, which had been formed in 1911, aided the blacks' in finding housing and in the other problems of resettlement.

JOB OPPORTUNITIES DECLINED for blacks after World War I. With war production ended and working forces reduced, blacks turned to such other fields as the auto industry, transportation and communications. But there they faced the problem of union membership. In 1920, the Friends of Negro Freedom was organized, hoping to form unions among black workers. Next came a National Association for the Promotion of Labor Unionism among Negroes, led by A. Philip Randolph and Chandler Owen. In 1925, an American Negro Labor Congress was held in Chicago. It hoped to join blacks and whites in the labor movement. That same year, Randolph organized the Brotherhood of Sleeping Car Porters and Maids.

NEW BLACK SOCIAL MOVEMENTS also were prominent during this period. Marcus Garvey of Jamaica organized a New York branch of his Universal Negro Improvement Association in 1916. By the end of the war, there were thirty U.S. branches.

PRESIDENT WILSON personally led America's huge treaty group to the peace conference at Paris. Wilson visited London and Rome, while on the way, and was greeted as a great leader who had brought peace to the world. The President took with him to Europe a group so large it used most of the space on the liner *George Washington*. Included were the peace treaty leaders, dozens of newspapermen, and a large number of advisors and experts. It rightly was called the world's largest diplomatic mission ever to cross the seas.

WILSON WAS DETERMINED to put his Fourteen Points into the treaty as the conference opened on January 18, 1919. The President and the other members of the Big Four—Prime Minister Lloyd George of England, Premier Georges Clemenceau of France, and Premier Vittorio Orlando of Italy—were the decision-makers. Wilson's official treaty team included Colonel Edward M. House, Secretary of State Robert Lansing, General Tasker H. Bliss and Henry White, a veteran of the foreign service. No members of Congress were included and there was only one Republican on the commission—White.

WILSON INSISTED that the peace treaty should be based on a League of Nations. His plan was fought by some of the twenty-six other nations attending the conference, which was held at Versailles near Paris. But Wilson won his argument and headed the group which prepared the League constitution. The draft, or written copy, of the constitution was laid before the conference on February 14, 1919. Wilson returned to the United States to present the League plan to his government leaders. Opposition had developed in America. A group of Republican senators told Wilson that the League, as presented to them, would be rejected by the Senate.

**President Wilson** led an American peace group to Paris. It was so large it needed most of the space on a big liner. The Big Four made all decisions at Paris.

WILSON TOOK his League of Nations fight to the people. Opposition to the League was growing in the Senate. Only loyal Democratic senators favored ratification, or approval, of the League. Wilson began his tour by special train on September 3, 1919. He traveled 9,500 miles, making thirty-seven speeches in twenty-nine states. The President's health broke down under the strain. He fainted on the train at Pueblo, Colorado, on September 26, and was taken back to Washington. The President suffered a stroke, or paralysis, on October 2, after returning to Washington. Wilson's left side was paralyzed and he never fully recovered. With the help of his wife, he ran the Presidency while still quite ill.

THE SENATE DEFEATED approval of the League of Nations with the help of Democrats. These Democrats would not accept changes offered by Senator Henry Cabot Lodge. From his bed, Wilson wrote that the changes would "nullify the treaty." The President said that Lodge's changes would take the strength out of both the League and treaty. The Senate took two votes and turned down both the League and peace treaty. Wilson then vetoed a declaration by Congress that World War I was at an end. America officially remained at war with Germany and the other Central Powers, even though the fighting in the war had ended many months before.

THE LEAGUE OF NATIONS opened in 1920 at Geneva, Switzerland, with fifty-four nations attending. One seat was left empty for the United States. The other nations still hoped America would have a change of heart. Since Wilson had started the League, America's former war allies felt deserted when the Senate refused to go along with the President.

**Thirty-seven speeches made** in twenty-nine states put too much of a strain on Wilson. The President collapsed in Colorado.

## *PROHIBITION ADOPTED—U.S. FINDS IT HARD TO ENFORCE*

PROHIBITION WAS ADOPTED when alcoholic drinks were outlawed in the United States by the ratification of the Eighteenth Amendment on January 29, 1919. The new law made it illegal to make, transport, bring into the country or sell alcoholic drinks. The passing of national prohibition marked the end of a century-old fight by the Anti-Saloon League, the Washingtonians and Women's Christian Temperance Union against the evils of alcohol. By the time the Eighteenth Amendment was ratified, nineteen states already had prohibition laws of their own in effect.

ENFORCEMENT OF PROHIBITION was another problem. Over President Wilson's veto, the Volstead Act was passed in October, 1919, establishing enforcement machinery under the Bureau of Internal Revenue. January 16, 1920, was set as the starting date. Prohibition lawlessness followed at once. Bootleg, or illegal liquor, empires arose under such ganglords as Al Capone of Chicago. The ganglords sold unlimited supplies of liquor to people who wanted to drink. Secret saloons called "speakeasies" sold drinks across the bar. Many people manufactured their own home-brew (beer) and gin in bathtubs. There were many gang slayings, often in broad daylight on crowded city streets.

SENTIMENT FOR REPEAL of prohibition developed. Problems of enforcement had turned prohibition into a noble, but losing experiment. A commission under George W. Wickersham, a former Attorney General, studied the problems connected with prohibition. In its report in January, 1931, the commission spelled out the difficulties of enforcement of the Eighteenth Amendment. Among the main problems of enforcement, the report said, was the lack of public acceptance of prohibition. Many patronized bootleggers and speakeasies.

**Prohibition made it illegal** to sell alcoholic liquors for drinking purposes, but many "speakeasies" (secret saloons) sold them.

## *WOMEN FINALLY WIN THE RIGHT TO VOTE IN ALL ELECTIONS*

**It had been a long fight,** but women won full voting rights at last. First women's rights convention was held 72 years before.

WOMEN'S RIGHT TO VOTE in all elections was added to the Constitution with ratification of the Nineteenth Amendment on August 26, 1920. Women's fight for these equal rights finally reached a triumphant climax. Seventy-two years had passed since Lucretia Mott and Elizabeth Cady Stanton held the first Women's Rights Convention. Wyoming was the first state to legalize women's voting—in 1869. By 1919, fifteen states had similar laws. In 1916, Montana elected Jeanette Rankin as the first woman member of Congress. But women did not enjoy full voting rights until the Nineteenth Amendment was passed, stating, "The right of citizens of the United States to vote shall not be denied or abridged (limited) by the United States or any state on account of sex."

TWO EARLIER AMENDMENTS to the Constitution brought important changes in America's economy and politics. The Sixteenth Amendment, ratified on February 25, 1913, established a permanent income tax on personal and corporate (company) earnings. The 1913 income tax law was not the first passed in America. During the Civil War, the Union had taxed incomes to help pay expenses of the war. During President Grover Cleveland's second administration, an attempt was made to establish a permanent income tax, but the Supreme Court ruled it was unconstitutional because it was not based on population. The Supreme Court's ruling made the Sixteenth Amendment necessary.

DIRECT ELECTION OF SENATORS by the people was adopted with ratification of the Seventeenth Amendment on May 31, 1913. Until then, U.S. senators had been chosen by the state legislatures, and there were many charges of seats being "bought" and "sold." Four times since 1894 the House supported amendments in Congress to change the system, but each time the Senate blocked the change. Voters in thirty states finally supported laws forcing their legislatures to hold primary elections for senators and then send to the Senate those who were elected.

# *U.S. MOVES TO HALT NAVAL RACE END IN FAILURE*

**America** asked other nations to end building up their navies and to scrap warships. The other nations agreed, but tore up only plans while America scrapped steel ships.

PRESIDENT HARDING called a conference to discuss naval disarmament, or the cutting down in the size, strength and costs of the world's navies. The conference opened in Washington on November 12, 1921, and nine nations attended—the United States, Great Britain, France, Japan, Italy, China, the Netherlands, Portugal and Belgium. Secretary of State Charles E. Hughes explained America's plan for naval disarmament. America, Great Britain and Japan were spending huge sums of money on their navies. Hughes said the time had come to halt the costly naval race.

HUGHES STARTLED the others by saying that America would scrap 845,000 tons of naval ships. America would scrap ships being built or already in the fleet, if England would scrap 583,000 tons and Japan would scrap 480,000 tons. Great Britain and Japan agreed in general. A treaty to reduce the size of the navies was worked out. It was based on the tonnage of capital ships, or those ships weighing more than 10,000 tons and carrying guns which fired shells larger than eight inches. Cruisers, destroyers, aircraft carriers and submarines were not included in the reduction.

A RATIO, OR SHARE, of capital ship tonnage to be kept by five big nations was decided upon. The ratio, or shares of warship tonnage, was set at 5 for the United States and England, 3 for Japan and 1.75 for France and Italy. A ten-year naval holiday was agreed upon, with no nation building any new capital ships.

NAVAL DISARMAMENT failed to develop as the United States had planned. The other nations scrapped only plans to build ships while the United States scrapped battleships already afloat. Also, England and Japan still built up their naval strength with the addition of cruisers, destroyers and submarines. America did not want to keep spending money to build new warships to keep up with Great Britain and Japan. Another naval conference was held in Geneva, June 20 to August 4, 1927, but nothing was agreed upon. In still another conference at Geneva in 1930, America's only gain was to have limits placed on all types of warships, instead of only capital ships. The United States gave up on disarmament.

PRESIDENT HARDING'S DEATH on August 2, 1923, shocked the world. The President died in a San Francisco hotel after returning from a good will trip to Alaska and Canada. He became sick with ptomaine poisoning from spoiled food. Pneumonia and death followed. Doctors said the President's death was caused by embolism, or blocking of a blood vessel. Harding's body was taken back to Washington on a special funeral train. Crowds totaling 3,000,000 met the train on its way to Washington, to pay their respects to the dead President. Harding was buried later in Marion, Ohio.

TRAGEDY AND MYSTERY marked the final days of Warren G. Harding. He was a saddened President when he left Washington on June 20 to start the trip to Alaska. Rumors of corruption, or dishonesty, in his administration had shaken him. The long-rumored corruption was revealed after Harding's death. The biggest scandal was the Teapot Dome deal in which Albert Fall, Secretary of the Interior, was sent to prison for taking bribes, or money, to give private leases on naval oil reserves, including Teapot Dome in Wyoming. Harding felt that he had been betrayed, or treated badly, by some of the Ohio friends to whom he had given Washington jobs. Charles F. Cramer and Jesse Smith, both assistants to important department heads, had committed suicide, or killed themselves. The day before he left Washington, Harding had a will drawn up for him by Attorney General Harry M. Daugherty.

THE TRIP WEST was hard for Harding. He struggled through many speeches and public appearances. The President's wife, Mrs. Florence King Harding, and his doctor warned Harding that he did not look well. The President refused to cancel his trip. Harding became ill after eating seafood. Arriving at San Francisco on July 29, he went to bed and soon died. Many said that Harding died because he no longer had the will to live.

CALVIN COOLIDGE, the Vice-President, was awakened at 2 A.M. to be told of Harding's death. His father, a notary public, swore him in as President by the light of a kerosene lamp in a quiet Vermont farmhouse. Coolidge was cautious, quiet and very careful with money. While governor of Massachusetts, he won national praise and attention with his firm action in handling a Boston police strike. He had never been to Washington, D.C. until his election as Vice-President.

**President Harding** was saddened from many dishonest acts by his friends in government.

# *AMERICA'S FORMER ALLIES FAIL TO PAY WAR DEBTS*

WAR DEBTS OWED to the United States from the Allies were disputed for many years. The war reparations, or damages, that the Allies claimed from Germany also were disputed. Almost every European nation, except Germany, owed America money. The debts came from war loans or from money advanced to help rebuild their war-torn lands. The total debt was ten billion dollars. The Allied Reparations Commission gave Germany a bill for thirty-three billion dollars. The two disputes became linked. The Allies said they would pay the United States only when Germany paid them. The United States said that debts were debts, and the Allies should pay up. In January, 1923, Germany failed to make its reparations payments to the Allies. As punishment, French and Belgian troops occupied the German Ruhr industrial district, rich in coal and iron mines.

THE DAWES PLAN was adopted to help solve the problem. At the reparations board's request, the United States named General Charles G. Dawes, Owen D. Young and Henry M. Robinson to work out the plan. The program finally was ready in April, 1924. Reparations were reduced, and Germany was loaned $200,000,000 to stabilize the mark, Germany's main unit of money. The United States still pressed the Allies to pay their debts. The Allies ignored the demands for payment, and only admitted that they owed the money.

THE WAR DEBT quarrel went on and in February, 1929, the Dawes Plan was changed. A new Young Plan took its place. This plan cut the German reparations bill to about eight billion dollars. As to the war debts, only Finland kept up its payments to the United States. The war debts of the other nations never were paid and the United States finally dropped its demands.

**All of America's demands** could wring little war debt money from her former Allies. The Allies wanted billions from Germany, but they never paid their debts to America.

**The Lone Eagle** nearly got his wings wet flying low over the Atlantic to Paris.

LINDBERGH FLEW ALONE across the Atlantic Ocean on a non-stop flight from New York to Paris on May 20-21, 1927. The 3,600-mile flight was made in 33½ hours, and all America cheered the daring of its new hero. Charles A. Lindbergh, Jr., was a pilot in the airmail service. A New York hotel owner in 1919 had offered a prize of $25,000 for the first pilot to fly solo, non-stop to Paris. Lindbergh took off in a little monoplane, the *Spirit of St. Louis,* to try for the prize. At 7:52 A.M. on May 20, Lindbergh raced his plane down the runway of Roosevelt Field at New York. He took off and headed into misty, cloudy skies in the direction of Nova Scotia and Newfoundland. He flew low, sometimes no more than ten feet above trees on land and the waves over water.

LINDBERGH FLEW ON as darkness fell over the Atlantic. He went up to 10,000 feet as fog and storm clouds gathered. Late in the second day, Lindbergh saw fishing boats. Then hills took shape in the distance, and he knew that he was on the right course. Lindbergh reached Ireland and set a compass course for Paris. The lights of Le Bourget Field, outside Paris, came into view. Lindbergh landed at Le Bourget at 10 P.M. as a crowd of thousands watched and roared a welcome. America called Lindbergh the "Lone Eagle."

AMELIA EARHART was the first woman to fly across the Atlantic Ocean. She and two men made the flight on July 17-18, 1928, from Trepassy, Newfoundland, to Burry Port, Wales. Wilmer Stultz was co-pilot and Louis Gordon was the mechanic. The crossing was made in a three-motored Fokker monoplane in twenty hours and forty-nine minutes. Miss Earhart later made solo flights across the Atlantic and Pacific Oceans. She was lost, and never found, during a flight over the Pacific.

## *U.S. JOINS OTHER NATIONS IN "LAW AGAINST WAR"*

WAR WAS OUTLAWED and war-seeking nations were called criminals in a Kellogg-Briand Peace Pact signed in 1928. The disarmament meetings of the 1920's had failed to end fears that new wars might break out. A desire grew among peace-loving people of the world for an international law against wars. Many leaders in the United States backed the idea, believing that a world peace pledge would put this nation beyond the danger of new foreign troubles.

ARISTIDE BRIAND, the French foreign minister, was approached by backers of the plan. He said he was interested. President Coolidge and Secretary of State Frank B. Kellogg were cool toward the idea. They saw a two-nation treaty with France as a promise by America to help France in case of war. Senator William E. Borah of Idaho was strongly in favor of a world peace treaty. He made speeches asking the "outlawing of war" and spread the idea of having all nations join in such an agreement. A petition, or request, which Borah wrote, was signed by 800,000 members of the National Grange, a farmers' organization. Some 2,000,000 Americans finally signed Borah's petition against war. The campaign spread from coast to coast and demands grew for America to do something about the new idea of a law against war.

COOLIDGE AND KELLOGG gave in, and the United States joined fourteen other nations in signing the Pact of Paris on August 27, 1928. The treaty said that war was an "instrument of national policy." It provided for all disputes, from whatever causes, to be decided in a peaceful manner. Many other nations signed later. The Senate ratified the Kellogg-Briand Pact, eighty-five to one. Many foes of the pact laughed at it. They said that it offered no plan for punishing nations which broke the law against war, and it did not rule out "self-defense" wars.

**A treaty to outlaw war** was signed by America and fourteen other countries.

## *HOOVER ADOPTS A GOOD NEIGHBOR POLICY*

A GOOD NEIGHBOR POLICY toward Latin America was Herbert Hoover's new idea. Soon after winning the 1928 election as President, Hoover left America on a good will tour of the Latin American countries. In a seven-week tour he visited eleven of them. In all of these countries, Hoover talked about America's friendship toward Latin America. He spoke of America's being a "good neighbor." All of the nations he visited gave him a warm welcome. In Brazil he was widely cheered.

HOOVER WAS A STRONG believer in friendship with other peoples. He had devoted much of his life to helping poor people in many lands. After working as a mining engineer in many continents, he had headed American food and relief projects for the victims of World War I.

A DECLARATION of America's new Latin American policy was written with Hoover's approval. It was the Clark Memorandum on the Monroe Doctrine written by Reuben J. Clark, Under Secretary of State. The memorandum canceled the Roosevelt Corollary to the Monroe Doctrine. That statement by Theodore Roosevelt in December, 1904, had said: "Chronic wrong-doing . . . may in America, as elsewhere, require intervention by some civilized nation, and in the Western Hemisphere adherence of the United States to the Monroe Doctrine may force the United States, however reluctantly, in flagrant cases . . . to the prompt exercise of an international police power."

THE UNITED STATES had used this power in several cases to step in and settle political and financial troubles in Latin America. In some cases only this United States action had stopped European nations from invading and taking over several republics. Warnings from America also had settled many border disputes. The Clark Memorandum said America had no right to interfere in Latin American affairs. It said the true purpose of the Monroe Doctrine was to "state a case of the United States versus Europe, and not the United States versus Latin America." The memorandum said the Monroe Doctrine was a weapon of defense and not of control of the rights of other countries.

HOOVER SAID he planned to "retreat from imperialism" and turn to "good neighborliness." He said, "We have no desire for territorial expansion, for economic or other domination of other people." Theodore Roosevelt's policy of "policing" Latin America was no longer in force.

**The Hoover administration** told Latin Americans that the United States had no right to interfere in their republics' affairs.

## *STOCK MARKET CRASH BRINGS SORROW TO MILLIONS*

**Millionaires became hungry** and some others became beggars and peddlers after the stock market crash. Billions of dollars in "paper" values were wiped out as stock prices fell.

A GREAT MARKET CRASH hit America in the fall of 1929 ending a period of wealth and big business. Americans had borrowed billions of dollars to gamble in the stock market. The first hint of a stock market crash came early in October when England raised the interest rates, or income, on British business and stock deals made at home. This was done to call back money which had been used to buy stocks in America. As a result, British holders of American stocks put them up for sale on the New York market to collect their money and use it at home. A general drop in stock prices began. American stock holders began to sell their stocks.

OCTOBER 29, 1929, was the darkest day ever to hit Wall Street, "home" of the stock market. A total of 16,800,000 shares of stock were sold. Prices fell swiftly. Many stocks which had been over-priced were wiped off the board. Even the trusted "blue chips," or most reliable stocks, were unloaded in a wild rush to sell before prices dropped further. Billions of dollars in the listed, or "paper," values of stocks vanished. Fortunes were lost with each click of the stock ticker. Stock holders begged their bankers, friends and relatives to lend them money to cover their losses. By evening, Wall Street was a street of doom.

THIRTY BILLION DOLLARS in stock "paper" values were wiped out in October. All efforts by the government, banks and people with money to recover from the blow failed. Trade came to a full stop; loss of jobs became general. Homes were lost. People who once had much money became hungry. Former stock holders who thought they were millionaires became broke almost overnight. Banks, business and factories closed. The Great Depression, or period of national poverty, had begun.

DEPRESSION AT ITS WORST had gripped America by the mid-1930's. The people cried for relief. Millions of workers were without jobs and had no money for food or clothing. Misery had taken the place of the happy days of wealth. The Hoover administration for months had refused to admit that there was a depression. The people were told that "prosperity was just around the corner." Soon, the people were told, there would be "business as usual." Finally, in October, 1930, Hoover admitted that the worst had happened and he began planning relief measures.

BUSINESS LEADERS were called to Washington for conferences in November. Hoover asked them to help bring back good times. He asked that the "first shock" fall on company profits and that wages not be cut and workers not be fired. But the businessmen already had lost their profits. They already had fired many workers and cut the wages of others. Hoover asked Congress for $150,000,000 for a program of public building which would provide jobs for those out of work. Included in the building plan were roads, public buildings, airfields, and river and harbor works. One project was Boulder Dam on the Colorado River, near Las Vegas. It watered vast farmlands and later was renamed Hoover Dam.

DIRECT FEDERAL AID to the needy was opposed by Hoover. The President thought it was the duty of the states, cities and volunteer groups to give direct help. He asked their support in a nation-wide relief effort. In many cities, food lines were formed, and soup and bread were given to hungry people. Hoover took two other steps to fight the depression, but without success. They were the Reconstruction Finance Corporation, which made it easier to obtain business loans, and an act providing federal loans for people who owned homes.

**Millions lost jobs** and could not buy food. Hoover admitted that the worst had come.

## *ROOSEVELT'S PROGRAM: RELIEF, RECOVERY, REFORM*

FRANKLIN DELANO ROOSEVELT was elected as the thirty-second President in 1932. He proposed a New Deal program to stop the depression. He had defeated Hoover in a landslide victory. Roosevelt, the governor of New York, won forty-two states. In his election campaign, Roosevelt told the nation: "I pledge you, I pledge myself, to a new deal for the American people." In his inaugural, or opening, address on March 4, 1933, Roosevelt said: "The only thing we have to fear is fear itself." On becoming President, Roosevelt at once launched a program of three "R's"—relief, recovery and reform.

ROOSEVELT CLOSED all American banks on the day after he took office as President. All business was halted for four days in the Federal Reserve System, trust companies, banks, credit unions, and building and loan associations. After examination, most were found sound and were permitted to reopen. Roosevelt called Congress into a special session. During this special session, known as the "Hundred Days," work was at top speed to put Roosevelt's recovery program into law. A Banking Act authorized the Treasury to call in all gold and gold bank notes. The saving of gold was prohibited. An Economy Act reduced government expenses with salary and spending cuts. The Federal Deposit Insurance Corporation was created, insuring a person's savings up to $5,000 (later $10,000).

A CIVILIAN CONSERVATION CORPS gave jobs in conservation, or forest saving, camps to men between eighteen and twenty-five. Codes of fair competition, set up by industry itself, were called for by a National Industrial Recovery Act (NIRA) and the National Recovery Administration (NRA) provided laws enforcing the codes. Quick relief for America's hungry millions was provided by a Federal Emergency Relief Administration. In the spring of 1933, the total of workers without jobs rose to approximately 13,000,000.

**Franklin Delano Roosevelt** became the man people looked to for relief. "The only thing we have to fear is fear itself," he said.

SEVERAL MILLIONS OF OTHERS were on relief lists. States and cities found the costs of relief were climbing beyond their ability to pay. The U.S. voted half a billion dollars for relief, to be handled by state and local governments. Farmers were helped by an act which reduced the amount of crops that could be grown, but paid the farmers for the crops they did not grow. A Farm Credit Act gave easier loans.

THE TENNESSEE VALLEY AUTHORITY (TVA) built dams, power plants and electricity lines throughout the Tennessee River Valley. Cheap electricity was provided for seven southern states. A Civil Works Administration gave jobs to 4,000,000 workers who built government projects. As he had promised in his election campaign, Roosevelt brought about the repeal of prohibition through the Twenty-First Amendment, which was ratified by enough states to go into effect on December 5, 1933.

**American troops** were called home from Nicaragua and Haiti. For the first time in eighteen years, no United States troops were stationed in Latin American countries.

"AMERICA, THE GOOD NEIGHBOR," became a fact during the first year of Roosevelt's administration. The United States had a long record of stepping into Latin American affairs. In 1901, changes in Cuba's constitution had given the United States some control over the island. In 1904, Theodore Roosevelt had declared that the United States had the right to use "police power" over Latin American "wrongdoers." In 1928, under Hoover, the Clark Memorandum on the Monroe Doctrine canceled Theodore Roosevelt's "policing powers." The Clark Memorandum had begun America's good neighbor policy.

FRANKLIN ROOSEVELT put the Good Neighbor Policy into action. In his inaugural, or opening, address he had said: "In the field of world policy, I would dedicate this nation to the policy of the good neighbor—the neighbor who resolutely respects himself and, because he does, respects the rights of others." Roosevelt's statement was pointed toward Latin America, where an unfriendly feeling toward the United States was building up. Secretary of State Cordell Hull put the new policy on record at a conference at Montevideo, Uruguay, on December 26, 1933. Hull supported a Latin American statement that "no state has the right to intervene in the internal or external affairs of another."

QUICK PROOF of America's new good neighbor policy followed. A treaty was signed with Cuba, freeing the Cubans from all United States control. The lease on the Guantanamo naval base was kept, however. United States Marines withdrew from Nicaragua in 1933 and left Haiti the next year. For the first time since 1915, no United States troops were stationed on Latin American soil. America's hand had been shown many times in the troubled lands of Central and South America. There had been money problems in the Dominican Republic and Nicaragua. Revolts in Mexico had drawn action by the United States.

## *GREAT DEPRESSION IS DEFEATED*

FOR THE NEXT FIVE YEARS, the New Deal fought depression and the country slowly recovered. Millions of jobless men and women were given jobs by the Works Progress Administration (WPA). Many of the men and women were taken off relief and put to work by this New Deal program. Most of the workers were unskilled laborers, but a program also was begun for professional workers, such as actors, musicians, artists and writers. Social Security was passed by Congress in 1935. Social Security provided pensions, or monthly payments, for workers and their wives (or husbands) at age 65. Payments also were provided for workers who lost their jobs through no fault of their own; this was called unemployment compensation. Social Security was paid for by taxes on workers and their employers during a man's working years.

LABOR WON GREAT GAINS with the passing of the National Labor Relations Act in 1935. A National Labor Relations Board (NLRB) was created with powers to hear and judge charges of unfair actions by employers. Collective bargaining was given its greatest boost. So-called company unions, those controlled by employers, faced many challenges by NLRB. Independently organized labor unions had a membership of more than 4,000,000. A dispute in the American Federation of Labor arose when John L. Lewis organized the Committee for Industrial Organizations.

WILD SPECULATION, or gambling, in stocks, such as brought on the great market crash of 1929, resulted in creation of a new Securities and Exchange Commission (SEC). This commission was given powers to regulate the activities of stock exchanges. A Wage and Hour law brought better living to millions of workers with more pay and fewer hours on the job. The work week was set at 44 hours, later 40 hours. Time-and-one-half was paid for overtime work.

**The Wage and Hour law** brought shorter working hours and more pay to many Americans. Shopping trips to the grocery store became a family treat, instead of a problem.

# COLLECTIVE BARGAINING BIG GAIN FOR LABOR

The federal government's strongest measure to promote collective bargaining by labor and management was the National Labor Relations (Wagner) Act of 1935.

**A National Labor Relations Board (NLRB) was created by the act. The board enforced workingmen's rights to organize and engage in collective bargaining. The workers bargained with their employers through representatives of own choice.**

**When requested by the workers of any company, the NLRB could supervise elections to determine which union would be the bargaining agent for the workingmen. The Wagner Act established limits on management's control of company unions.**

**When it found an employer to be guilty of unfair labor practices, the NLRB could give "cease and desist" orders. The NLRB could appeal to the courts, if necessary, to enforce its order when it was ignored.**

**Collective bargaining helped the rise of a Committee for Industrial Organization (CIO). Under John L. Lewis, the CIO soon rose to power. The committee, while still part of the A.F. of L., organized 300,000 steelworkers and more than 100 contracts were signed. A major victory was won in 1937 when General Motors agreed to recognize the United Automobile Workers as bargaining agent for its members. The CIO withdrew from the A.F. of L. in 1938.**

# THE WINNING OF WORLD WAR II

**Hitler and Mussolini** walked side by side in what they planned to be a march through the free world. The dictators of Germany and Italy formed the Rome-Berlin Axis.

STORM CLOUDS OF ANOTHER WAR gathered over Europe. Adolf Hitler's speeches dared the world to stop him as he rearmed Germany. The German people took up the cry, "Heil Hitler!" Hitler headed a new German national party called the Nazis. Hitler's rule of Germany was harsh. He formed a private army called the "Storm Troopers." This army threatened, beat up and murdered those who were against Hitler. People not considered "pure" German were badly treated and plans were made to get rid of them. Political enemies, Jews, Gypsies, and other non-German minorities were to be rounded up in concentration camps and reduced to slave labor, or were put to death.

IN ITALY, Benito Mussolini planned to build up a new Roman Empire. Europe's democracies were alarmed, but the depression kept them busy. They took no steps to halt the rise of the two dictators.

ITALY ATTACKED ETHIOPIA as Mussolini put his dream of a Roman Empire into action. On October 3, 1935, the new and modern Italian army drove into weak Ethiopia in East Africa. Ethiopia's Emperor Haile Selassie, known as the "Lion of Judah," fled to England. Addis Ababa, the Ethiopian capital, was captured and Italy's seizure of the country was completed. The League of Nations protested Italy's attack and tried to punish Mussolini with trade penalties, but Mussolini held Ethiopia.

A SPANISH CIVIL WAR broke out and threatened to draw outside nations into the fight. General Francisco Franco led a revolt to overthrow Spain's Loyalist government. Hitler and Mussolini gave Franco help in the form of planes, guns and supplies. Russia gave the same kind of help to the Loyalists. Many American citizens went to Spain to fight for the Loyalists, even though the United States government declared neutrality. Spain's government was overthrown, and Franco became dictator.

GERMANY AND ITALY formed the Rome-Berlin Axis, or partnership, in October, 1936. The Axis was a military pact and agreement to fight Communism. In 1937, Japan joined in a three-way military and anti-Communist treaty with Germany and Italy. The treaty bound together three powerful military nations, all looking to take over their neighbors. Japan had been the first to go to war. In 1931, Japan had invaded Manchuria and in 1937 launched an attack on China. The United States refused to recognize the Japanese government in Manchuria, and warned Japan to stop fighting in China. Japan saw that America was a threat to her new empire. In December, 1937, Japan attacked and sank the U.S. gunboat, *Panay,* in China. A crisis drew nearer.

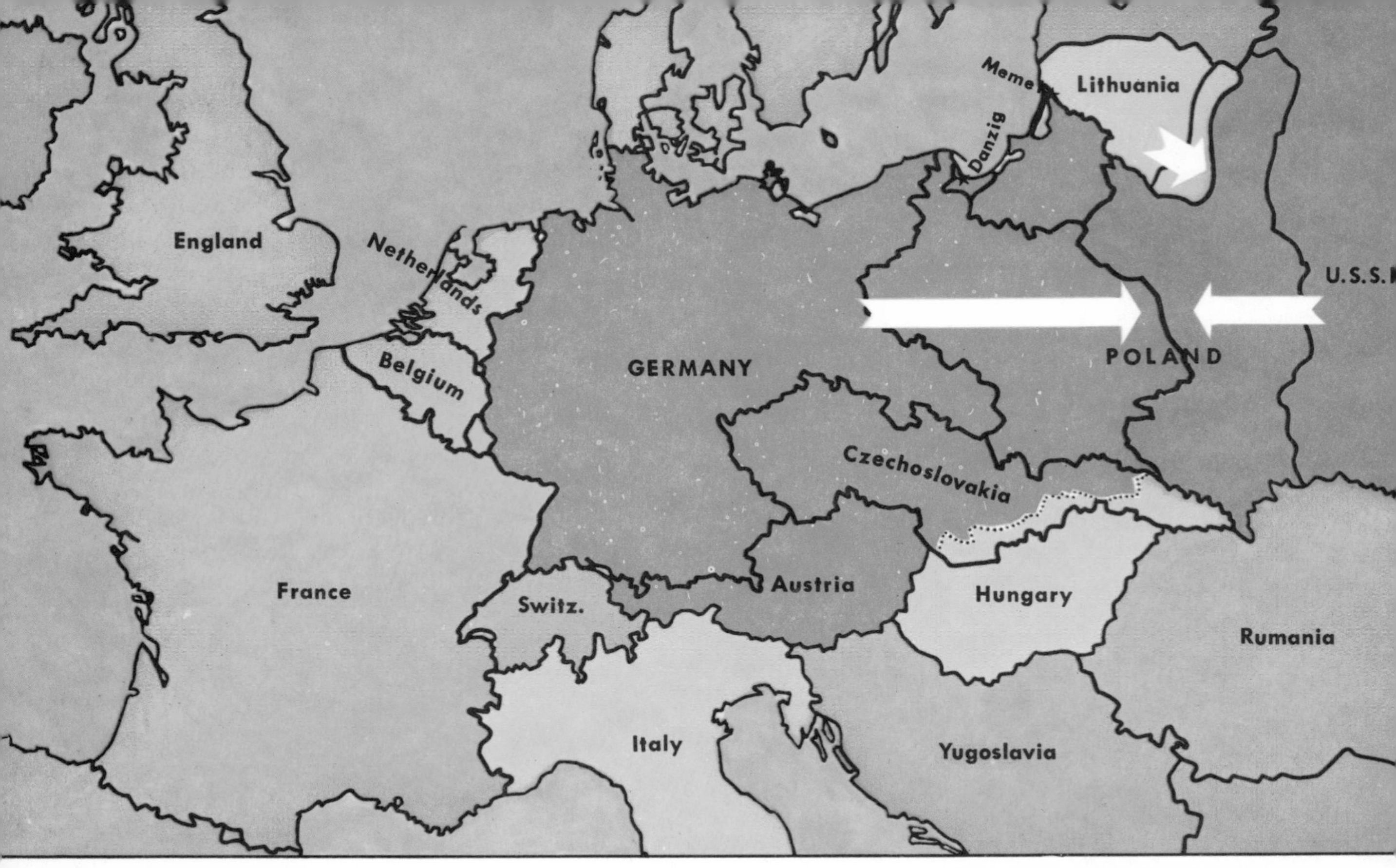


**Poland** took the first deadly blows as Hitler started World War II. Stalin, now Hitler's "friend," sent Russian armies to seize the eastern portion of Poland.

WORLD WAR II FINALLY CAME! Hitler occupied Austria and parts of Czechoslovakia in 1938. In 1939 he seized the remainder of Czechoslovakia and signed a "friendship" pact with Joseph Stalin, dictator of Communist Russia. With Stalin's agreement, Hitler turned on Poland. He wanted to build a highway and railroad across the Polish Corridor, Poland's outlet to the Baltic Sea. When Poland, supported by France and Britain, refused, Hitler invaded Poland on September 1, 1939, and World War II began.

A BRAVE AND WELL-TRAINED Polish army of a million men met the attack. But it did not have the strength or the guns and planes to stop the Nazi "blitzkrieg." The "blitzkrieg" was a lightning combined-attack by warplanes, tanks and land troops. Great Britain and France demanded that Hitler withdraw his forces from Poland. On September 3, after Hitler turned down the demand, Britain and France declared war on Germany. The second great World War in Europe had begun!

IN THREE WEEKS of fighting, the Nazis destroyed the Polish army. The terror of the Germans' Stuka dive bombers spread over the land. The Nazi bombers dropped bombs on many of Poland's cities. Nazi tanks rolled in and the troops followed. Thousands of civilians were killed. By mid-September western Poland was conquered, and its proud city of Warsaw was in ruins.

STALIN SENT his Red, or Communist, armies into eastern Poland on September 17, to seize a share of the now helpless land. Stalin next demanded and got sites for Baltic Sea bases in Latvia, Estonia and Lithuania. But Finland refused the demand. On November 30, the Soviet Union's forces attacked Finland. For three months, little Finland put up a heroic defense. But Russia's great strength won out, and a treaty was signed on March 12, 1940, ending the war. America's sympathy for Finland was great. Little Finland had fought valiantly.

THE WESTERN HEMISPHERE united for common defense against possible attask by outside nations. The rise of Nazi and Fascist dictators frightened the countries of North and South America. Through a series of agreements, unity of the Western Hemisphere was established. Many were written before the war in Europe. Later, other treaties were written.

PLANS FOR UNITED ACTION in case of attack by non-American nations already had been made by the time the war began. At a Buenos Aires Conference in December, 1936, President Roosevelt said in his opening speech that any attack would find the Western Hemisphere "wholly prepared to consult together for our mutual safety and our mutual good." Leaders of other nations of the Americas supported the idea and signed an agreement for defense meetings should any attacks occur.

OPPOSITION TO OUTSIDE threats was pledged at a Lima Conference in December, 1938. The American states signed the Declaration of Lima, agreeing that they would "resist vigorously all foreign intervention or activities that may threaten them." Consultations, or talks, would be held should the "peace, security, or territorial integrity" of any American republic be threatened. Secretary of State Cordell Hull, leader of the United States group, pledged full support of this policy in case of any such event taking place.

A WARNING WAS ISSUED to warring nations to keep their naval battles away from home waters on this side of the Atlantic Ocean. The foreign ministers of the American nations adopted this policy at a meeting in September, 1939, during an Inter-American Conference. The Declaration of Panama was issued. Areas called sea safety zones were outlined in the hemisphere's waters south of Canada. All warring nations were warned not to fight any naval battles within these zones. The Declaration of Panama later was to be tested as Great Britain and Germany sent their warships over wide areas. The United States was the natural leader in the Western Hemispheric unity moves. Also, this nation had greatly improved relations with such republics as Mexico, Brazil, Haiti and Panama. Panama had been granted the rights of a sovereign republic in the canal zone.

**Roosevelt** told Latin Americans that any attack would find Western Hemisphere nations ready to act together for defense.

# LEADERS IN THE WORLD STRUGGLE BETWEEN FREEDOM AND DICTATORS

President Franklin Roosevelt recognized the rising threat of the dictators and their plan to dominate, or rule, the rest of the world. Roosevelt asked Congress to change America's neutrality laws to permit the sale of arms and supplies on a cash and carry plan to nations at war.

Winston Churchill, great soldier and statesman, soon was to become Britain's prime minister in World War II. Churchill had served as the first lord of the admiralty, or navy department, and minister of munitions (arms) during the first World War. In 1940 he headed the admiralty.

Benito Mussolini, Italy's dictator, was allied with Adolf Hitler in the Rome-Berlin Axis. Mussolini had seized Ethiopia and Albania. He waited for a favorable time to join Hitler in war on Britain and France. The Italians were called Fascists.

Hitler, the German dictator, already had annexed Austria, seized Czechoslovakia and overrun western Poland. Hitler had broken the promises he made to Neville Chamberlain in the Munich Pact.

Charles De Gaulle, patriotic French general, refused to accept the coming fall of France as final. De Gaulle and some of his staff fled to England and set up headquarters in London for Free French forces.

Joseph Stalin, dictator of the Soviet Union, signed a friendship pact with Hitler before the Nazi invasion of Poland. Stalin seized the eastern half of Poland, but did not trust Hitler.

Emperor Hirohito of Japan was the Japanese leader of the new order in Asia—"Asia for Asiatics." The Japanese people believed that Hirohito was of divine origin, and obeyed him without question. The Japanese political leaders wanted war.

Chiang Kai-shek rose to power in China as the leading force against Japanese war plans. Chiang Kai-shek headed the Chinese Nationalists. During 1938, American engineers helped build the Burma Road, Chiang Kai-shek's main supply line.

**England's Royal Air Force** turned back Hitler's Luftwaffe after eight weeks of attacks. "Never have so many owed so much to so few," Churchill said of the R.A.F.

A SUDDEN STRIKE by Germany's lightning "blitzkrieg" war turned the so-called "phony" war into a 1,000-mile fighting front. For six months, the German army had stayed behind its Siegfried Line, a chain of concrete "forts," many of them underground on the German borders. The French had waited behind their Maginot Line, the same kind of defense line on the French borders. The British Expeditionary Force had stood by in France. The rest of the world said, "It's a phony war." But, on April 9, 1940, Hitler struck. Without warning, 50,000 Nazi troops poured into Denmark, and German warships steamed into Norwegian harbors. Denmark could put up no fight, and surrendered. The Nazis drove out a British-French expeditionary force and defeated Norway in twenty-four days. Three small nations next fell to the Nazis—the Netherlands, Luxembourg and Belgium.

THE "BLITZKRIEG" drove the Belgians and French back toward the English Channel. The Germans took Boulogne and Calais. On May 28, King Leopold III surrendered the entire Belgian army. The British army was trapped by the swift advance of the Nazis. It was saved by a military miracle at Dunkirk. Every British ship—large and small—that could be used, was sent to Dunkirk. With enemy planes roaring overhead, 340,000 British troops were rescued and taken back to England. Meanwhile, Churchill became British prime minister.

THE FALL OF FRANCE marked the Nazis' sweep to the English Channel. As France was about to fall, Mussolini chose this as the time to declare war on France and England. France surrendered on June 22, 1940, and a Nazi-ruled French government was set up at Vichy. Hitler began heavy air attacks on the British Isles on August 8. For eight weeks, Britain's Royal Air Force fought off and actually defeated Germany's huge Luftwaffe, or air force. Hitler then invaded the Balkans, capturing Rumania, Bulgaria, Hungary and Yugoslavia.

FIFTY OVER-AGE DESTROYERS remaining from World War I were traded to Great Britain by President Roosevelt. In return, the United States was given land for military bases in eight British-held areas of the Western Hemisphere. With Britain fighting Hitler and Mussolini alone, Roosevelt wanted to give her all the help possible. Guns, planes, ammunition and supplies began flowing to England. British warships were permitted to use United States ports and shipyards. British air pilots were trained and attended civil air schools in America. Britain needed escort and patrol ships and the destroyer trade was made.

MANY WORLD WAR I destroyers had been tied up in American naval yards. They were the old four-funnel, or four-stacker, type. Roosevelt made a personal deal with England, trading the fifty destroyers for ninety-nine year rent-free leases on air and naval base sites in Newfoundland, Bermuda, the Bahamas, Jamaica, St. Lucia, Trinidad, Antigua and British Guiana.

LEND-LEASE HELP to Britain and other foes of the Axis was passed by Congress as the next move. This act permitted the United States to lend, lease or otherwise supply arms and military supplies to Britain, or any other nation whose defense was important to America's security. Seven billion dollars was voted to start the program. American isolationists, opposed to taking any part in the war, said the destroyer trade broke the neutrality law.

**America's** old four-stacker destroyers of World War I came out of retirement and rode the oceans again. America traded 50 of them to Britain for eight new bases.

THE WAR CAME TO AMERICA! Pearl Harbor in Hawaii was bombed by the Japanese in a sneak attack on Sunday morning, December 7, 1941. Even while peace talks were being held in Washington with the Japanese, Japan's fleet had sailed for Hawaii. At 2 P.M. (Washington time) that Sunday, Japan's peace talkers handed Secretary of State Cordell Hull a note turning down America's peace offer. Hull already had received news of the attack on Pearl Harbor, which began thirty minutes earlier. The attack began at 7:50 A.M. (Honolulu time) when Japanese dive bombers flew in low from the Pacific Ocean. The enemy planes bombed Army and Navy airfields. Almost all of the American planes were caught on the ground and many were destroyed. Then came more dive bombers and torpedo planes from the Japanese aircraft carriers many miles at sea. Between 150 and 200 planes took part in the attack. Eight American battleships were anchored at the naval base. Japanese pilots singled them out and sank the *Arizona, California* and *West Virginia*. The five other battleships were damaged.

OF EIGHTY-SIX American warships in Pearl Harbor, nineteen were sunk or heavily damaged in the two-hour attack. Plane losses were 177. American casualties were 2,341 killed and more than 1,000 wounded. American pilots who managed to get planes into the air and anti-aircraft gunners shot down fifty Japanese planes. A few hours after they hit Pearl Harbor, the Japanese also attacked the Philippines, Guam, Wake, Midway, Hong Kong and the Malay Peninsula. In his war message to Congress the next day, Roosevelt called it a "day of infamy." Congress declared war on Japan. Germany and Italy declared war on America and America declared war on them.

## *PHILIPPINES FALL*

THE PHILIPPINES FELL to the Japanese after five months of heroic but hopeless defense. The small force of Americans and Filipinos under General Douglas MacArthur was cut off from help. The first Japanese troops landed in the Philippines on December 10, 1941, after two days of bombing. The Japanese took Guam on December 13, and Wake on December 22. Bombing, cannon and land troop attacks made possible the capture of Manila and Cavite on January 2. MacArthur withdrew his forces to the Bataan Peninsula and set up headquarters on Corregidor, "The Rock" in Manila Bay.

MACARTHUR WAS ORDERED to leave secretly for Australia to become commander in the Southwest Pacific. General Jonathan Wainwright, who was left in command, chose to defend Corregidor when forced to get off Bataan on April 9. Corregidor fell on May 6, and Japan's victory in the Philippines was complete.

THOUSANDS OF AMERICAN and Filipino prisoners were forced by the Japanese to make a Death March from Bataan to inland camps. The eighty-five mile march was made by different groups in six to twelve days. Many prisoners were beaten and clubbed. Some were shot, bayoneted or beheaded. Thousands died on the Death March. General Wainwright was one of those who lived. Japanese air, land and sea forces drove through the Western Pacific. Two of Britain's strongest warships, the *Prince of Wales* and the *Repulse,* were sunk by torpedo planes in the South China Sea. Hong Kong, Singapore and Rangoon fell. The Chinese supply line over the Burma Road was cut. Other Japanese invaders captured the Netherlands East Indies. The Japanese invaders were spreading out over the Pacific Ocean.

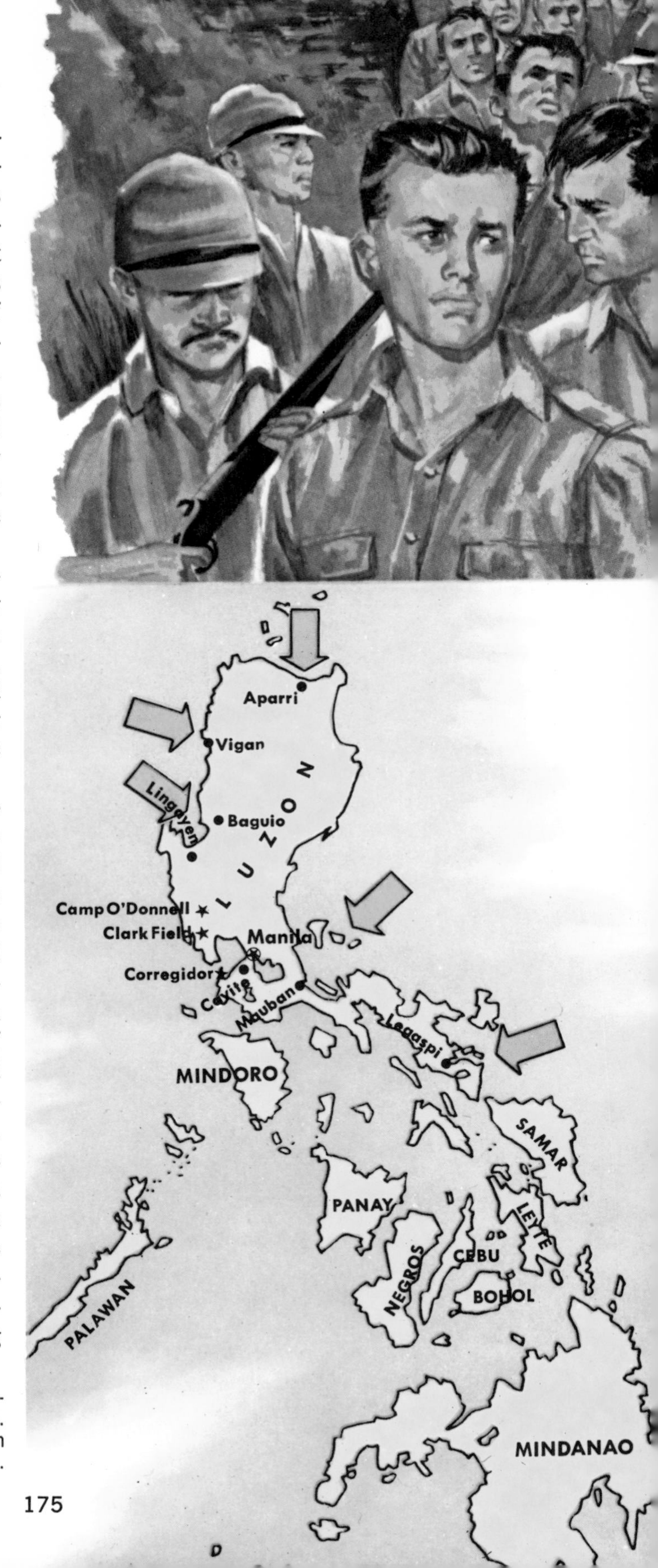


**The Japanese made five landings** on Luzon when they invaded the Philippines. Americans and Filipinos taken prisoner on Bataan were forced into a Death March.

# AMERICA BECAME UNITED IN ALL-OUT EFFORT TO WIN THE WAR

The armed services were unified under the Joint Chiefs of Staff. Admiral William D. Leahy was chief-of-staff for President Roosevelt. Commanders of the armed services were General George C. Marshall of the Army, Admiral Ernest J. King of the Navy, and General Henry H. Arnold of the Army Air Force. Admiral Chester W. Nimitz was commander of the Pacific Fleet.

Americans put aside their private quarrels after the Japanese attack on Pearl Harbor. The nation became united in a mighty war effort. Isolationists, who had fought against America going to war, declared, "Now that we have been attacked, we must crush our enemies of the Axis."

Organized labor joined in the effort. Union strife was put aside and a "no strike" policy was followed, with some exceptions. A National War Labor Board was established by the government with William H. Davis as chairman.

The War Production Board was established under Donald Nelson to speed the production of materials needed for victory. The War Manpower Commission, under Paul V. McNutt, was created to put America's manpower to the best use.

The Red Cross Blood Donors Service was widely supported by Americans who themselves could not fight on the battlefields. Ten million blood donations were made to the Red Cross service. Hundreds of thousands of wounded fighters were helped and countless lives were saved by America's blood donors.

The United Service Organizations (USO) helped keep up the morale of servicemen. The USO established thousands of centers, maintained by volunteer workers. The centers provided off-duty activities. Some of America's most popular entertainers led USO shows into war zones all over the world.

The people responded generously to war bond drives. Patriotic citizens led rallies. Companies had payroll plans among employees, asking that ten per cent of their pay be used to buy bonds.

The citizens willingly accepted wartime hardships. When a shortage of gasoline developed, auto pools were formed to reduce the number of autos in use. Rationing, or limiting sales, of some goods was supported. With the rationing of food, "victory gardens" were planted by many citizens.

**Dorie Miller,** a black messman aboard the *Arizona,* manned a machine gun. He shot down four Japanese planes during Pearl Harbor attack to win the Navy Cross.

**Large numbers** of blacks won commissions as officers in World War II. They attended the same candidate schools as whites and won rank under same rules.

**President Truman** in 1948 ordered integration speeded in America's armed services. The Korean War saw white and black soldiers often fighting side by side.

WORLD WAR II SAW MANY RACES united in America's fight against the Axis powers. It was not a war defending the freedom of any one race, but for all. About one million black men and women saw service in America's armed forces. Dorie Miller was a black crewman aboard the U.S. battleship *Arizona.* When the Japanese planes roared over his ship, the young black manned a machine gun and shot down four enemy planes. The *Arizona* was sunk, but Dorie Miller was one of those who got off safely. He was awarded the Navy Cross for his bravery under fire.

FOR THE FIRST TIME, black soldiers won the rank of general. Benjamin O. Davis, Sr., in 1940 was named as America's first black general. By the end of World War II, he was commander of Godman Field in Kentucky. His son, Benjamin O. Davis, Jr., was a fighter pilot in the war and later became a general. Frederic Davison, who led black infantry in World War II, became a general in Vietnam. American Indians also contributed to World War II victory, although their numbers were limited, because of smaller population. A group of Navajo Indians won fame in the Pacific. Used as lookouts, and spies, on small enemy-held islands, they gave military information over radio by talking to each other in their native Navajo language. The Japanese never "broke" the "code."

ON THE OTHER HAND, the war brought no glory to thousands of Japanese civilians living in America. Government orders removed 110,000 Japanese, many of them born in America, from their West Coast homes to a dozen inland camps, where they were kept under military guard. This government order was put into effect to avoid any possible spying or sabotage which the Japanese might attempt. Japanese bank funds were frozen and their property taken over. After the war, some Japanese won damages in court suits.

LATIN AMERICA JOINED in the fight on the Axis—all except Argentina and Chile. The Good Neighbor Policy paid dividends, or rewards, soon after Pearl Harbor. Twelve Latin American republics either declared war, or broke with Axis powers. The United States invited the Latin Americans to a conference at Rio de Janeiro, opening on January 15, 1942. All twenty-one of the republics sent groups. A resolution was offered, calling for a general Latin American break with the Axis. Only Argentina and Chile refused. All of the other republics, which had not already done so, broke relations with the Axis.

ARGENTINA OPENLY favored Germany. President Roosevelt was worried over the growing Nazi and Fascist sympathy in that country. Argentina had a large trade in Europe and did not want to make Hitler angry at a time when the Nazis appeared to be winning. Also, Argentina was a rival of the United States in its wheat and meat trade. The Rio de Janeiro conference closed on January 28 with Argentina and Chile still on friendly terms with America's enemies. Later on, both broke with the Axis.

RELATIONS BETWEEN the United States and the other Latin American republics were good throughout the war. Brazil was very helpful in the war on Germany's submarines. Brazil also provided airfields from which the United States flew men and supplies across the Atlantic Ocean. Brazil was the first of the Latin American republics to declare war, and the only one to send troops.

A DECLARATION of the United Nations had been adopted at an earlier meeting at Washington. Two weeks after Pearl Harbor, Roosevelt and Churchill met with the delegates from twenty-six nations. On January 1, 1942, the declaration was announced. It pledged all to fight until the Axis was defeated. All agreed not to make a separate peace. This was the start of the United Nations Organization.

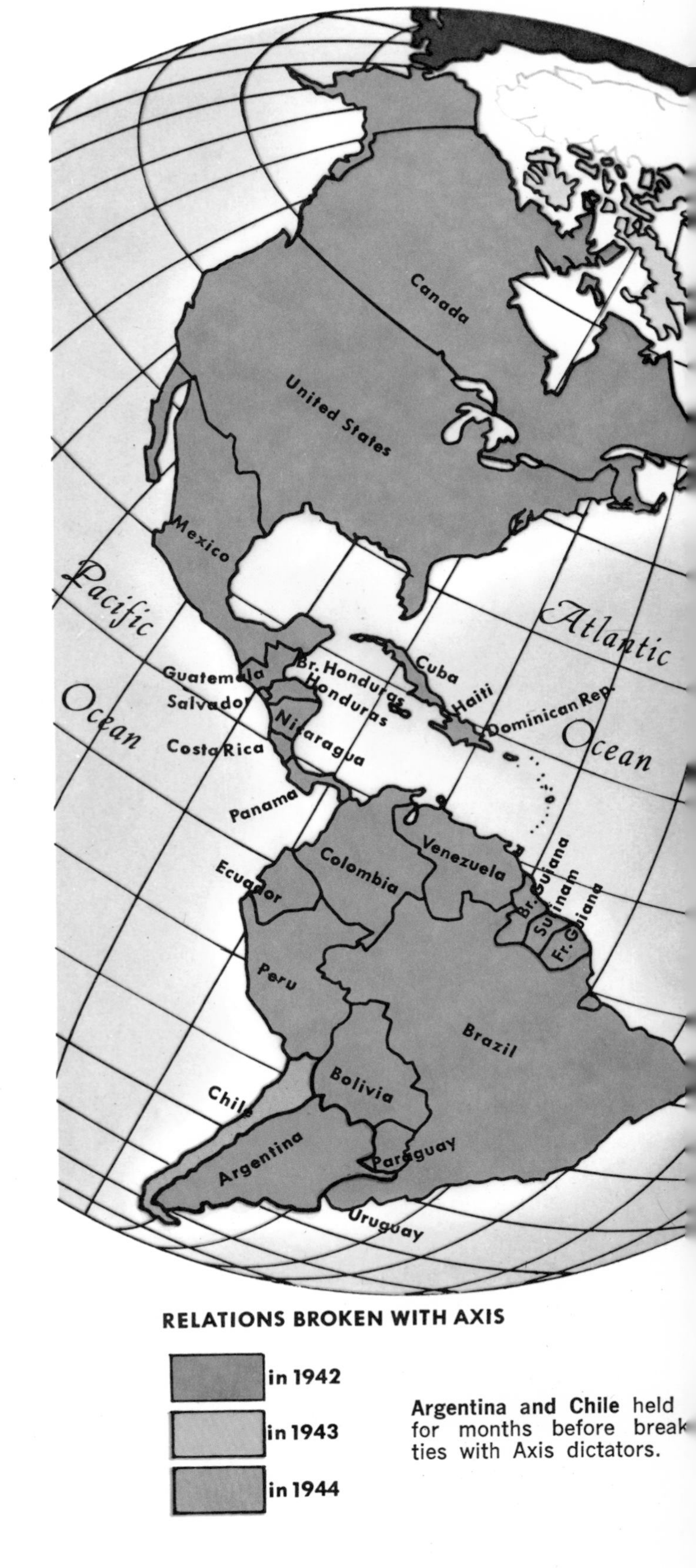


**Argentina** and **Chile** held for months before break ties with Axis dictators.

# WOMEN OF AMERICA WENT TO WAR IN UNIFORM AND IN FACTORIES

Nearly 100,000 women served in the WACS—Women's Auxiliary Army Corps. Organized on May 14, 1942, the WACS were commanded by Colonel (Mrs.) Oveta Culp Hobby. Later, renamed Women's Army Corps, it was taken into the regular army. About 15,000 WACS went overseas.

The Navy had its WAVES—Women Accepted for Voluntary Emergency Service. With Captain Mildred H. McAfee as commander, the WAVES were organized on July 30, 1942. More than 85,000 women volunteered for the WAVES and 4,000 served outside the United States.

The Coast Guard was another service to enroll women as regular members, approving the branch on November 23, 1942. They were known as the SPARS. More than 10,000 women joined the SPARS, who were commanded by Lieutenant Commander Dorothy C. Stratton.

A women's unit of the Marine Corps was organized on February 13, 1943, under the command of Colonel Ruth Cheney Streeter. The more than 18,000 women who joined were full members of the corps and adopted no nickname. They proudly called themselves Marines.

The largest women's army of all was the vast group of war factory workers. Women helped make the planes, guns and all other materials needed by the men fighting on the war fronts. Slacks became the familiar working uniform of this equally proud group of American women who went to war.

Nurses served with all branches of the fighting forces—often under fire. The Red Cross enrolled 60,000 women to serve in the Army and Navy nurse corps. Many were decorated for brave services in zones of great danger.

Thousands of women volunteered for services in the war zones. The Red Cross took in a large number for duty in first aid stations, canteens, and service centers overseas. Women entertainers toured the battle zones to appear in shows for America's servicemen. The USO had people serving at centers in the United States and overseas.

THE PACIFIC WAR SPREAD as the Japanese pressed their opening gains. The Battle for Java was marked by two fierce fights by American naval forces—one a victory and the other a defeat. On January 24, 1942, units of Admiral Thomas C. Hart's forces attacked a large Japanese convoy in Macassar Strait between Borneo and Celebes. Nineteen Japanese troop ships were sunk. The Japanese, on the way to invade Java, were met again on February 27 in the Java Sea. An allied naval force, including several American warships, was defeated in a three-day battle. The American seaplane tender *Langley* was among the ships sunk. Only four United States destroyers came out of the battle with slight damages. The Japanese landed large troop forces on Java and captured Batavia, capital of the rich Netherlands East Indies.

TOKYO WAS BOMBED in a daring American air raid on April 18, 1942. Led by Colonel James H. Doolittle, sixteen B-25 bombers took off from the deck of the aircraft carrier *Hornet,* 800 miles from Japan. They bombed factories and military targets in Tokyo, Yokohama, Kobe, Nagoya and Osaka. Of the eighty-four Americans who made the raid, sixty-four landed safely in China. Some of the others were shot down and captured in Japan. Others landed in Russia and were held. The Japanese received another shock early in May when two Japanese fleets were pounded by American ships under Admiral Jack Fletcher in the Battle of the Coral Sea. It was entirely a naval air battle, with no fighting between ships. American carrier planes destroyed an enemy troop convoy in the Solomon Islands. In other Coral Sea actions, American planes sank one Japanese carrier and crippled two others. The American carrier *Lexington* was sunk.

THE JAPANESE MADE a double thrust eastward across the Pacific Ocean—one aimed at the Aleutian Islands and the other at Midway Island. Japanese troops landed in the Aleutians on June 3, 1942, and for months held Kiska Island against almost daily American bombing attacks. The Battle of Midway was a costly defeat for the Japanese and made America almost even in Pacific naval strength. Army, Navy and Marine planes based on Midway hit the Japanese battleships and carriers as they neared the island on June 4. Admiral Raymond A. Spruance's carrier planes sank four Japanese carriers and a heavy cruiser. The Japanese lost more than half of their fleet. About 275 enemy planes were destroyed or lost when they fell into the sea after their carriers were sunk. The American carrier *Yorktown* was sunk. Japan's Pacific advance was ended.

**Japanese bombed** the Aleutian Islands and landed on Kiska and Attu. In an attack on Midway at the same time the Jap fleet lost four aircraft carriers to U.S. planes.

## *ALLIES BEGIN INVASIONS OF AXIS STRONGHOLDS*

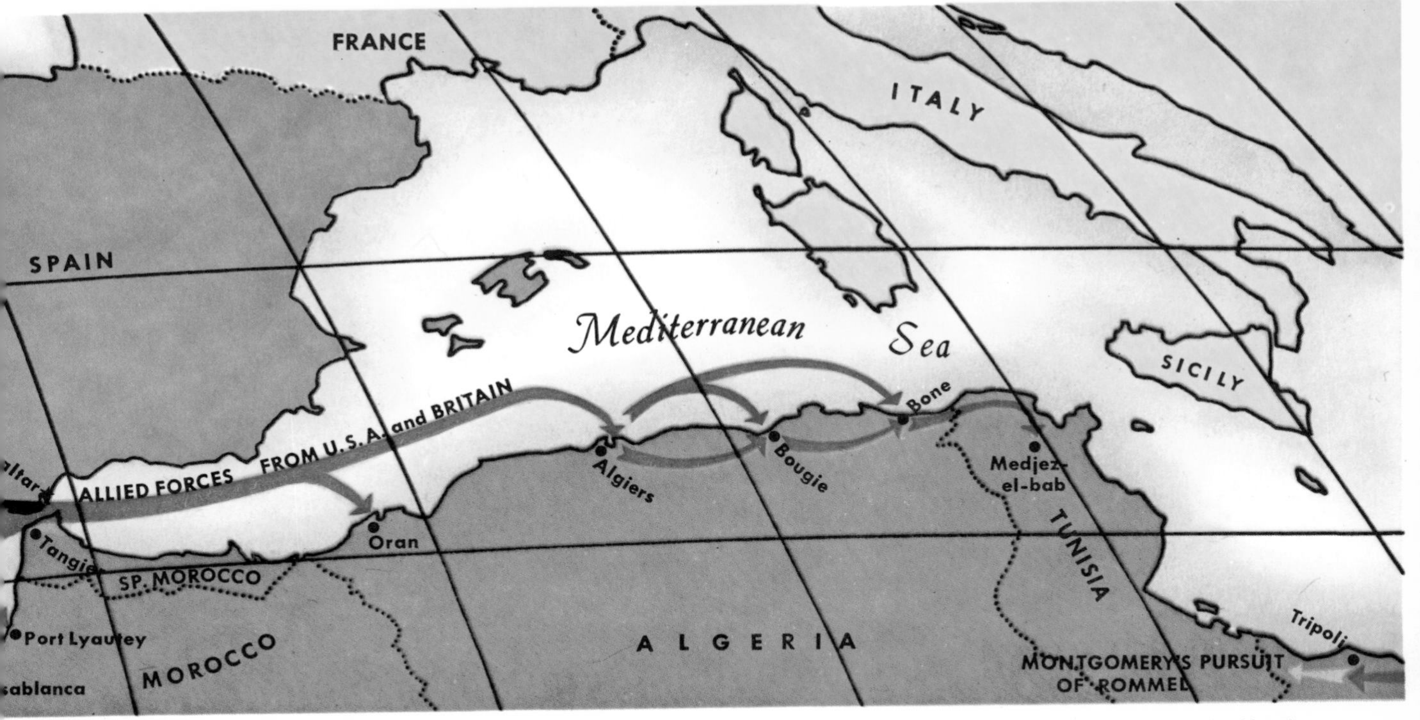


**British-American invaders** landed in North Africa and later drove Axis off continent.

THE ALLIES BEGAN a series of invasions which were to lead them to the shores of France. A blistering war was being fought across North Africa's desert sands by the armies of Great Britain and the Axis. General Bernard L. Montgomery commanded the British Eighth Army. General Erwin Rommel, the "Desert Fox," commanded Germany's Afrika Korps. A German-Italian offensive drove the British back into Egypt. Then Montgomery hit with an offensive of his own that drove Rommel out of Egypt and into Libya. Italy's army under General Rodolfo Graziani already had been destroyed in Libya.

NORTH AFRICA was invaded by a huge British-American army under the command of General Dwight D. Eisenhower. On November 8, 1942, an Allied fleet of more than 350 warships and 500 troop transports appeared off French Morocco. Casablanca and the Algerian ports of Oran and Algiers were captured in a few days. The Axis was driven out of Africa in spite of the additional troops and planes Hitler sent to his Afrika Korps. General Jurgen von Arnim took over the Axis' African command from Rommel. General George S. Patton, Jr., became commander of American forces. With the British, they trapped Arnim on Cape Bon Peninsula and forced him to surrender on May 13, 1943. The Allies took 250,000 Axis prisoners.

ON TO EUROPE drove the Allies. Sicily was invaded on July 10, 1943, when 2,000 Allied ships moved against the island. Patton and Montgomery led 160,000 troops ashore and attacked the Axis defenders. The enemy was heavily bombed and shelled. The Axis fought bitterly but, group by group, was defeated. The battle ended on August 18 with the enemy having lost 167,000 men. Italy was invaded on September 3 and on that same day, a new government which had been formed, surrendered. Mussolini had been jailed, but Nazis helped him escape. The main battle for Italy began with an attack on Salerno.

A HUGE PRODUCTION MACHINE arose in America's factories and spread its power across the world. A flow of arms and other war supplies reached American and Allied fighters in all the war zones. Workers in the United States did a huge job in the production, or making of war goods. This made it possible for the fighting men to do their job. America's war production was called the greatest single reason why the Allies won World War II. War production first had been under the Office of Production Management (OPM), created in January, 1941, under William Knudsen. In January, 1942, the War Production Board, under Donald Nelson, took over direction of the war industries.

AMERICA'S PLANTS worked at top speed, night and day. The guns, ammunition, planes, tanks, ships and other tools of war poured out. But the fact that several government offices were doing the job, all working on their own, created a problem. A central office, in control over all, was needed. The Office of War Mobilization was established on May 27, 1943. Supreme Court Judge James F. Byrnes was named as the director by Roosevelt. Byrnes was put in charge of nearly the entire war program and became known as the "Assistant President." Under Byrnes, the Office of War Mobilization unified efforts and the war machine became even larger.

LABOR TROUBLES developed in spite of an agreement by unions and management to reduce strikes. In January, 1942, a National War Labor Board (NWLB) was created to settle labor disputes. A Little Steel plan was adopted. This made wages rise as the cost of living went up. But there were strikes, including a walkout by 500,000 of John L. Lewis' coal miners. A War Labor Disputes Act was passed, ordering thirty days' notice before a strike could be called in a war industry. It was made illegal to strike in government-operated industries. The President was given the power to take over factories making war goods when workers went on strike.

**The giant of American** war production was turned loose on the Axis at full speed. Patriotic American workers kept war goods flowing to Allied forces in all war areas.

# *ALLIED LEADERS SET WORLD WAR II COURSE AT CONFERENCES*

**Joseph Stalin of Russia**, Franklin D. Roosevelt of the U.S. and Winston Churchill of Britain were the "Big Three" in strategy conferences held during war.

ALLIED LEADERS PLANNED the strategy to win World War II in conferences held during the last three years of the war. Roosevelt and Churchill held the first meeting at Casablanca, French Morocco, opening on January 14, 1943. They set "unconditional surrender" by the Axis as their terms for ending the war. The term "unconditional" aroused criticism in Allied countries. Roosevelt explained that it did not mean destruction of the peoples of enemy countries, but of their governments.

ROOSEVELT AND CHURCHILL met again at Quebec, Canada, from August 11-24, 1943. They agreed that France would be invaded late in the spring of 1944. Foreign ministers of the Big Three powers met at Moscow, Russia, October 19-30—Secretary of State Cordell Hull of the U.S., Foreign Secretary Anthony Eden of Britain, and Foreign Commissar V. M. Molotov of the Soviet Union. Stalin pledged Russia to enter the war against Japan soon after the European war ended.

THE BIG THREE FINALLY MET — Roosevelt, Churchill and Stalin. They held a conference at Teheran, capital of Iran, opening on November 28, 1943. All pledges were repeated. Stalin promised that a Russian offensive against Germany on the eastern front would be timed with the invasion of France. On the way to Teheran, Roosevelt and Churchill met with Chiang Kai-shek of Nationalist China at Cairo, Egypt. He was promised that all lost territories would be restored to China and Japan would lose all Pacific Islands obtained since 1914.

THE YALTA CONFERENCE was the last meeting of Roosevelt, Churchill and Stalin. The meeting opened on February 4, 1945, after Roosevelt had been elected to a fourth term as U.S. President. Many decisions were reached—some of them secret—and Yalta became a bitter postwar issue. After heated debate, Stalin finally agreed to the rebuilding of Poland as a free and independent state. All Polish groups, both Communist and non-Communist, would be included in a new government. Stalin promised to hold free elections in occupied countries of Eastern Europe. After the war, Stalin was accused of breaking his promises. A final conference remained to be held at Potsdam, Germany. At this conference Harry S. Truman, who had become President upon Roosevelt's death, was to make the decision to A-bomb Japan.

## *ALLIED ARMIES INVADE FRANCE, LIBERATE PARIS*

LONG-PLANNED D-DAY ARRIVED! An Allied invasion of France and a drive toward Berlin began, under the supreme command of General Eisenhower. For many months, Allied bombers had been pounding Germany. Factories, railroads and highways had been hit. On June 5, 1944, the greatest invasion fleet ever gathered steamed out of many ports into the English Channel and headed for the French coast. The first landing units of 176,000 troops were carried by 4,000 ships and protected by 3,000 planes.

THE FIRST ALLIED UNITS landed along the Cotentin Peninsula in Normandy early on June 6. Opposition at that point was light. But at Omaha Beach the Allied invaders met fierce opposition. The Allies fought savagely to hold only 100 yards of beach. More than a million men were landed in the first three weeks. Vast supplies were poured into France. Included were 170,000 trucks, jeeps, or small military cars, and tanks.

THE ALLIED INVADERS spread out along the Normandy coast. Cherbourg was captured on June 27. St. Lo fell on July 18. The American armored Third Army under Patton drove its tanks from St. Lo and cut off the Brittany Peninsula. Meanwhile, a supporting Allied invasion of southern France had begun. The American Seventh Army, under General Alexander Patch, landed between Marseilles and Nice. The Allies drove up the Rhone River Valley. On June 23, the Russians had begun an offensive and moved west in great force on an 800-mile line. They threw the Germans back all along the eastern front.

PARIS WAS LIBERATED, or freed, on August 25. The Battle of the Bulge was the Nazis' final struggle to break out of the Allied ring closing around them. The Nazis broke through for forty miles near Saint Vith, Belgium. Americans under General Anthony McAuliffe made a heroic stand at Bastogne. Allied troops and planes rushed to the rescue and Bastogne was freed with thousands of Germans killed.

**Two Allied invasions** hit Hitler's European fortress. First landings were made in Normandy—the second in Southern France.

THE MARINES LANDED on Guadalcanal, as America took the offensive in the Pacific with an invasion of the Solomon Islands. The Japanese had seized these British islands early in 1942 and were developing Guadalcanal as a major base. On August 7, 1942, Marines under General Alexander A. Vandegrift landed on Guadalcanal. They captured the new airfield and drove the enemy into the jungles. Navy Seabees, or construction battalions, quickly put the airfield in shape for use by Marine planes. For fifteen months American land, sea and air forces fought their way up the chain of Solomon Islands. In November, 1943, they took Bougainville, and all of the Solomons were captured. Both the Americans and Japanese lost heavily in naval battles. So many ships were sunk that Guadalcanal waters became known as "Iron Bottom Bay."

AMERICA'S PACIFIC DRIVE spread early in 1943. The Pacific Fleet, commanded by Admiral Chester Nimitz, began an island-hopping campaign to the west. Admirals Raymond A. Spruance and William Halsey led the Navy's task forces in these invasions. General MacArthur captured New Guinea and drove toward the Philippines. The Japanese were bombed out of the Aleutians. Americans and Canadians landed on Attu and re-captured the island in a week of fighting. The Japanese evacuated Kiska.

A COSTLY SEIZURE of the Gilbert Islands by Pacific fleet amphibious, or sea-land, invasion forces opened a Central Pacific offensive. American casualties on Tarawa were 3,500. The Marshall Islands were captured next, then Saipan and Guam in the Mariana Islands were taken by Marines and Army troops. The Marine First Division, heroes of Guadalcanal, took Peleliu in the Palau Islands on September 15-17, 1944. Meanwhile, MacArthur landed on Leyte in the Philippines on October 20, and moved on to Mindoro Island. On January 9, 1945, MacArthur returned to Luzon, main Philippine Island on which Manila was located. Admiral Thomas C. Kincaid's amphibious forces landed the Sixth Army under General Walter Krueger. MacArthur recaptured Manila on February 5 and freed the Death March survivors.

**Marines landed** and drove the Japanese into the jungles. Then came the Seabees to put airfields in shape for Marine fighter planes.

IWO JIMA AND OKINAWA were seized. A bloody three-week battle by the Marines in February took Iwo Jima; America's losses were 4,189 killed and Japan's 23,000 troops on Iwo Jima were nearly wiped out. After landing on April 1, American forces won Okinawa in eighty-two days of fierce fighting. They stood on the doorstep to Japan, in position for an invasion.

# G.I. BILL OF RIGHTS PROVIDED POST WAR BENEFITS

POST-WAR PROBLEMS of America's millions of men and women in the armed services came in for consideration in the last year of World War II. Congress passed the G.I. Bill of Rights, which provided help and benefits for those who soon were to return to civilian life after the war was won. The benefits were outlined in the Servicemen's Readjustment Act, passed on June 22, 1944. After Pearl Harbor, Congress changed the Selective Service Act to send drafted men overseas. Terms of service were to end six months after the end of the war. An Allotment Act gave payments to the wives and children of servicemen. The G.I. Bill of Rights was the next step. It provided payments for those who couldn't get jobs after the war, hospital benefits, loans for businesses and homes, and money for college educations and vocational courses, or training in trades. More than 16,000,000 American men and women served during the war in the Army, Navy and Marine Corps.

The veterans hospital system was built up to provide better health services for disabled veterans.

The government guaranteed loans for building homes and businesses.

Jobless pay of $20 a week for fifty-two weeks was provided for veterans who could not obtain jobs after their discharge from the services.

Money was provided for college educations or vocational courses.

## *WAR'S BURDEN FALLS ON PRESIDENT TRUMAN*

PRESIDENT ROOSEVELT DIED just as the victory for which he had fought so hard was about to be won. The President's death came suddenly at Warm Springs, Georgia, on April 12, 1945. Roosevelt collapsed and soon died after getting a headache while having his portrait painted. His death was due to a cerebral, or brain hemorrhage, doctors said. Vice-President Harry S. Truman became President, and the great war burden which Roosevelt had been carrying fell on him. One of Truman's first tasks was to open the organization meeting of the United Nations. Fifty nations were present when Truman opened the U. N. conference at San Francisco on April 25, 1945.

TRUMAN HAD TWO-PARTY SUPPORT. He had been a forceful Missouri senator, but was a newcomer to world politics. Truman received the voluntary support of forty Republican senators. Secretary of State Edward R. Stettinius, Jr., went to San Francisco with Truman. Leaders from other leading countries who attended the U.N. conference were Foreign Minister V. M. Molotov of the Soviet Union, Foreign Secretary Anthony Eden of Great Britain, and Foreign Minister T. V. Soong of China. The rights of veto, or denial, caused a major dispute early in the conference. Russia insisted that the Big Five members of the proposed Security Council have the right to veto any issue, including even the veto of talks on the subject. The Soviet Union gave in only after Harry Hopkins visited Stalin in Moscow on Truman's orders. It was agreed that the Big Five would have the power to veto any decision of the Security Council, but not to veto talks on the issue.

MOLOTOV AND EDEN flew back to Europe as the surrender of Germany neared. In the next two months, the final draft of the United Nations Charter was completed. The United Nations Charter was signed on June 25, 1945

**Harry S. Truman** took over war burden with President Roosevelt's death. He opened a meeting which formed the United Nations.

THE FINAL ORGANIZATION provided for a General Assembly made up of all member nations. The Security Council had eleven members. Five were to be permanent members—the United States, Britain, France, Russia and China. The six other members were to be elected every two years. The Big Five had veto powers. A single veto killed any Security Council action. A secretary-general was to be chief officer of the U. N. An International Court of Justice included all member nations. A Trusteeship Council took over countries that had no governments of their own.

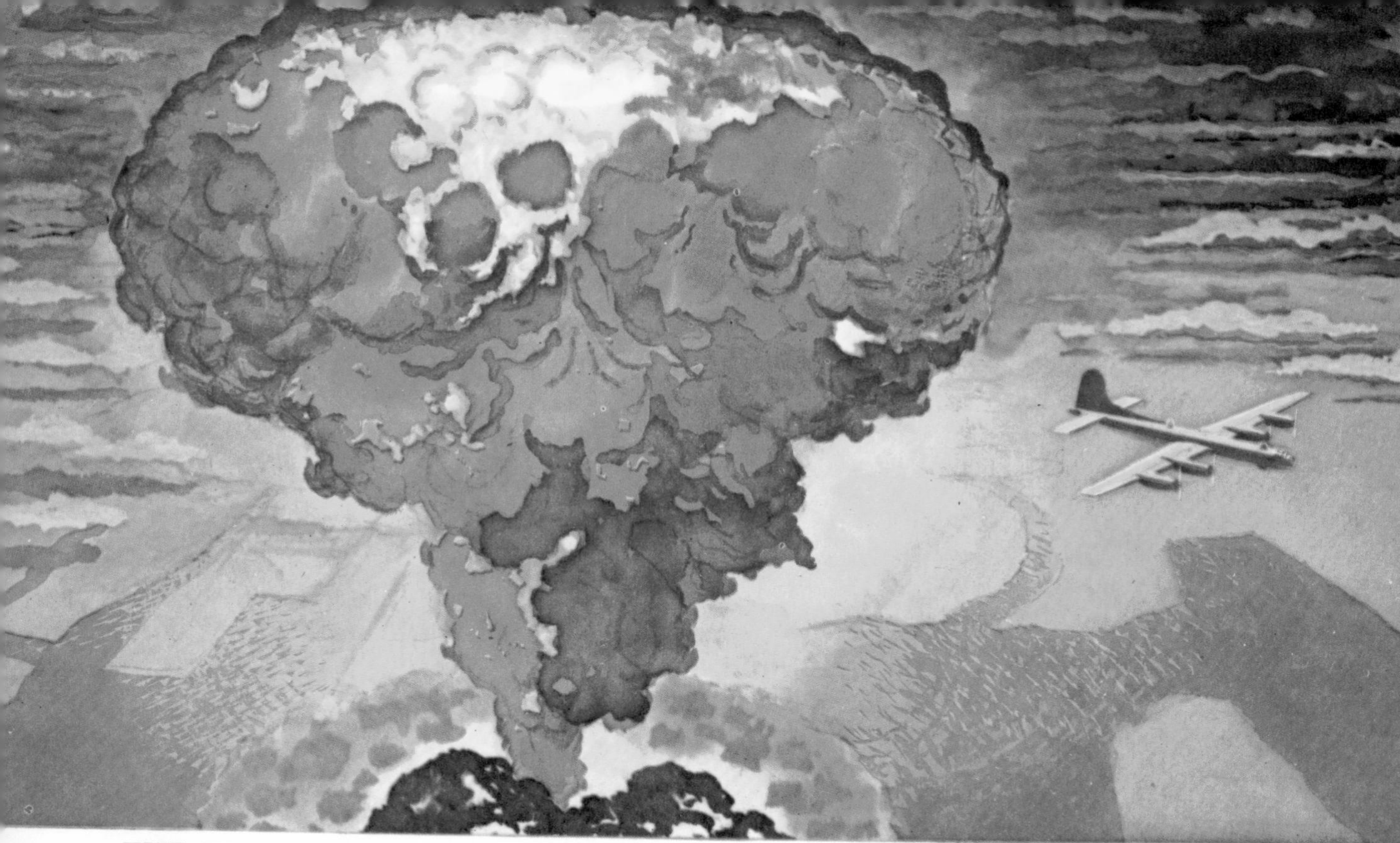

The atomic bombs' mushroom of death rose over Japan. After Hiroshima and Nagasaki were A-bombed, the Japanese surrendered.

THE FINAL DEFEAT OF GERMANY saw Hitler's once mighty army pounded into bits. After the Battle of the Bulge, the Allies, led by Patton's Third Army, drove into the Ruhr Valley and crossed the Rhine River. The American army raced across Germany. To the east, 2,000,000 Russians under Marshal Georgi X. Zhukov drove back the Nazis and took Warsaw. The American Fifth and Seventh Armies made big gains in Italy. Doom closed in on Hitler from all sides. In the Ruhr Valley, 325,000 Germans surrendered to Allied forces. The first Russian troops entered Berlin on April 25, 1945. The next day, the American and Russian armies met at the Elbe River. Berlin fell to the Russians on May 2. The Germans surrendered in Italy under pressure by the American Fifth and Seventh Armies. Then they surrendered in the Netherlands and Denmark. Admiral Karl Doenitz, head of a provisional government in Germany, officially surrendered the nation. V-E Day or Victory in Europe, came on May 7. Hitler committed suicide and Italians captured and hanged Mussolini.

ATOMIC BOMBS WERE DROPPED on Japan! America had successfully exploded an A-bomb in a test and Japan was given an ultimatum, or demand for surrender. Japan refused and Truman decided to use the A-bomb. On August 6, a single B-29 Super Fortress plane dropped the bomb on Hiroshima. A mushroom cloud of death rose over the city. More than 80,000 of Hiroshima's 340,000 residents were killed. Still no surrender came. Russia chose this timely opportunity to declare war on Japan and invade Manchuria. On August 9, a second A-bomb was dropped, this one on Nagasaki. About 70,000 Japanese were killed. Japan surrendered on August 14, 1945, with Emperor Hirohito keeping his throne. Warfare had entered a new and more fearful age—that of nuclear weapons. Formal signing of surrender papers took place on the battleship *Missouri* in Tokyo Harbor on September 2. MacArthur signed for the Allies. World War II was over.

# COLD WAR AND THE ATOMIC BUILDUP

PART 9

**Five of America's leaders** attended opening of the United Nations in London. The U. N. chose New York City as its home.

THE WORLD'S HOPE for lasting peace was bright as the United Nations held its first meeting in London. Created at San Francisco, the U.N.'s first purpose was to prevent future wars. Five well-known Americans were sent as this nation's group when the London meeting opened on January 10, 1946. They were Secretary of State James F. Byrnes, former Secretary of State Edward R. Stettinius, Jr., Senators Arthur H. Vandenburg and Tom Connally, and Mrs. Eleanor Roosevelt, the widow of Franklin D. Roosevelt.

FIFTY NATIONS had signed the United Nations charter. They had joined together to outlaw war. At a second meeting in 1946, the United Nations chose New York City as its permanent headquarters. John D. Rockefeller, Jr., gave $8,500,000 for eighteen acres of land for the United Nations' home, which was built on the East River in New York City.

TRYGVE H. LIE of Norway was chosen as the first Secretary-General of the U.N. The General Assembly elected Paul Henri Spaak of Belgium as its first president. Mexico, Egypt, the Netherlands, Brazil, Poland and Australia were chosen as two-year members of the Security Council. The five permanent members were the United States, Great Britain, France, China and the Soviet Union. In spite of high hopes and a good start, disputes developed only nine days after the first meeting began.

IRAN PROTESTED to the Security Council about Russian troops that refused to get out. Iran, a large oil producing country on the border of Russia, had agreed with the United States, Britain and Russia on the withdrawal of troops after the war. Russia refused to vote on bringing up the issue. But the other nations discussed it anyway. Pressure was put on Russia, and the troops were finally taken out on May 6, 1946. Another dispute with the Communists came about over Greece. Russia's Ukranian delegation complained that British troops stationed in Greece were a threat to the Balkan, or southeast-European area. Russia had already taken over the countries of northeastern Europe. Britain protested that the Communists were trying to take over Greece. Fighting between the Greek government and local Communists had been going on since the end of the war. A United Nations report said this war was being supported by Communist Albania, Yugoslavia and Bulgaria. The Russians objections blocked action by the Security Council.

SOVIET EFFORTS to block other U.N. actions developed. The Soviet Union's use of the veto power became a problem.

**The great day** had come for Filipinos. America granted them freedom and voted $620,000,000 to help Philippines rebuild.

THE PHILIPPINES had been promised by the United States that one day they would be given their freedom. In March, 1934, Congress passed a Tydings-McDuffie Act which provided for independence of the Filipinos within twelve years. A program was begun to give the Philippines the training they needed to prepare for self government. At the end of the twelve years, World War II had been won and the Philippines were cleared of Japanese invaders. On July 4, 1946, America kept the promise it had made. President Truman declared "the independence of the Philippines as a separate and self-governing nation."

CONGRESS ARRANGED for the Filipinos to become independent without being deserted by the United States. The war had brought much damage to the islands. Half of Manila had been destroyed. On April 30, 1946, a Philippine Rehabilitation Act was passed. It gave the Philippine government $620,000,000 to repair war damage. On the same day, a Philippine Trade Act was passed. For a long time the island's goods had been sent for sale in the United States without the payment of duties, or taxes. The Trade Act continued free duties for eight years. After that duties would be charged on a scale starting low and rising slowly over twenty years. The United States was granted use of twenty-three military and naval bases in the islands for ninety-nine years. Manuel Roxas was the first president of the new Philippine republic.

PUERTO RICO BECAME a commonwealth of the United States in 1953. As residents of a commonwealth, Puerto Ricans ruled their own island, made their own laws, had full self-government, and controlled their own trade. Through their own choice, they kept ties with the United States. Louis Munoz Marin was the governor. Truman approved a life sentence instead of execution for Oscar Collazo, one of two Puerto Ricans who tried to assassinate him. The other man was killed in the attempt.

## *TRUMAN DOCTRINE*

TRUMAN DECLARED A DOCTRINE to help democratic nations keep the Communists from taking over their governments. A Cold War with Russia began. In February, 1947, England announced that she could no longer support the Greek Government in its war with the Communists. England needed the men and money to rebuild her own country. The Greek government could not hold off the Communists without help. Russia also demanded complete control of the Turkish waterway leading from the Mediterranean into the Black Sea. If Greece fell, Turkey would have to give in. Then Russia would have military and naval bases in the eastern Mediterranean Sea.

AMERICA HAD STOOD BY as Russia had taken over the countries of eastern Europe after the war. At first the Americans had trusted the Russians as their allies. But when the Reds threatened Europe and the Middle East, America began to see the danger of Russian expansion. Truman decided the time for trust had gone. Now was the time for action. On March 22, 1947, he announced his "Truman Doctrine."

TRUMAN TOLD CONGRESS: "One of the primary objectives of the foreign policy of the United States is the creation of conditions in which we and other nations will be able to work out a way of life free from coercion (other nations forcing their ideas upon them). We shall not realize our objectives, however, unless we are willing to help free peoples to maintain their free institutions and their national integrity against aggressive movements that seek to impose upon them totalitarian (one-party) regimes. This is no more than a frank recognition that totalitarian regimes imposed on free peoples, by direct or indirect aggression, undermine the foundations of international peace and hence the security of the United States." Truman then asked Congress for money to give help to Greece and Turkey.

**Congress backed** Truman's Doctrine and voted $400,000,000 to help Greece and Turkey fight against Communist attacks.

CONGRESS APPROVED the Truman Doctrine by voting $400,000,000 in aid for the two nations. General James A. Van Fleet was sent at the head of a military group to help Greece train its army. With the Truman Doctrine, America began a policy of trying to "contain" the Communists, or keep them from spreading into democratic countries. Americans at first called the Truman Doctrine dangerous. But many soon supported it. The Soviet Union already had taken its stand, with Foreign Minister V. M. Molotov speaking against America's foreign policy before the United Nations. America and Russia faced each other . . . the Cold War was on!

**America's foreign aid began.** In the twenty years after the start of the Marshall plan, more than 107 billion dollars was given.

THE MARSHALL PLAN next was adopted by the United States to help European nations recover. George C. Marshall, who was Army Chief-of-Staff in World War II, was the new Secretary of State. He suggested his plan in a talk at Harvard University on June 5, 1947. The plan offered to help European nations rebuild their cities, farms, and factories. In a huge program, the United States would supply them with the money, machinery and goods needed. The Marshall Plan was a program to spread over several years. The plan went beyond the United Nations Relief and Rehabilitation Administration (UNRRA), in which the U.S. had taken part. The Truman Doctrine was aimed at the Communists, but Marshall's plan included the Communists.

MARSHALL SAID at Harvard: "Our policy is not directed against any country or doctrine, but against poverty, desperation and chaos. Its purpose should be the revival of a working economy in the world so as to permit the emergence of political and social conditions in which free institutions can exist." The Soviet Union, however, saw the Marshall Plan as a move to block Communism. The Russians refused to attend a conference to decide on Europe's needs under the Marshall Plan. The Soviet satellites, or smaller nations which were taken over by Communists under Russian control, also refused to attend.

A GROUP OF SIXTEEN nations set Europe's four-year needs at 16.4 to 22.4 billion dollars. Congress passed the Foreign Aid Act of 1947 in December. In April, 1948, Congress voted 5.3 billion dollars for the first year of the European Recovery Program (ERP). Truman named Paul Hoffman as director of the Economic Cooperation Administration (ECA) to grant money and make loans under the rules of the ERP. Huge cargo ships loaded tons of wheat, rice, steel, machinery and equipment and sailed to Europe. Farm lands were replanted and new, modern factories were constructed. By 1970, America had spent more than 112 billion dollars on aid to foreign countries.

# TAFT-HARTLEY ACT AFFECTS LABOR AND INDUSTRY

AMERICA'S INDUSTRY WAS HIT by a wave of strikes after World War II ended. War plants rushed into reconversion, or return to making peace-time goods, when war production was stopped. Wartime wage controls ended and, with the cost of living rising, labor demanded higher pay. Also, much overtime pay was lost with the end of war production. In 1946, approximately 2,000,000 workers went on strike. By 1947, unions had 14,000,000 members and management accused the leaders of using high-handed, or dictator, methods. Over President Truman's veto, Congress passed the Labor-Management (Taft-Hartley) Act on June 23, 1947. The act, sponsored by Senator Robert A. Taft of Ohio, established labor controls. Management could seek injunctions to prevent strikes. Union leaders strongly opposed the controls and ending of the closed shop. They called the Taft-Hartley Act a "slave labor act."

**Unions were ordered to prepare statements of finances and keep them open for public inspection, upon request. Officials of unions were required to take oaths that they were not Communist Party members.**

**Labor's right to strike was lessened. In some cases, an eighty-day "cooling-off" period could be ordered. Management could sue for any damages resulting from strikes, either to property or business.**

**The Taft-Hartley Act ended the closed shop, which required employers to hire only union members. The union shop was kept, permitting the hiring of non-union men, who would have to join the union later. States were permitted to pass "right-to-work" laws, allowing the hiring of any worker, regardless of any connection with labor unions or obligation to join one.**

**Changes were made in the "check-off" system, where union dues were taken out of a worker's wages. The worker's written consent was needed for dues to be taken out before a "check-off" could be made.**

**Latin American leaders** gathered at Bogota and studied the Western Hemisphere's map. They formed the Organization of American States, their strongest alliance.

THE ORGANIZATION OF AMERICAN States (O.A.S.) was formed at Bogota, Colombia, in 1948. It was the strongest group yet formed by the republics. A charter for the O.A.S. was drawn up and signed at the Ninth International Conference of American states. The treaty came within the lines drawn up by the United Nations for such agreements in various regions, or areas, of the world. Other such organizations were to follow. The charter outlined the duties of its members. The new organization decided to make its headquarters at the Pan-American Union building in Washington. The O.A.S. was seen as a bright spot in the world's cloudy outlook.

COLLECTIVE SECURITY, or safety for all, was one of the strongest points in the Organization of American States charter. United action would be permitted to prevent war and guard security. A defense council was established and plans for mutual defense were made. A resolution against Communism was adopted at Bogota. During the conference, a local revolt broke out at Bogota which gave a first-hand example of revolutionary disorders. The revolt came after the assassination of the leader of the anti-government party. Several hundred Bogota residents were killed and much property was damaged in the Colombian capital. The conference was forced to halt its meeting during the riots. When the conference was reopened, the resolution against Communism was approved by the delegates.

SECRETARY OF STATE Marshall worked hard to unite the Latin American people against Communism. He had trouble in making the Latin American republics understand that the Marshall Plan for economic aid to Europe did not include them. Although South America had suffered no property damage or other war losses, the republics wanted some of America's dollars. A "Little Marshall Plan" was offered. President Truman said that a half-billion dollar loan could be made through the Export-Import Bank at Washington. But this had no appeal to the Latin Americans. The conference ended with good feelings all around, however, and by October, 1948, the Organization of American States was established and ready for business. In the many years of international discord that were to come, the Organization of American States was to face many tough situations. America tried to work closely with the O.A.S. at all times.

## *EAST-WEST SPLIT OVER GERMANY OPENS COLD WAR*

A BREAK OVER GERMAN RULE developed between the Western Allies and the Soviet Union. After the war, American, British and French occupation, or control, zones had been established in West Germany. Russia occupied East Germany. Berlin was divided east and west. Located deep in the Soviet zone of East Germany, Berlin was more than 100 miles away from West Germany. America and Britain wanted a federal type of government in Germany. Russia wanted a centralized state. The West felt sure that this would lead to a totalitarian, or one-party, rule and objected. The East-West break became wider in a series of meetings by the Council of Foreign Ministers, held at Moscow. The United States and Britain rejected a demand by Russia for ten billion dollars in reparations from Germany. Russia was angered and the dispute became more heated in the struggle between democrary and Communism.

RUSSIA BLOCKADED all land and canal travel between Berlin and the West's zones, on June 24, 1948. This shut off West Berlin and its 2,000,000 people from Allied supplies, 100 miles away. The Communists hoped the West Berliners might be starved into going over to the Reds' side . . . and that all of West Germany might follow. With all land routes closed, the Allies began a huge airlift to relieve West Berlin. American and British planes flew supplies in a steady stream between West Germany and West Berlin. When going at top speed, the airlift delivered 4,500 tons of supplies each day. The Russians lifted the blockade on May 12, 1949.

TWO GOVERNMENTS were set up in divided Germany. The Western Allies formed a German Federal Republic in West Germany. It was the beginning of democratic government in West Germany. Soviet leaders formed a German Democratic Republic in East Germany. The East German government was Communist and was controlled by the Russians. Bernard Baruch, a noted American statesman, warned the nation: "We are in the midst of a Cold War which is getting warmer."

**Russia's Communists** in East Germany blockaded West Germany from all land travel. The Allies kept West Berlin supplied with a huge airlift using hundreds of planes.

# *FREE WORLD LEADERSHIP FALLS UPON AMERICA*

**Homeless and displaced** people wandered over Europe. Truman signed a Displaced Persons bill admitting thousands to U.S.

LEADERSHIP OF THE FREE WORLD by now had fallen upon America's shoulders. War's costs and damages had left many lands needy and hungry. Almost all of Europe had to be rebuilt and America's huge foreign aid program was begun with the Marshall Plan. The threat offered to the Free World by the Communists led to the Truman Doctrine. Now the problem of displaced persons arose. Families were separated, many never to see each other again. The Germans killed 6,000,000 Jews in the countries they seized.

COMMUNISTS MOVED INTO eastern European countries after World War II and shut them off behind an Iron Curtain. As a result of war's human wreckage, many former residents who had been displaced from these countries were afraid to return to their old homes. The new rulers killed non-Communists as freely as the Nazis had killed non-Germans. A movement began in the United States to admit displaced persons. Nationality groups asked the government to give liberal, or easy, entrance permission to their own peoples in Europe. Opposition was voiced by some native-born American groups who remembered the bitter jobless days of the Great Depression. Nevertheless, America opened its doors and on June 25, 1948, President Truman signed the Displaced Persons Bill. The act permitted the admission of 205,000 displaced persons, in addition to 3,000 orphans. Congress later increased the total to 341,000. Displaced Persons Bureaus were set up to help families adopt European war orphans and to help the "D.P.'s" solve their problems on reaching America. All of the Free World, its governments and peoples, looked to America for leadership.

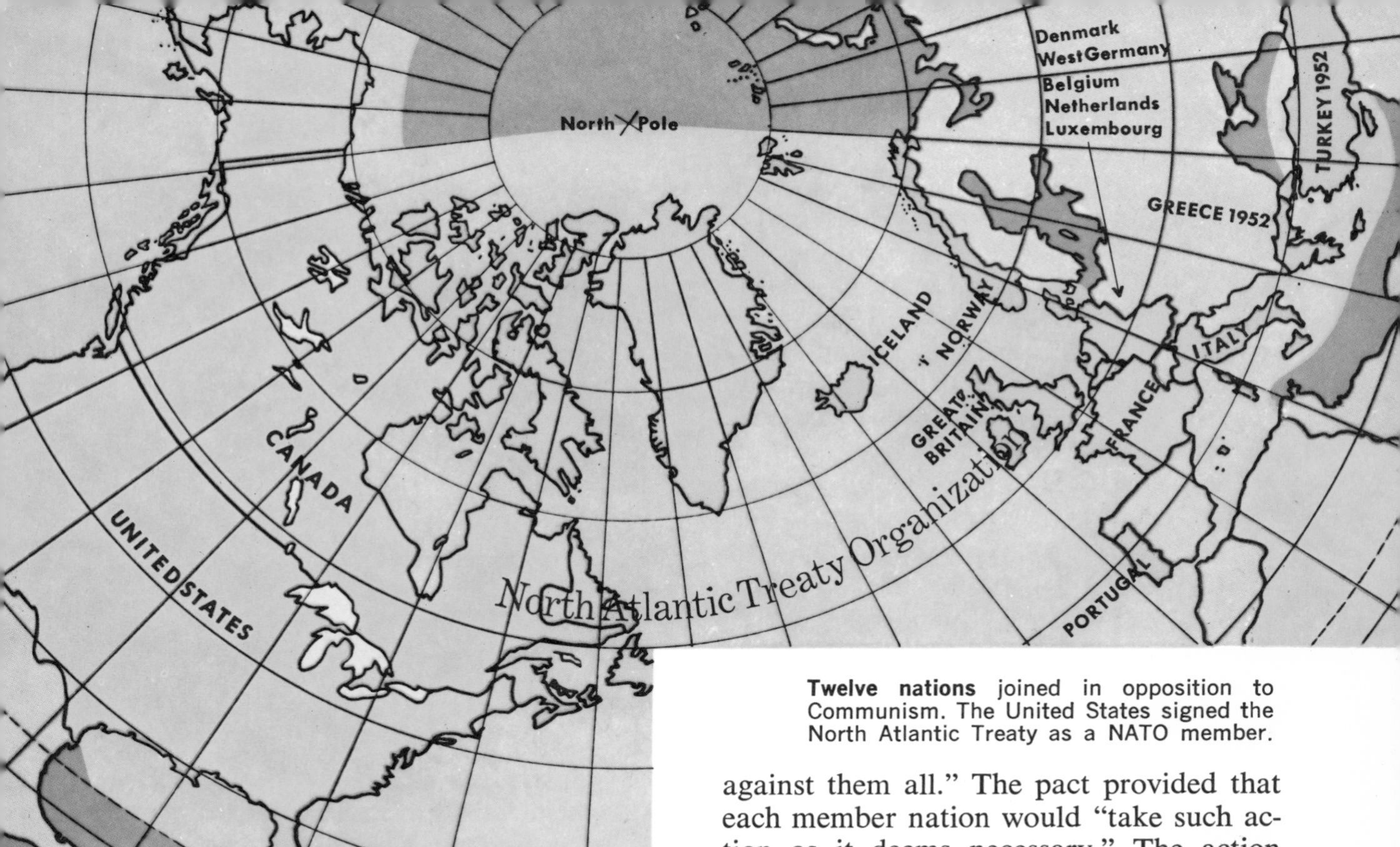


**Twelve nations** joined in opposition to Communism. The United States signed the North Atlantic Treaty as a NATO member.

A NORTH ATLANTIC TREATY opposing Communism was signed by twelve nations, including the United States. It was a twenty-five-year defense pact and was the first such peacetime pact ever made by the United States. Dean G. Acheson, who took over Marshall's post as Secretary of State, faced troubles in Berlin as soon as he took office. The Soviet Union had made no move to ease the Cold War. A defense agreement among the North Atlantic anti-Communist nations had been planned for some time. Acheson had the United States included as the pact took shape.

THE FOREIGN MINISTERS of the twelve nations met at Washington and on April 4, 1949, signed the North Atlantic Treaty. Article Five of the treaty said: "The parties agree that an armed attack against any one or more of them in Europe or North America shall be considered an attack against them all." The pact provided that each member nation would "take such action as it deems necessary." The action would include use of "armed force" if necessary. Nations signing the treaty were the United States, Britain, Canada, France, Belgium, the Netherlands, Luxembourg, Denmark, Norway, Iceland, Italy and Portugal. This built a western defense wall.

A NORTH ATLANTIC TREATY Organization (NATO) was set up for united defense under a Council of Ministers. The treaty did not commit the United States to military action, but treaty opponents in America protested that it carried a moral pledge. The Senate, however, approved the treaty in July by an 82 to 13 vote. General Dwight D. Eisenhower in 1950 was named Supreme Commander of NATO armed forces. He asked for six divisions of American troops to be sent to Europe. The North Atlantic Treaty followed three other pacts which already had been signed under collective security rules of the United Nations. The others were the Brussels Pact in Europe, and the Treaty of Rio de Janeiro and the Organization of American States, agreements signed in Latin America.

RUSSIA DEVELOPED AN A-BOMB! On September 23, 1949, President Truman told the nation: "We have evidence that within recent weeks an atomic explosion occurred in the Soviet Union. This probability always has been taken into account." America's atomic experts figured that the Russian explosion took place about September 1. Russia said later that her atomic testing grounds were in Novaya Zemla, an island off western Siberia in the Barents Sea, close to the Arctic Circle. The atomic rivalry had begun and the Americans were greatly worried. The chance that some day there might be an atomic war was seen by many as a great threat to mankind.

A HYDROGEN BOMB was exploded by the United States on November 1, 1952, in a successful test off Eniwetok in the Marshall Islands. The most powerful blast man had ever known was set off by United States Joint Task Force 132. In the tremendous explosion that followed, a part of the island—an atoll, or coral reef—completely disappeared. The blast was seen more than fifty miles away. The new hydrogen bomb was twenty-five times as powerful as the atomic bomb dropped on Hiroshima. In August, 1953, the Soviet Union also exploded its first hydrogen bomb. In March, 1954, the United States set off two more bombs. In one explosion, a B-29 bomber, flying twenty miles away was hit by the blast. The force of the explosion flipped the plane over on its back as it flew along.

A NEW TERROR was brought to the world. Included was the fear of atomic "fallout," or spreading through the upper air of harmful chemicals thrown out by an atomic bomb explosion. This was called radioactivity. Many feared that when the radioactive "fallout" finally settled on the earth, a threat would be presented to man's health. A plea for atomic controls grew. America and Russia agreed to halt atomic tests above the ground, but underground testing was continued by both.

**America exploded** a hydrogen bomb so powerful it could destroy an entire city.

# COMMUNIST WARS AND MEN IN SPACE

WAR BROKE OUT IN KOREA and armed fighting with the Communists finally came. Communist North Korean troops crossed the thirty-eighth parallel dividing line and attacked South Korea on June 25, 1950. The North Koreans were well supplied with modern Soviet-made arms. South Korea, named the Republic of Korea, was weak and its defense quickly was beaten down. The United Nations backed South Korea against the attack, which was made without warning. Military help for South Korea was ordered by the U.N. The job of giving quick aid to South Korea fell on the United States. President Truman ordered air and naval forces to go to South Korea at once. Some of America's troops on duty in Japan were landed at Pusan, closest South Korean port. Truman called it a "police action" so that no action by Congress was needed. General Douglas MacArthur was named U.N. commander.

SOUTH KOREAN-AMERICAN forces were too small to stop the fully equipped North Korean Army. They fell back to the port of Pusan in the southeastern corner of Korea. The Americans dug in and the Communists were stopped only thirty miles from the last port. More soldiers were needed and the United States called up many of its military reservists. Thousands arrived and went to the front lines to stop the Communists.

MACARTHUR HAD A BOLD IDEA. He told his staff that he would invade Inchon, 200 miles up the coast and behind the enemy lines. On September 15, Navy ships landed 25,000 Marines at Inchon, and they soon swept to Seoul, the capital. The North Korean army was trapped and defeated. The American armies drove across the border and invaded North Korea.

**South Koreans** fled from their farms in fear. They led cattle, carried bundles on their heads and babies on their backs.

## *CHINESE REDS ENTER WAR IN KOREA*

COMMUNIST CHINA ENTERED the war as U.N. forces, now on the offensive, pushed the North Koreans back across the thirty-eighth parallel border. The Chinese government had warned that it "could not stand idly by." MacArthur drove on and took Pyong-yang, North Korean capital. The North Korean army was broken and was in full retreat. The U.N. forces drove on toward the Yalu River, the boundary between Korea and China. American bombers paved the way. On October 26, 1950, Red China made good its threat. An army of 200,000 Chinese Communists crossed the Yalu and met the U.N. forces.

THE BLOODY BATTLE of Yalu Valley followed. The 1st Marine Division, at the Chosin Reservoir, was completely surrounded by the Chinese. The Marines fought on all sides. They "attacked to the rear," and fought their way to the coast. The Navy took 100,000 Marines and 90,000 Korean civilians to safety. On the other side of Korea, the Army was pushed back into South Korea again. By mid-January the Communists had made a second invasion of South Korea. Russian-made MIG jet fighters flew in from China and attacked American troops and bombers.

MACARTHUR WANTED PERMISSION to bomb the MIG bases in China. He also wanted to blockade the coast of China. Truman did not want to take these steps. America's allies in the war did not want the war to spread to other lands beyond Korea. MacArthur and the President differed on how to run the war. When a letter, written by MacArthur, critical of the President's handling of the war, was read in Congress, Truman took away his command and called him home. General Matthew B. Ridgway, the new commander of the 8th Army, was named to replace him. Ridgway saw that the U.N. troops could not attack the strong Chinese army. His plan was to trap and destroy large units of the Chinese. When enough had been destroyed, Ridgway would attack and push them back to the border again. "Operation Killer," as this was called, got underway. Ridgway destroyed large parts of the Chinese army. American fighters and bombers hit their troops and line of supplies. Meanwhile the U.N. army got stronger. The Chinese were pushed back across the border. The U.N. army was poised to invade North Korea.

**General MacArthur** was called home. "He went too far," President Truman explained.

# *ARMISTICE BRINGS UNEASY PEACE IN KOREA*

**Long after the fighting ended,** American troops stayed on guard duty in South Korea. They held lonely posts, watching for attacks which might come from North Korea.

PEACE CAME TO KOREA. A Communist bid for armistice talks was made on June 23, 1951. The U.N. agreed and the talks began on July 10 at Kaesong, near the border line. They were shifted to Panmunjon and two years of argument and delays followed. Finally, on July 27, 1953, an armistice agreement was signed. North Korean prisoners who refused to return to Communist territory would be freed as civilians after 120 days. President Syngman Rhee of South Korea wanted the war to continue until all of Korea was united. On June 17, he permitted 25,000 prisoners to "escape"—far ahead of the agreed upon date for their release.

THE TRICK FAILED to block the armistice, however. The final terms gave South Korea about 1,500 more square miles of land than it had before being invaded. A neutral commission took over the prisoner exchange. Thousands of prisoners held by the U.N. refused to return to North Korea. A total of 3,597 Americans were freed by the Reds. As no peace treaty had been signed, American troops were kept stationed on guard duty in Korea for many years.

A FEW AMERICAN prisoners chose to remain with the Communists. Other Americans who had been prisoners told of "brain washing" by their captors. "Brain washing" was a form of mental torture. The Communists tried to get military information and "confessions" from the victims. The Reds also tried to talk prisoners into becoming Communists. Americans had deep sympathy for the South Koreans. American soldiers gave the South Koreans much help in food, clothing, blankets and money. Many Korean orphans were adopted in the United States. Congress voted $200,000,000 for South Korean relief and rebuilding. The "police action" in Korea cost America's armed forces a total of 157,530 casualties, 33,629 of them battle deaths.

# MANY CHANGES IN AMERICA'S LIVING IN THE MID 20TH CENTURY

Many changes in America's way of living had taken place by the mid-way point in the Twentieth Century. The nation had taken a strong hand in foreign affairs. Its armed forces were stationed at bases in many lands around the world. Democracy and Communism clashed over world policies in the Cold War.

National defense had become a top program. Huge sums were spent on defense on a permanent basis. The advancing power of atomic weapons created a constant threat of nuclear war at any time. The fight for civil rights was pushed.

America's population rose to 150.6 million. This was a gain of 14.5 per cent in ten years. The birth rate increased—as compared to the decrease during the Great Depression years. Size of the average American family increased. The West had the most population gain.

Slum conditions spread as living space in large cities became more crowded. Many new suburbs sprang up and the old suburbs became heavily populated. A "Flight to Suburbia" from the cities grew.

More than 34,000,000 Americans attended schools and colleges each year. The post-depression children reached school age and the G.I. Bill of Rights helped large numbers of former servicemen return to their educations. Teacher shortages were a large problem at all school levels.

Television made great gains as home entertainment. More than 15,000,000 sets were in American homes. Attendance at motion picture theaters was reduced and the movie industry specialized in producing super color films as multi-million-dollar "spectaculars."

Congress established the National Science Foundation in May, 1950. Wartime development of radar and similar devices led to peacetime uses of electronics. Many new electronic products improved the way of doing things and America's methods became faster and better.

War novels became popular reading with the public. Among them were *Tales of the South Pacific*, by James E. Michener, and *The Young Lions*, by Irwin Shaw. Popular religious works included *Peace of Mind* by Rabbi Joshua Liebman and *The Robe* by Lloyd Douglas.

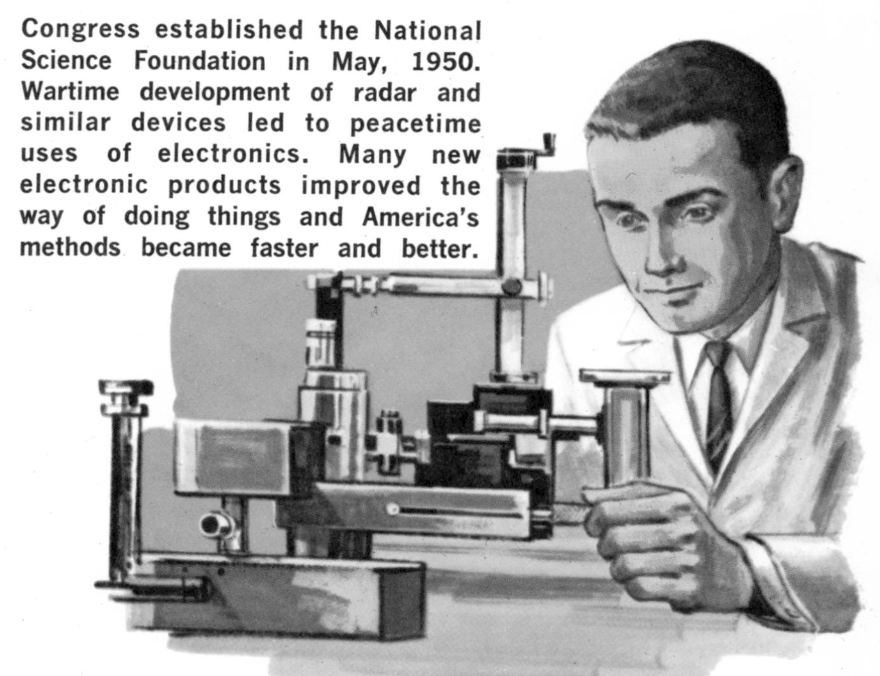

# *SEATO PACT PROVIDES MUTUAL DEFENSE TALKS*

A PACT IN SOUTHEAST ASIA was the next block placed in the path of Communism. While holding parts of Korea and Vietnam, the Reds wanted still more gains. Chiang Kai-shek had been forced to move with his army to Formosa. There were threats that Chinese Communists might invade Formosa. The United States called a Manila Conference of Far Eastern states. The United States, Great Britain, France, Australia, New Zealand, Pakistan, Thailand and the Philippines attended. Burma, Ceylon, India and Indonesia, who called themselves "neutralists," refused to attend.

THREE DAYS AFTER the meeting began, a treaty for mutual help and defense talks was signed. The pact, adopted on September 8, 1954, was not a military agreement. But it did say that in case of threats by an outside power the treaty members "would consult immediately." The new organization took the name of the Southeast Asia Treaty Organization. The initials were used to create the short name of SEATO.

A Pacific charter similar to NATO was signed, pledging each member to defend its own self-rule against a take-over by outsiders. This was in answer to charges by the Communists that the democratic nations planned seizures of colonial lands. This, the Communists said, was the true purpose of the formation of SEATO in the Southeast Asian area.

THE UNITED STATES had helped create defensive treaties in both of the great ocean areas of the world. In the Atlantic it was NATO and in the Pacific it was SEATO. In another move, the United States signed a mutual defense treaty with Chiang Kai-shek's Chinese Nationalists on Formosa. A new trouble spot had developed. Indo-Chinese Communists had defeated the Vietnamese Loyalists and the French. The country was divided at the Seventeenth parallel into North and South Vietnam.

**Eight nations** on four continents joined in forming SEATO to stop Asian Communism.

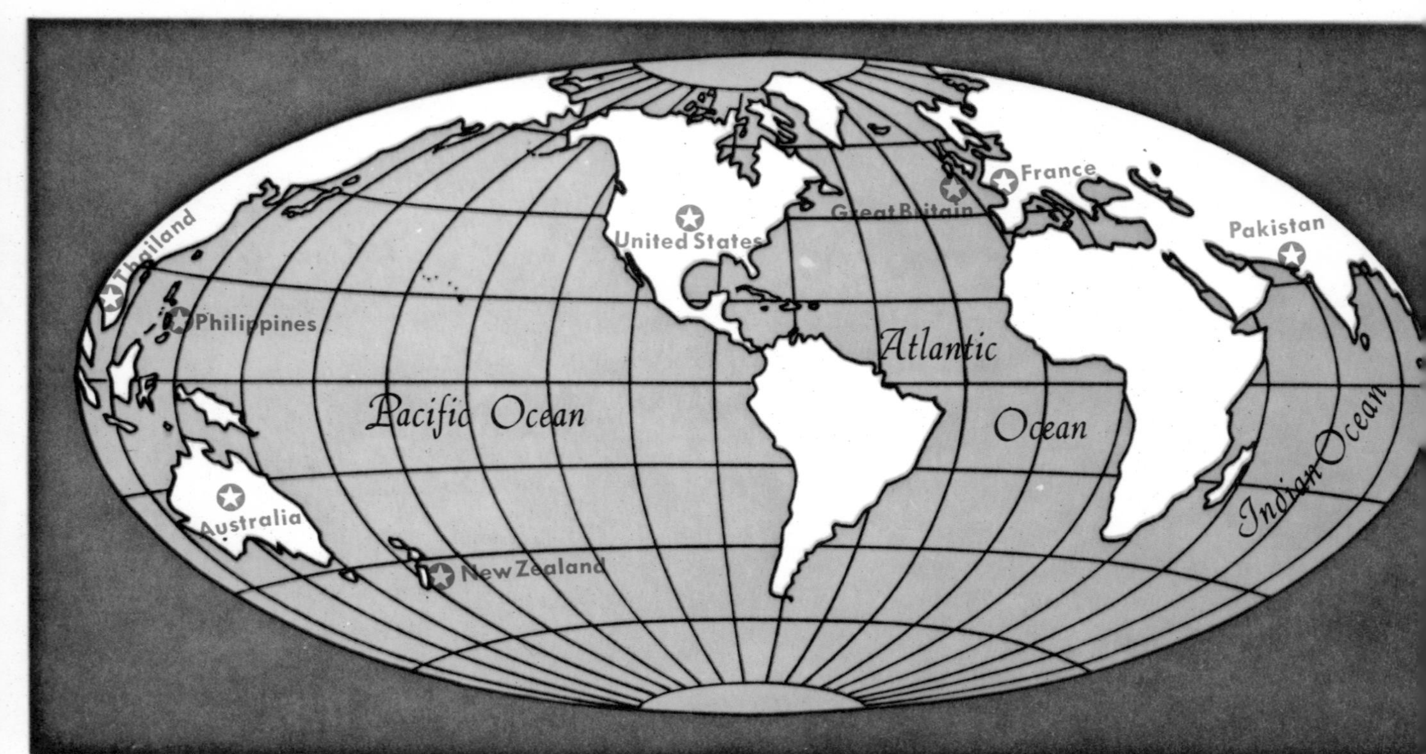

# *HUGE LABOR MERGER JOINS A.F. of L. and C.I.O.*

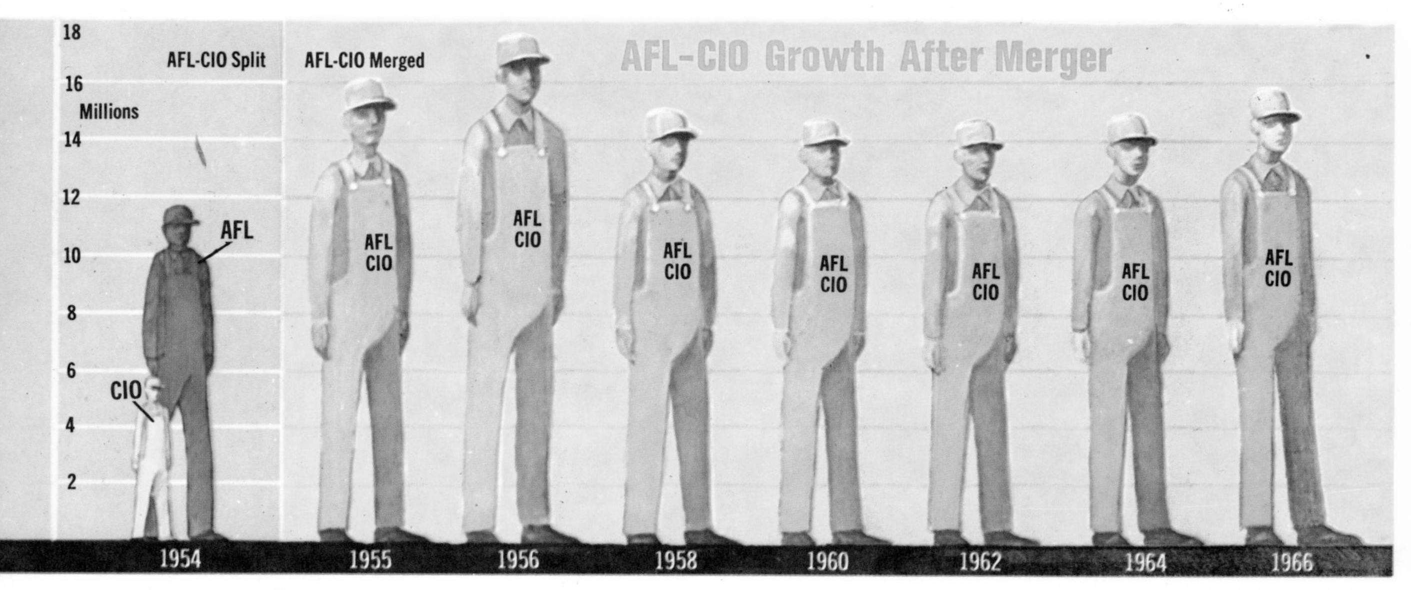


**Before their merger,** the A.F. of L. and CIO had been bitter rivals. After joining forces, the AFL-CIO passed 16,000,000 members in 1956, then leveled off at 15,000,000.

A HUGE LABOR MERGER, or joining together, gave the workingmen of America a united front of 15,000,000 organized members. The American Federation of Labor and the Congress of Industrial Organizations joined forces after almost twenty years of rivalry. The A.F. of L. and the C.I.O. had followed different ways of unionism. The Federation was made up of single independent unions of skilled workers. In 1935, John L. Lewis had formed a Committee for Industrial Organization, within the American Federation of Labor. Lewis' group organized large over-all unions for individual trades. Under this new system, all workers of any industry, such as steel, belonged to one big union.

THE LEWIS GROUP was suspended by the A.F. of L. in 1936. Two years later, the leaders, including Lewis, were expelled from the A.F. of L. Under Lewis' leadership, the former Committee for Industrial Organizations was reorganized as the Congress of Industrial Organizations. This new organization was called the C.I.O. The two groups—A.F. of L. and C.I.O.— gained in strength and the sizes of their memberships. By its aggressive ways, the C.I.O. gained recognition in many industries. But the rival groups both had the same goal of more benefits for workingmen.

LEWIS, THE LEADER of the C.I.O., became a fighting figure on the national scene. He opposed Franklin Roosevelt and supported Wendell Willkie for the Presidency in 1940. When Willkie was defeated, Lewis led his United Mine Workers out of the C.I.O. The miners went back to the A.F. of L., but withdrew again in 1947. Labor's ranks were split by quarrels during the 1940's and early 1950's. But both had the same post-war problems, and a movement for uniting of the A.F. of L. and C.I.O. began and gained strength.

THE MERGER was completed on December 5, 1955, in a meeting of the two organizations in New York City. The two groups voted to combine their memberships as the AFL-CIO. George Meany, head of the A.F. of L., became president of the united organization. Walter Reuther, C.I.O. leader, became the vice-president. From that point on the AFL-CIO exercised increasing influence in America's affairs.

# SUPREME COURT RULES SCHOOL SEGREGATION ILLEGAL

**Federal troops guarded** black students as they entered an all-white high school at Little Rock. School integration had begun.

PUBLIC SCHOOL SEGREGATION, or the sending of white and black children to different schools, was declared unconstitutional by the Supreme Court in May, 1954. This ruled out a "separate but equal" school policy which had been upheld by the Supreme Court in 1896. In the 1954 ruling, the court said that laws which forced blacks to attend separate schools were against the Fourteenth Amendment. This amendment guaranteed civil rights and the Supreme Court said that segregation denied blacks equal rights to education. State and local school boards were ordered to end school segregation, and federal courts were ordered to enforce the new ruling "with all deliberate speed."

SCHOOL INTEGRATION, or sending white and black children to the same schools, was fought in many areas. This not only included the South, but some large cities in the North. The first big test came in Little Rock, Arkansas, in Sepember, 1957. The first blacks were to be admitted to the all-white Central High School. Governor Orval M. Faubus of Arkansas called out the national guard to "prevent disorder." Black students were turned away as they tried to enter the school. Rioting broke out when the school finally admitted nine black students. President Eisenhower sent 1,000 United States paratroopers to Little Rock and placed the state guard under federal command. The black students were guarded entering and leaving the school. Integration was enforced in Little Rock.

RIOTS AGAINST INTEGRATION marked the entry of James H. Mededith as the first black student at the University of Mississippi in 1962. President John F. Kennedy ordered federal troops to the college town of Oxford. When the riots were at their worst, September 30 and October 1, 1962, about 15,000 troops were in Oxford. Tear gas and bayonets were used to break up the riots. Guns were fired over the rioters' heads. Meredith, heavily guarded, was enrolled in the university.

**Lebanon** asked America for help, and President Eisenhower sent Marines. The Marines were on guard in Lebanon for two months.

PERMISSION TO USE FORCE if necessary to stop Communism in the Middle East was given President Eisenhower by Congress in March, 1957. Middle Eastern nations had to ask for help before the President could act. This new policy was called the Eisenhower Doctrine. The President used his doctrine to make a show of force during troubles in Jordan in April. Communists were behind efforts to overthrow King Hussein's government. Although help was not asked, Eisenhower sent America's Sixth Fleet to that area of the Mediterranean Sea. Included were 1,800 Marines. No attempt was made to use the forces. Hussein put down the revolt himself and accepted a grant of $10,000,000 financial aid from the United States.

GAMAL ABDEL NASSER, president of Egypt, led in the organization of a United Arab Republic (U.A.R.) with himself as president. Egypt and Syria were the members. Nasser had seized the Suez Canal in 1956. States around Egypt and Syria accused Nasser of backing revolts which tried to gain control of their governments. The Communists also were accused.

AMERICAN TROOPS landed in Lebanon in July, 1958, as revolts broke out in the Middle East. King Feisal II and Crown Prince Abdul Illad of Iraq were murdered in a pre-dawn raid on their palace. With the Middle East in an uproar, President Camille Chamoun of Lebanon asked for help, and, on Eisenhower's order, United States Marines landed there on July 15. Within a week more than 10,000 troops had landed.

ANOTHER REVOLT in Jordan threatened King Hussein's rule and Hussein asked England for help. Two thousand British paratroopers were flown into Jordan. The American and British troops remained in Lebanon and Jordan for several weeks. Dag Hammarskjold, secretary-general of the United Nations, visited the Middle East and said that dangers had ended in Lebanon and Jordan. The American and British troops were withdrawn in September.

**Russia's man-made "moon"** circled the earth when a rocket fired it into space.

NEW GAINS IN SCIENCE began as the International Geophysical Year opened on July 1, 1957. All nations were invited to take part in scientific study and experiments. The program included study of the earth, the seas, the atmosphere, the sun and outer space. Congress voted $35,000,000 for America's part in the Geophysical Year.

THE FIRST ARTIFICIAL satellite, or small model of a space object, was put into orbit by the Russians on October 4, 1957. The satellite, circling the earth, was called a man-made "moon." The Russians named it *Sputnik I*. For days, *Sputnik I* spun in elliptical, or egg-shaped, orbits around the earth every hour and a half. *Sputnik I* was an aluminum ball twenty-two inches in diameter and weighing 184 pounds. It was blasted into outer space by a huge rocket and continued to orbit until it fell into the earth's denser air and burned. Russia put *Sputnik II* into orbit in November.

AMERICA'S FIRST satellite was put into orbit less than four months after the Soviet feat. The space race was on! On January 31, 1958, the Army sent *Explorer I* circling the earth. *Explorer I* weighed thirty pounds and was blasted into orbit from the nose of a Jupiter-C rocket. In March, the Navy orbited *Vanguard I*. This satellite was small, weighing only three and one-quarter pounds. But it had a "life expectancy," or period of continued orbiting, of from two centuries to 1,000 years. In October, an Air Force *Pioneer* rocket was fired into outer space in an effort to orbit the moon. *Pioneer* failed to reach the moon, but it did streak 79,173 miles into space.

THE SPACE RACE picked up speed as America and Russia fired many other satellites into orbit. The Soviets fired three moon rockets in 1959. One passed the moon and went into orbit around the sun. The second hit the moon, and the third took pictures of the moon's hidden side. Radio and weather satellites were launched, or sent into orbit, by the United States in 1960. In July, 1962, *Telstar,* built by the Bell Telephone system, was orbited. It soon relayed, or sent along, telecasts from continent to continent.

THE MILITARY POSSIBILITIES of rockets developed. In November, 1958, America fired an Atlas missile that hit its ocean target area 6,325 miles away.

# *CUBAN REVOLUTION BRINGS PROBLEMS 90 MILES FROM U.S.*

**Castro at first was cheered as a hero.** But when he revealed himself as an active Communist, he lost America's support.

FIDEL CASTRO SEIZED POWER in Cuba after more than five years of revolt against President Fulgencia Batista's rule. Castro's final victory came on January 2, 1959, when his rebel army marched into Havana. From his mountain headquarters, Castro had led guerrilla warfare against Batista's forces. Castro dropped his guerrilla attacks and began a full-scale drive on Havana from Oriente Province. His army grew as thousands of other Cubans, who hated Batista, joined along the way. Batista resigned and fled as Castro and his army entered Havana and took over rule of Cuba. The United States recognized Castro's government and many thought the bearded leader was a hero.

THE REAL CASTRO soon was revealed. After gaining power in Cuba, Castro began killing many former Batista followers. Hundreds were tried on charges of torture and murder of Cubans who had opposed Batista. During the first five months of Castro's rule, more than 500 died before firing squads. The United States Senate called the killings a "Cuban blood bath." Castro became a cruel dictator. He seized American-owned oil refineries and other businesses in Cuba. He threatened America's continued use of the Guantanamo naval base. Castro demanded that the American embassy staff in Havana be reduced to eleven. On January 3, 1961, retiring President Eisenhower broke off relations with Cuba.

AN ATTEMPTED INVASION of Cuba by refugees who had fled to America ended in failure. Early in April, 1961, the Cuban Revolutionary Council made an appeal in New York for all Cubans to join in an effort to overthrow Castro. President John F. Kennedy declared that the United States planned no invasion. On April 17, an invading force of 1,400—most of them Cuban refugees and exiles—landed from Bahia de Cochinos, or Bay of Pigs. Air support from America was expected but it did not arrive. The invaders were captured by Castro's troops after a short fight. A Freedom Committee in America finally traded farm equipment to Castro for the release of many of the prisoners.

# *THE FIRST MEN IN SPACE*

MEN IN SPACE! The Soviet Union won the race to put the first man into orbit, or a circling of the Earth. On April 12, 1961, Major Yuri Gagarin was sent into orbit and circled the globe once before landing safely. Gagarin's spacecraft *Vostok,* weighing five tons, was shot into space by a huge rocket. Gagarin, the pilot, called a cosmonaut by the Russians, traveled at a speed of 17,000 miles an hour. On May 5, America put Commander Alan B. Shepard, Jr., of the Navy into space. America called her spacemen astronauts. A Redstone rocket carried Shepard into space. The firing, or blastoff, of the rocket was seen by 50,000,000 Americans watching on television. Shepard did not circle the earth, but made a sub-orbital flight. He rode in a Mercury spacecraft, called a capsule, which was named *Freedom 7.* It weighed two tons and its flight continued for fifteen minutes. In July, Captain Virgil I. (Gus) Grissom made a second sub-orbital flight.

THE FIRST AMERICAN to orbit the earth was John H. Glenn, a Marine Corps lieutenant colonel. Glenn circled the earth three times on February 20, 1962. Glenn rode a Mercury capsule named *Friendship 7*. Glenn's flight was made in four hours and fifty-six minutes. He landed in the Atlantic 700 miles east of Cape Canaveral, America's space launching base. In May, 1962, Malcolm Scott Carpenter, a naval lieutenant commander, was the second American to orbit the earth. He also circled three times. After Carpenter came down, it was feared that he was lost. But he was found sitting on a life raft.

MANY SPACE FLIGHTS by both Americans and Russians followed. Soviet Major Gherman S. Titov made seventeen orbits in twenty-five hours and eighteen minutes. Major Leroy Cooper, Jr., of the American Air Force, made twenty-two orbits in Mercury capsule *Faith 7*. Cooper's flight required thirty-five hours. His top speed was 17,500 miles an hour. Earlier, Commander Walter M. Schirra, Jr., had orbited six times. He parachuted his capsule *Sigma 7* into the Pacific Ocean within 9,000 yards of the main recovery ship, the aircraft carrier *Kearsarge*.

**Alan Shepard** became America's first astronaut as 50,000,000 watched on television.

## *BERLIN WALL SHUTS OFF EAST BERLINERS*

**Many East Berliners** trying to cross the wall to West Berlin were shot by guards.

THE REDS BUILT A WALL dividing Berlin in an effort to stop East Berliners from crossing into West Berlin. Since 1949, some 2,000,000 East Germans had fled from the Communist-held areas to West Germany. The Berlin Wall arose overnight. Shortly after midnight on August 13, 1961, the Communists ordered border controls established. Before dawn, East Berlin workers had built the first part of a border wall dividing the city. The wall kept East Berliners from crossing into West Berlin without first obtaining special permits.

MORE THAN 50,000 East Berliners awoke that first morning to find they could not cross to report for jobs which they held in West Berlin. Families were torn apart. East German rulers said the wall was meant to control the crossing of East Berliners only. But sixty-eight of the eighty crossing points were closed. This was cut to seven crossings and Western army forces were permitted to use only one crossing point. The United States, Britain and France protested that a promise of free movement in Berlin and Germany was broken. Moscow replied that only East Germany could settle it.

THE SOVIETS TURNED down all pleas that the wall be torn down. Building of the wall continued until it became a five-foot high stone and wire wall along nearly the entire twenty-five mile East-West border. President John F. Kennedy ordered a 1,500-man battle-group sent to join the 5,000 Americans already on duty in West Berlin. Some refugees trying to cross the wall and escape into West Berlin were shot to death by East Berlin guards. The refugees dug tunnels, leaped over wire fences, and even swam the canal in their efforts to reach West Germany. In August, 1962, the Soviet leaders withdrew their commanders from East Berlin. They turned the city over to the East German government. America was angry with this Russian move. America did not have any official relations with the East German government. This was seen as a move to force the United States to deal directly with the East Germans. Even after the Russians withdrew from East Berlin they kept tight control.

## *U.S. BLOCKADES CUBA TO STOP MISSILES*

CUBA WAS BLOCKADED by the United States to stop Russia's sending of atomic rockets, called missiles, to the island. America and Russia stood face to face in a test of courage and will power. Atomic bases were being built and armed in Cuba by the Russians. President Kennedy demanded that they be removed and for a week the world feared that atomic warfare was at hand. America's distrust of Fidel Castro had been building up. American planes found and took pictures of the Russian missile bases in Cuba. The bases were for the firing of rockets with a 1,200-to-2,000-mile range. This was a threat to all the Americas.

ON OCTOBER 22, 1962, Kennedy announced that the United States Navy would turn back any ship carrying atomic rockets to Cuba. He said that any missile fired from Cuba against any nation in the Western Hemisphere would be seen as "an attack by the Soviet Union on the United States, requiring a full retalitory response"—the firing of American rockets against Russia.

AN AMERICAN FLEET rushed to Caribbean waters to carry out Kennedy's blockade order. Marines were flown to the Guantanamo naval base in Cuba. Forces of all armed services were gathered at Key West. Air Force troop transports were included. America was ready to invade Cuba, if necessary, to destroy the missile bases. Two ships carrying Soviet cargoes were stopped by the blockading fleet. The Soviets drew back from war's threat. Russian Premier Nikita Khrushchev ordered the Cuban bases taken apart and the rockets returned to Russia. Castro refused to permit United Nations inspection of the tearing down of the bases. But Khrushchev agreed to United States inspection of Soviet ships carrying the rockets home. After the bases and missiles were gone, Kennedy ordered the blockade lifted on November 20, 1962.

**American warships** stopped Russian cargo ships. Russia took back the Cuban missiles.

**President Kennedy** fell back in his seat. Mrs. Kennedy took her husband in her arms.

PRESIDENT KENNEDY WAS KILLED by an assassin who shot him down with a sniper's rifle as the President was riding in a motor parade in downtown Dallas, Texas. Shortly after noon on November 22, 1963, Kennedy had been waving to a cheering crowd from the back of the Presidential limousine. With him was Mrs. Jacqueline Kennedy. Texas Governor John Connally and Mrs. Nellie Connally were sitting in the limousine's extra seats.

A CROWD OF 5,000 had met Kennedy at the Dallas airport. Many thousands lined the streets as the motorcade, or parade, passed by. Then three quick shots were heard and the President fell back into his seat, blood pouring from a wound in the head. "Oh, no!" cried Mrs. Kennedy, taking the limp form of her husband in her arms. Governor Connally also was wounded.

THE PRESIDENT lived only thirty minutes. Both he and the governor were taken to Parkland hospital. Kennedy's death was announced at 1 P.M. A reporter had seen a rifle being withdrawn from a window of a nearby building after the shots were fired. Police found a mail order rifle in the building. Lee Harvey Oswald, a Marxist, or Communist, and a Castro follower, was arrested as the leading suspect in the assassination. Oswald was shot and killed by Jack Ruby, a night club owner. Ruby was convicted of murder and died in jail while awaiting an appeal.

**Lyndon Johnson,** the new President, began the Great Society and a War on Poverty. Congress voted billions for his programs.

LYNDON BAINES JOHNSON became America's thirty-sixth President upon the death of Kennedy. Johnson, the Vice-President, was sworn in as President at 2:38 P.M., ninety-eight minutes after Kennedy's death was announced. He took the oath aboard *Air Force One,* the Presidential jet plane, at Love Field in Dallas. The plane's "living room," where the event took place, was crowded with twenty-seven people, including Mrs. Johnson, Mrs. Kennedy and members of the White House staff.

LYNDON JOHNSON, 55 years old, had been a strong candidate for the Democratic nomination for President in 1960. When the party chose Kennedy, Kennedy then personally picked the Texan, Johnson, to be his Vice-Presidential running mate. "John F. Kennedy's policies will be followed," Johnson announced after taking office. During the fourteen months in which he filled out Kennedy's term, Johnson stuck to Kennedy's plans. Then Johnson defeated Senator Barry Goldwater of Arizona in 1964 to win his first full term as President. Johnson had the greatest popular vote margin in Presidential history, 15.8 million. He won forty-four states to Goldwater's six, for 486 electoral votes to 52. Senator Hubert Humphrey of Minnesota was elected Vice-President in the Democratic landslide.

NOW PRESIDENT in his own right, Johnson began a huge welfare, or relief, program which he called the "Great Society." A War on Poverty was a leading program. Huge sums were voted by a strongly Democratic Congress to pay for all of the Great Society's programs. A "head start" program gave young children training before they entered school. This program was for children from poorer families and neighborhoods who needed some training in studying so they could do better in school. Job training courses were begun. Johnson strongly backed equal rights for Negroes. He had been elected on a Democratic platform which promised to make America the most powerful nation on earth, raise wage minimums, or the lowest wages that could be paid, and increase medical aid for citizens reaching sixty-five years of age.

## *1964 ACT BOOSTS MINORITY GROUPS' FIGHT FOR EQUAL RIGHTS*

EQUAL RIGHTS FOR BLACKS were made stronger by the Civil Rights Act of 1964, which became law on July 2. The new act called for blacks to have equal rights in getting jobs, in voting, and in being served in public places. The act outlined rights which had been passed before as laws. A new part of the act said that blacks were to be given equal rights to rent hotel rooms, to be served in restaurants, and to be given seats in theaters and other public places. A later voting rights law gave the Attorney General the power to take over and control the signing up of blacks on voting lists. This power was to be used in states which denied blacks some of their voting rights.

A MODERN REVOLUTION FOR CIVIL RIGHTS had swept across America. It started with a "sit-in" at a restaurant at Greensboro, North Carolina, on February 1, 1960. Four students from the Agricultural and Technical college for blacks at Greensboro entered a store, made some purchases, and ordered coffee at the lunch counter. On being refused service because they were blacks, the students "sat in" at the counter until the store closed. The revolution for civil rights spread.

BLACK FREEDOM RIDERS were attacked at Birmingham, Alabama, in 1961 while riding buses to test the U.S. law that outlawed segregated seating in interstate buses. On August 28, 1963, a freedom march on Washington carried to the nation's capital a direct civil rights plea. Approximately 200,000 took part in the march. Among the leaders were Martin Luther King, Jr., and A. Philip Randolph, campaigners for civil and labor rights.

**Blacks' rights** to be served in restaurants were guaranteed by a new law in 1964.

# EQUALITY ORDERED IN SERVICES AND JOB CHANCES

A major step in the fight for equality was taken in the Civil Rights Act of 1964. The act was based on legislation submitted to Congress in 1963 by President Kennedy. Lyndon Johnson, upon becoming President after Kennedy's assassination, urged Congress to pass the bill to honor Kennedy's memory. Congress passed the bill and Johnson signed it on July 2, 1964.

Also ordered was equal opportunity in obtaining jobs, regardless of race, color or sex. Discrimination in labor unions was forbidden. An Equal Employment Opportunity Commission was created. Many businesses began including in their employment advertisements the statements that "equal opportunity" jobs were offered.

The new law outlawed discrimination in public services on grounds of race, color, religion or national origin. Blacks were guaranteed equal services in such public places as hotels, restaurants, lunch counters, theaters and halls for entertainment.

The Attorney General was authorized to file court suits to enforce school desegregation. The law did not authorize courts or U.S. officials to order transportation of students from one school to another merely for purposes of integration. But schools were ordered to find best ways.

If the laws against racial discrimination were broken, any program or activity receiving financial, or money, assistance from the federal government faced the loss of money until violations ended.

# 1965 ACT HELPS MORE AMERICANS CAST BALLOTS

Methods being used to deny blacks and others an opportunity to vote came under fire of the Voting Rights Act of 1965. In signing the bill into law on August 6, President Johnson said the act "strikes away the last major shackle (slavery chain)." Campaigns to register black voters spread in the South. Many civil rights leaders from the North helped.

**The "examiners" could talk with those wishing to vote. If those talked to were found to be qualified as voters, the "examiners" would order their registration.**

**The law authorized the appointment of federal "examiners," or registrars, to assure the enrollment of all qualified voters in federal, state and local elections—regardless of voters' race, creed or color.**

**Unfair literacy tests which were used to deny blacks their voting rights were ordered stopped. The day after the act became law, the U.S. Justice Department entered court suits to stop such tests in seven Southern states and also Alaska.**

**The poll (voting) tax, as a requirement for voting in national elections, was ended by the Twenty-Fourth Amendment, ratified in 1964. The 1965 voting act declared that such taxes denied an individual his constitutional right to vote in any election, including state elections. Suits were filed to stop poll tax laws then in effect in Mississippi, Alabama, Texas and Virginia.**

**Nearly 1,000,000 more black voters were registered in eleven southern states from 1964 to May, 1968. In 1964, there were 2,164,000 blacks registered. The total increased to 2,189,000 in 1967 and rose to 3,072,000 in time for 1968 elections.**

**Defense Secretary** Robert S. McNamara said Vietnam controlled the gateway between the Pacific and Indian Oceans. He saw rule by the Communists as a threat.

THE U.S. BECAME DEEPLY involved in war in Vietnam, eight thousand miles from America. After four years of giving South Vietnam limited help in the form of huge amounts of money and materials, U.S. military advisors were sent to help the South Vietnamese in their fight against attacks by Communist forces from North Vietnam. The North Vietnamese military machine was strengthened by its successful fight to drive the French from Indo-China in 1954. But it was not until late 1964 that the U.S. began giving South Vietnam full military support. On August 2 and August 4, 1964, the U.S. destroyers *Maddox* and *C. Turner Joy* were reported as attacked by North Vietnamese PT, or patrol-torpedo, boats while the U.S. warships were on patrol in the Gulf of Tonkin off Vietnam. On August 7, Congress approved President Johnson's proposal by passing the Tonkin Resolution. The resolution gave the President powers to "take all necessary measures to repel (stop) any armed attack against U.S. forces."

FIGHTING BECAME A REAL WAR for the U.S. after the Tonkin affair. Hundreds of air force, navy carrier and Marine fighter-bombers began attacking in North Vietnam. America's giant B-52 bombers soon joined in the fight, first from bases on Guam and then from Thailand. General William C. Westmoreland, U.S. commander in Vietnam, spread American forces from the Mekong Delta, in southeast Vietnam, to the Demilitarized Zone (DMZ), the Seventeenth Parallel dividing North and South Vietnam. U.S. Marines, commanded by General Lewis M. Walt, held a big base at Da Nang, not far from the DMZ.

"SEARCH AND DESTROY" methods were used against the Communist Viet Cong throughout 1965-1966. The Viet Cong were guerrillas, or bandit-type forces, which attacked villages. The Viet Cong killed many thousands of South Vietnam's villagers and farmers were driven from their lands. Civilian officials were executed. U.S. Army troops, Marines and South Vietnamese soldiers hunted down the Viet Cong. Meanwhile, Viet Cong terrorists repeatedly attacked Saigon, South Vietnam's capital.

NORTH VIETNAMESE REGULAR TROOPS slipped across the Demilitarized Zone and joined the Viet Cong in attacks in South Vietnam. America's strategy shifted in 1967 from "search and destroy" missions to planned military campaigns. Major battles were fought in the Mekong Delta, one of the great rice-producing areas in Asia. By the end of 1967, more than half a million Americans were serving in land, sea and air forces in Vietnam.

## *U.S. TROOPS SENT TO DOMINICAN REPUBLIC*

AMERICAN ARMED FORCES were sent to the Dominican Republic when a revolt and rioting broke out. On April 24-25, 1965, an army revolt overthrew the government. The United States had backed this government which was a three-man rule headed by Donald Reid Cabral. Colonel Francisco Caamano Deno, a leader in the revolt, tried to bring back to power former President Juan Bosch. Dominican navy, air force and some army units under General Wessin y Wessin met the rebels in armed clashes. The revolt was put down and a three-man military junta, or council, was named to govern the country.

AS FIGHTING CONTINUED, President Johnson sent 405 United States Marines to the Dominican Republic on April 28 to protect Americans there. Navy ships already had taken 1,172 Americans from Santo Domingo, the island capital. Fighting and rioting spread and Johnson sent a large force to the island. By May 5, a total of 12,439 Army troops and 6,924 Marines were in the Dominican Republic. Eight United States soldiers had been killed and forty-nine wounded. On that date, May 5, the rival Dominican forces signed a truce, or "cease-fire," agreement arranged by an Organization of American States commission. But fighting continued.

THE ORGANIZATION of American States sent an inter-American army to Santo Domingo to keep the peace. The O.A.S. patrolled the areas controlled by a five-man junta, headed by General Antonio Imbert Barreras. The O.A.S. peace commission resigned and its place was taken by O.A.S. Secretary Jose A. Mora. The first American troops were withdrawn on May 26. By then nineteen Americans had died in the Dominican fighting.

AGREEMENT FOR AN ACTING government was signed on August 31 by an O.A.S. peace group and the rebel leaders. Hector Garcia-Godoy was chosen acting president. A general strike was called and new rioting began when 600 students fought against a cut in student council money. Garcia-Godoy ordered some top military officers to foreign posts and the fighting eased. In June, 1966, Joaquin Balaguer won a free election to become president of the Dominican Republic. Balaguer received strong support of the United States.

**American troops** were rushed to the Dominican Republic. They set up guns and bases at main points to protect Americans there. About 20,000 troops were sent to the island.

**White used a rocket gun** to steer himself around *Gemini 4* during "walk" in space.

A WALK IN SPACE was made by Lieutenant Colonel Edward White on June 3, 1965. With James McDivitt as command pilot, White stepped out of *Gemini 4* and for twenty-one minutes floated in space attached to a lifeline. He worked his way around the spacecraft using a hand rocket gun. White traveled nearly a quarter of the way around the world during his "walk." Frank Borman and James A. Lovell broke all space flight records on December 4-18, 1965. In *Gemini 7* they orbited the earth 206 times in a flight which lasted for fourteen days. During this flight, Thomas Stafford and Walter M. Schirra rode *Gemini 6* into orbit and rendezvoused, or met, with *Gemini 7*. The craft came within one foot of each other.

TRAGEDY HIT AMERICA'S space program. Three astronauts died in a fire which broke out in their spacecraft while they were inside during a test on the ground. Edward White, who had lived through the "walk" in space, was one of those who died in the fire. The two others were Lieutenant Colonel Virgil Grissom and Lieutenant Commander Roger Chaffee. Doctors said smoke killed the astronauts. The fire started from electric wires under Grissom's seat. Oxygen in the spacecraft burst into flames and the astronauts were unable to open the escape door. The tragedy also set back America's plans to land men on the moon.

# *REBELLIONS AND RIOTS MARK 1967*

**Bloody rioting in Newark and Detroit** from July 12 to July 30, 1967, resulted in 69 deaths. Hundreds were injured. Fire bombings and shootings marked both outbreaks.

MARTIN LUTHER KING WARNED America that the summer of 1967 might bring bloody disorders. The warning came true in massive riots at Newark, New Jersey, from July 12-17 and at Detroit, Michigan, from July 23-30. Fire-bombing, shootings, property damage and many arrests took place in both cities. In the riots at Newark, 26 were killed, 1,500 injured, and 1,000 arrested. At Detroit, 43 blacks and whites were killed and 2,000 were injured. Dr. King, the leader of the Southern Christian Leadership Conference, had spoken to warn his countrymen, not to threaten. His warning came true.

EVER SINCE 1964, racial violence had been increasing. In the summer of 1964, three young men were killed while working on a voter registration program in Mississippi. Two were whites and one was a black. Their bodies were later found buried under a dam site near the town of Philadelphia, Mississippi. A federal jury convicted seven suspects, including a Ku Klux Klan leader.

KING LED CIVIL RIGHTS GROUPS in a three-months voter registration campaign at Selma, Alabama, in 1965. Several persons were killed during the campaign, including Mrs. Viola Gregg Liuzzo, a white civil rights worker from Detroit. In August, 1965, serious rioting took place in Watts, a black neighborhood in Los Angeles. Thirty-five persons, including policemen, were killed. James Meredith, the first black student to enroll at the University of Mississippi, was shot on June 6, 1966, while making a personal voter drive march in Mississippi. He received several wounds, but recovered and continued his march. Other riotings and disorders also had taken place in the North during the summer of 1966. Two were killed in Cleveland and two died in Chicago during demonstrations in a racially restricted neighborhood.

IN COMPLETE CONTRAST to the rioting was a peaceful campaign at Resurrection City, also called Poor City. Resurrection City was a camp built alongside the reflection pool near the Lincoln Memorial in Washington. From May 5 to June 25, 1968, thousands of poor peoples' campaigners—mostly blacks—led by the Reverend Ralph D. Abernathy, sought new relief laws for America's poor. A delegation appeared before a congressional group.

# DISORDERS REPORT CALLS FOR REFORMS

President Johnson in 1967 appointed an Advisory Commission on Civil Disorders. A report was made in March, 1968. The commission, headed by Governor Otto Kerner of Illinois, said: "Our nation is moving toward two societies, one black, one white—separate and unequal." A multibillion dollar program of reforms was proposed by the Kerner report.

The building of 6 million units of decent housing for lower-income groups was recommended. Another proposal was an "open occupancy" law.

Total desegregation and more pre-school and vocational courses were urged as educational goals for the program.

Two million equal opportunity jobs should be created, the commission said. The report set welfare standards at a "minimum poverty" level of $3,335 annually. A voice for blacks in neighborhood policy-making was also urged.

An open occupancy law was passed soon after the report was issued. It barred racial discrimination in the sale and rental of 80 per cent of U.S. housing. The act authorized housing law suits.

## *STUDENT PROTESTS BRING DISORDERS TO CAMPUSES AND STREETS*

STUDENT DISORDERS hit some of the nation's largest universities and colleges in 1968-1969. Campus activities were upset and fighting took place in streets. The protesting students had a variety of complaints. Some demanded more academic freedom, or voice in college affairs. They claimed the right to help choose college faculty members. Opposition to the Vietnam War and the military draft were other reasons given. Black students wanted courses in black history. Some student protests and demonstrations were sponsored by the Students for a Democratic Society.

HUNDREDS OF COLUMBIA University students were arrested during disorders which took place at New York from April to June, 1968. The protests began with an argument over a gymnasium on the Columbia campus. On May 3, 1968, Negro students seized the administration building of Northwestern University at Evanston, Illinois. This protest concerned black housing units and a meeting place. The University of California at Berkeley had a series of student disorders, extending into 1969. Some of the most violent disorders took place at San Francisco State College, with bombings, fires, building damage, and fights with police and troops.

THE NATIONAL GUARD was called out twice in 1969 to put down student disorders at the University of Wisconsin at Madison. Police threw tear gas bombs and the guardsmen used bayonets to drive back mobs rioting in the streets. Passive resistance was used to end student seizure of the administration building at the University of Chicago, in protest to the dismissal of a teacher. President Edward E. Levi refused to call on the police, but some Chicago students later were suspended or expelled for their part in the disorders.

HARVARD STUDENTS SEIZED the university's administration building at Cambridge on April 9, 1969. The students demanded that Harvard discontinue the Reserve Officers Training Corps (R.O.T.C.). Four hundred helmeted policemen forced their way into the building and removed the protesters. In the fighting, 30 persons were injured and 196 were arrested. Later, some of the leaders were suspended or expelled. At Cornell University, about forty black student members of the Afro-American Society seized the student union building on April 19, 1969. They left the building only when promised that no action would be taken against them. The black students were armed with 17 rifles and shotguns and a supply of ammunition, which they said they carried to protect themselves against threats.

**Crowds of University students** took part in demonstrations and disorders. Some lasted as long as three months. Hundreds of arrests were made, but few were jailed.

**Stokely Carmichael explained** that Black Power was to "provide a community with . . . strength . . . to make its voice heard."

**Floyd McKissick said:** "Black Power seeks power in the areas of politics, economics, self image, leadership, law enforcement."

**Charles Hamilton**, a professor, said "Black Power is talking about a drastic change in nature of the social-political system."

**The Black Muslims** sought a complete separation of white and black communities. They had their own restaurants and stores.

BLACK POWER BECAME a powerful force in civil rights. The phrase "Black Power" was first used during a 1966 civil rights drive in Mississippi. The term was used in many newspaper headlines over stories reporting developments in the drive. It attracted much attention. Some blacks soon called for the removal of all whites from their organizations. Leaders of black groups defined Black Power in their own way. Stokely Carmichael, chairman of SNCC, a civil rights organization, said: "Black Power is to provide a community with a position of strength from which to make its voice heard . . . to win political power . . . This is what blacks seek: control. Ultimately, the economic foundation of this country must be shaken if black people are to control their lives."

FLOYD MC KISSICK, president of the Congress of Racial Equality, said: "Black Power seeks power in the areas of politics, economics, self image, leadership, law enforcement, and consumer buying. United, the black man can fight the evil of white supremacy." Charles Hamilton, college professor and writer, said: "Black Power is talking about a drastic change in the nature of the social-political system — its values as well as institutions. For the black people of the ghetto, the system is no longer legitimate. The fact is that black people have the power to deny peace and stability to the larger society. Only when black people feel a personal stake in the society will they protect it. Only then will it be legitimate."

THE BLACK MUSLIMS, one of the oldest Black Power groups, called for complete separation of white and black communities. The Muslims used only their own restaurants, grocery stores and police to avoid any need of the white man. Muslims took new names and gave up all alcohol and tobacco. Women wore special dress and the Muslims had special schools.

# *THOUSANDS MARCH IN PROTEST TO U.S. WAR IN VIETNAM*

**Thousands of protesters** against the U.S. fighting in Vietnam stormed the Pentagon. The demonstrations took place for two days and troops and police arrested 647.

ANTI-WAR FEELINGS AROSE in America and brought huge protest marches. As the fighting continued in Vietnam and the total of Americans killed increased, thousands demanded, "End the War!" On April 15, 1967, twin marches were held in New York and San Francisco. Police estimated the New York crowd at 100,000 and San Francisco's at 50,000. On May 13, a counter-march was made at New York by 70,000 members of veterans' groups, fraternal and religious organizations and labor unions. These marchers said they were "supporting our men in Vietnam." They protested "attacks on our nation and the impression given of a people who oppose their country."

THE PENTAGON WAS STORMED by thousands of anti-war protesters on October 21, 1967. An estimated throng of 35,000 demonstrated for two days before America's military headquarters building in Washington, D.C. The goal was to reach Defense Secretary Robert McNamara's headquarters and other military leaders' offices and demand in person: "End the war in Vietnam now!" Army troops and police drove back protesters trying to enter the Pentagon. During the two days, 647 were arrested. Again, thousands marched in a counter-demonstration at New York and other thousands drove throughout the day with their cars' headlights on to signal their support of America's war effort.

DRAFT CARD BURNINGS and violence marked some protests. But on April 5, 1969, peaceful anti-war marches were held by 35,000 in New York and 20,000 in Chicago. On October 15, 1969, the first of two Moratorium Day demonstrations took place. "M-Day" rallies, as they were called, were held in many large cities and small towns—all generally peaceful. On November 13-15, 1969, the largest anti-war demonstration up to that time—the Second M-Day—was held at Washington. It was estimated that 250,000 persons—most of them young Americans—marched in the national capital on November 15. Nearly 10,000 U.S. troops were on standby alert, but were not needed.

**Robert Kennedy was slain** by an assassin, as his brother President Kennedy had been. Kennedy was shot at Los Angeles after winning California primary election.

THE 1968 PRESIDENTIAL campaign brought political storms and a tragedy. On March 31, President Johnson announced that he would not run for re-election. Controversy and public dissent, or difference of opinion, had developed during his administration. The Democratic Party was split. Senators Robert F. Kennedy and Eugene McCarthy became the leading rivals of Vice-President Hubert H. Humphrey for the Democratic nomination. Kennedy had just won the June 4 California primary when tragedy struck. He was shot in a Los Angeles hotel. Kennedy died on June 6 and America was stunned by the slaying of the brother of President John F. Kennedy, who also was assassinated. Sirhan B. Sirhan, a Jordanian, was convicted of Robert Kennedy's murder.

MASSIVE DISORDERS marked the 1968 Democratic national convention, held at Chicago from August 26-29. While political fighting was taking place in the convention hall, mobs demonstrated outside. Chicago had been warned that plans to "wreck" the convention had been made. Chicago was prepared, but the disorders raged as threatened.

CONVENTION WEEK BROUGHT MOB scenes. Disorders began when several thousand were prevented from camping overnight in Lincoln Park because the park closed at 11:00 p.m. On the final night, 2,000 demonstrators and some convention delegates stormed around the convention headquarters hotel. In all, 641 demonstrators were arrested during the week. Many demonstrators and police were injured, but none was killed. Cries of "police brutality" were heard. Later, eight demonstrators were indicted and tried on charges of conspiring to incite the riots.

THE DEMOCRATS NOMINATED Humphrey for President and Senator Edmund S. Muskie for Vice-President. Earlier, at a convention in Miami Beach, the Republicans had nominated former Vice President Richard M. Nixon for President and Governor Spiro T. Agnew of Maryland for Vice-President. On November 1, five days before the election, President Johnson ordered U.S. forces to stop all bombing of North Viet Nam—a main campaign issue.

**Great disorder** marked the 1968 Democratic convention at Chicago. Demonstrations in a park, in the streets, and before headquarters hotel led to 641 arrests.

## *NIXON ELECTED—CALLS FOR PEACE, UNITY, EQUALITY*

RICHARD M. NIXON WAS ELECTED on November 5, 1968, as America's thirty-seventh President. He won a close victory over Vice-President Hubert H. Humphrey. Not until the next morning, when Nixon was assured of Illinois' 26 electoral votes, was the election decided. The final electoral vote totals were: Nixon, 302; Humphrey, 191, and George C. Wallace, the American Independent (third) Party candidate, 45. Nixon won 32 states, Humphrey 13, and Wallace 5. Humphrey won the District of Columbia. In the popular voting, Nixon had 31,770,237, Humphrey 31,270,533 and Wallace 9,906,141. Nixon's popular vote margin over Humphrey was 499,704. Because he did not win a majority of the total popular vote, Nixon was a minority President.

NIXON'S ELECTION as President was hailed as a great political comeback, coming after he had lost the 1960 election to John F. Kennedy. In his inaugural address on January 20, 1969, Nixon outlined peace, unity and equality as his goals. He said: "The greatest honor history can bestow is the title of (world) peacemaker. This honor now beckons America." On unity, he said: "What has to be done (in America), has to be done by the government and people working together." On equality, Nixon said: "No man can be fully free while his neighbor is not. To go forward at all is to go forward together. This means black and white together."

AMERICA'S NEW PRESIDENT lost no time in beginning a search for world peace. Nixon started an eight-day trip to European capitals on February 23, 1969, to "meet the leaders and the people of our allies." He visited Brussels, London, Bonn (West Germany), West Berlin, Paris and Rome twice. He held conferences with the nation's leaders on each visit. On his return, Nixon said he had found "a new trust in the United States." From July 26 to August 3, Nixon made a nine-day tour of Asian capitals, including a visit with American soldiers at Saigon. The President told the Asians that they must play a greater part in their own defense, but the U.S. would keep present commitments. The Asians were told they must deal with their own Communist troubles at home. These policies, outlined by the President, were called the Nixon Doctrine.

**After taking office,** President Nixon began a search for world peace. He visited European capitals and "found new trust in the U.S." Nixon next made a tour of Asia.

DEMOCRATS KEPT CONTROL in both houses of Congress in the 1968 election. The Republicans gained five seats in the Senate, but the Democrats still had a 58 to 42 majority. In the House of Representatives, the Republicans gained four seats, but the Democrats retained strong control, 243 to 192. In an election highlight, the voters of Arizona returned Barry Goldwater to the Senate, after his 1964 Presidential defeat by Johnson. Mrs. Shirley Chisholm of Brooklyn was elected to the House as the first black woman to become a member of Congress. Blacks increased their representation in Congress by reelecting six House members and adding three newcomers.

# BLACK LEADERS GAIN SUPPORT AND RECOGNITION

American voters at an increasing rate supported political candidates regardless of color or race. In many cities, black candidates were fully accepted and won elections with substantial support of white voters when they appeared best qualified.

**Black candidates had strong voter support to win in congressional and local elections. Mrs. Shirley Chisholm of Brooklyn, New York, was elected in 1968 as the first black woman to become a member of Congress. In 1967, Cleveland voters elected Carl B. Stokes as mayor, and Gary, Indiana, elected Richard G. Hatcher as mayor. In 1969, Charles Evers was elected as the first black mayor of Fayette, Mississippi.**

**In 1966, Massachusetts with less than 2% of black voters elected Edward W. Brooke as the first black member of the U.S. Senate in the Twentieth Century. Brooke, a Republican, defeated former Governor Endicott Peabody to win the Massachusetts election and Senate seat.**

**Thurgood Marshall was sworn in on October 2, 1967, as the first black member of the U.S. Supreme Court. Marshall was appointed by President Johnson while serving as Solicitor General of the United States. Marshall had once served as special attorney for the National Association for the Advancement of Colored People.**

**Tragedy struck on April 4, 1968, when Doctor Martin Luther King, Jr. was assassinated at Memphis, Tenn. James Earl Ray shot King as he stood on the balcony of his motel room planning a march by the Memphis garbage workers. The Reverend Ralph Abernathy was with King at the time of King's shooting. Abernathy became the new leader of the Southern Christian Leadership Conference. Ray was tracked down in an international manhunt and confessed to the slaying of King.**

# "CONTINUING POVERTY" CALLED INDIANS' GREAT PROBLEM

**The U.S. government** turned to new efforts to provide better opportunities for Indians. A 1962 act by Congress began a public works program on and near reservations. Included was the building of facilities on reservations. A 1969 act provided funds for an education and economic program for Great Lakes tribes.

AMERICAN INDIANS' FIGHT for better living continued into the 1970's with some progress made, but much still not made. At an Indian Conference at Boise, Idaho, in March, 1968, Robert L. Bennett, U.S. Commissioner of Indian Affairs, said: "The overriding Indian problem is continuing poverty." In the 1960 census, America's Indian population was shown as 552,000, with more than 300,000 living on reservations. The Indian population when warfare in the West ended in the 1890's was 240,000. Despite this gain, Bennett said: "Indian communities are no further advanced economically than was rural America in the 1930's."

LACK OF JOB OPPORTUNITY was blamed by Bennett. He explained: "Indian unemployment averages close to 40 per cent, and may range as high as 70 per cent in some places and in some seasons." A major cause, he said, was the scarcity of industrial jobs near the reservations. A public works program for the Indians was begun by the U.S. in 1962. It provided jobs for Indians in road building, forestry work and the building of community facilities. Low-cost public housing was provided on some reservations, and tribes were authorized to establish their own housing authorities. Field Employment Assistance Offices for Indians were opened in some cities.

INDIANS BEGAN AN ACTION CAMPAIGN of their own to win the rights they claimed America owed them. On November 20, 1969, a group of Indians representing twenty tribes seized Alcatraz Island, abandoned federal prison in San Francisco Bay. They claimed the island under an 1868 treaty between the U.S. government and the Sioux, stating that unused federal lands would be returned to Indian ownership. On seizing Alcatraz, the Indians moved into the old prison buildings and set up a community of their own. On February 8, 1970, the government removed its one-man security guard, John Hart, and the Indians remained in possession of Alcatraz. They called it "free Indian land" and flew a "Red Power" flag at the dock.

LOUIS R. BRUCE, AN INDIAN, was appointed in 1969 as the new U.S. Commissioner of Indian Affairs. Bruce was born in the Sioux country of South Dakota. He became an attorney in New York Mohawk country. Bruce reorganized the Bureau of Indian Affairs, naming Indians to seventeen of nineteen top positions. Anthony Lincoln, a Navajo, was named to head economic programs. The Navajos won a major claim in 1970 when the U.S. agreed to pay them for lands lost in 1868.

## *UNION LABOR COVERS A WIDE FIELD OF WORKERS*

**By 1970, organized labor** covered many fields. Some public service workers had their own unions. Black labor leaders formed a Negro American Labor Council.

BY 1970 ORGANIZED LABOR represented workers in many fields. Union membership now included public service workers, teachers, actors, TV and radio employees, entertainers, and athletes in some professional sports. Some state and local employees were among public service workers who formed unions. Even some fire departments were organized. Bus drivers and elevated and subway motormen and conductors were organized in many cases. Public service strikes occurred from time to time. In 1962, President Kennedy by executive order granted federal employee unions the right to bargain collectively with government agencies.

THE TWO LEADING TEACHERS' UNION federations were the American Federation of Teachers (AFT) and the National Editorial Association (NEA). The United Federation of Teachers (AFT) had 53,000 members in New York. The Chicago Teachers Union (AFT) had 20,000 members. Teacher strikes took place in New York in 1968-1969 and in May, 1969, schools were closed for two days by Chicago's first teacher strike. A major league baseball strike was averted as 1969 spring training was about to begin when club owners increased pension benefits.

IN THE TRADE-INDUSTRIAL union field, the United Auto Workers split with the AFL-CIO and became an independent union. Walter Reuther, head of the Auto Workers, had disagreements with George Meany, president of the AFL-CIO. After the Auto Workers' withdrawal, Reuther turned to expanding his Alliance for Labor Action. He lined up with the independent Teamsters union and invited others to join.

A NEGRO AMERICAN LABOR COUNCIL was organized in May, 1960. A Philip Randolph was the first president. He was succeeded by Cleveland Robinson. The council said it wanted to help 1,500,000 black union members solve problems.

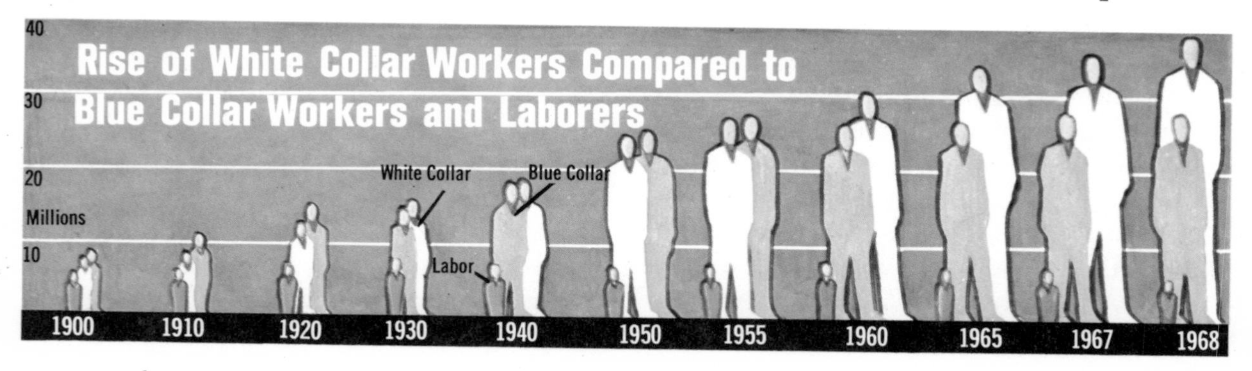

**America's industrial plants** were blamed for much air and water pollution. Steel plants in the Great Lakes area were accused of putting leftover matter in lakes.

AMERICA'S INDUSTRY GREW to giant size and contributed greatly to a better standard of living. But industry also brought a major problem. Air and water pollution had become a national threat by the 1970's and many of the causes were traced to pollution. In the Great Lakes area, steel and other plants were blamed for dumping into the lakes the refuse, or leftover matter, from their steel manufacturing. Much river pollution also was blamed on the dumping of refuse. The complaint arose in big cities that the burned gases piped from automobile motors polluted, or made impure, the air that millions had to breathe. Industrial smokestacks also were blamed. Steel, oil and other big industries joined with federal, state and local governments in a fight on pollution.

AMERICA'S AUTO AND STEEL industries were among the world's leaders in production and sales. In the oil industry, petroleum deposits were discovered in 1968 on Alaska's North Slope. In September, 1969, the state of Alaska sold 179 leases on land in the oil fields for more than 900 million dollars. Alaska began a program to build highways, airports, hospitals and schools. Timed with the Alaska oil land sale was a successful attempt by a 150,000 ton oil tanker-ice breaker, the *S.S. Manhattan,* to make the first commercial voyage through the Northwest Passage around the upper end of North America.

BIG BUSINESS ADVANCED with industry's growth. Franchising by 1970 was an 80-billion dollar system of selling goods and services. Franchising consisted of a parent company, or franchiser, which sold its products or services through an independent store or agency owned by an individual. The individual was called the franchisee and used the franchiser's name or patent. Some 4,000 companies were engaged in business as franchisers and the franchisees numbered nearly 500,000.

CONGLOMERATES WERE ANOTHER big business system. The conglomerate was a corporation which gained control of several companies, from different fields, and put them under one control. One leading conglomerate's holdings included a large seller of sporting goods, a leading meat packer, a large auto rental firm, a commercial air line and several companies producing jet fighter planes, aerospace equipment, electronic controls and aircraft parts. The stock market continued as one of the biggest businesses of all—about 12 of every 100 persons in America owned shares of stock in the nation's industry or business investments.

# *FIRST MOON LANDINGS MADE BY AMERICAN ASTRONAUTS*

**First men on the moon!** Neil Armstrong, Michael Collins and Edwin Aldrin, Jr., rode *Apollo 11* to the moon. Two landed and raised the American flag there.

THE FIRST MEN TO LAND on the moon were American astronauts—and they did it twice in 1969! July 20, 1969, was the date of America's first moon landing. Astronauts Neil Armstrong, Michael Collins and Edwin E. Aldrin, Jr., took off on July 16 and flew *Apollo 11* to the moon. Armstrong and Aldrin landed in a lunar module and walked on the moon's surface for 2 hours and 16 minutes. They planted the American flag on the moon. After 20 hours on the moon, the lunar module returned to *Apollo 11,* which Collins had kept in orbit around the moon.

APOLLO 11 SPLASHED DOWN in the Pacific Ocean on July 24, to end one of the world's greatest explorations. President Nixon greeted the astronauts aboard the recovery aircraft carrier *Hornet.* Armstrong, Collins and Aldrin, on August 13, traveled across the nation and millions hailed them in New York and Chicago. They made a world tour of 22 nations and were cheered by huge crowds.

AMERICA'S SECOND MOON LANDING was made on November 19. Charles Conrad, Jr., Richard Gordon, Jr., and Alan Bean manned *Apollo 12* during its flight from November 14-24. Landing on the moon, Conrad and Bean found the picture-taking robot, *Surveyor 3,* which America had soft landed on the moon in 1967. They placed scientific instruments on the moon and a nuclear power generator to operate them. The astronauts remained on the moon for 31½ hours, with two walks.

A NARROW ESCAPE FROM DISASTER marked an unsuccessful attempt by *Apollo 13* to make America's third moon landing, April 11-17, 1970. As they neared the moon, astronauts James Lovell, Fred Haise and John Swigert faced great danger when an oxygen explosion ripped their service module. The landing attempt was canceled and *Apollo 13* circled the moon and headed home. Using only the landing module's power, Lovell, Haise and Swigert managed a safe landing in the Pacific. America hailed the skill and courage of the spacemen and their ground crew.

# MAN'S FIRST WALKS ON THE MOON'S SURFACE

Neil Armstrong and Edwin Aldrin were the first men to walk on the moon's surface. Armstrong used tools to collect rock and soil samples to be brought back to earth for chemical testing. Meanwhile, Aldrin unwrapped an antenna to send messages.

Aldrin set up a solar windshield to measure rays and detect possible bits of matter thrown off by the sun. Not far away, the lunar landing module rested where it had settled down on the moon's surface in a soft landing. Astronauts left footprints.

A moon seismograph, called a seismometer, was placed on the moon's surface. The astronauts' footsteps began registering at once. The seismograph's sounds were received on the earth. Scientists studied the possibility of moonquakes taking place. They awaited later data.

The lower part of the lunar module, resting on the surface, was used as the platform from which the module was blasted off to return to Apollo 11. The launching rockets started the astronauts safely on the way back home. On their return, they were hailed both in America and abroad.

**The order to integrate schools** "at once" was issued in the first landmark case to come before the Supreme Court under the new U.S. Chief Justice, Warren E. Burger.

SCHOOL INTEGRATION "AT ONCE" was ordered by the Supreme Court on October 29, 1969. The Supreme Court's decision was unanimous in overruling a delay which had been granted to fourteen Mississippi school districts. The "integration at once" order abolished the "all deliberate speed" doctrine which the Supreme Court established in 1955. In 1954, the court had ruled that school segregation was unconstitutional. Segregation foes charged that the word "deliberate" had been considered by the officials of some school districts to mean "whenever they could get around to it."

THE "AT ONCE" DEADLINE established in the latest Supreme Court ruling brought new integration controversies in the South. Some schools insisted they could not fully integrate on such short notice. Some Southern congressmen pressed for the same integration rules to be enforced in the North. The Supreme Court's broad language covered all school systems in which segregation existed. No exact time limit was given for "integration at once," but federal orders began going out to some schools within forty-eight hours. The matter of expenses, such as busing pupils, was brought up by most schools under fire.

GREATER EFFORTS TO INTEGRATE fully the U.S. armed services were ordered by the top commanders of the Marine Corps and army. On September 3, 1969, General Leonard F. Chapman, Jr., commandant of the Marine Corps, announced that he had instructed Marine commanders to make "positive and overt (obvious) efforts to eradicate (wipe out) every trace of discrimination." On October 13, Secretary of the Army Stanley Resor said the army must "give more recognition to the Negro's presence in the army and the fact that he has a long military heritage."

GENERAL CHAPMAN SAID that racial problems "are almost unheard of among Marines in combat," but "Negro Marines apparently are encountering what they regard as discrimination when they return to this country or to rear areas in Vietnam." Secretary Resor said: "Military leaders must reexamine policies and practices in terms of their impact on the soldier as an individual" . . . the black soldier "needs to know from his leaders where they stand, whether he can expect help from them, whether they are willing to accept him without asking that he reject his heritage."

## *FEDERAL ANTI-RIOT LAW TESTED IN CHICAGO CONSPIRACY TRIAL*

**Courtroom disorder** marked the conspiracy trial. All defendants were sentenced for contempt of court. Defense Attorney William Kunstler drew a heavy sentence.

A NEW FEDERAL ANTI-RIOT LAW was tested in 1969-1970 in a stormy court trial which grew out of the 1968 Democratic convention in Chicago. Eight defendants were the first to be tried under the 1968 anti-riot law. The law made it a federal crime to cross state lines with the intention of stirring up, organizing, or taking part in a riot. A riot was defined by the law as any public disorder involving three persons or more, and producing one act of violence endangering other persons and property. The penalty upon conviction was $10,000 fine, five years in prison, or both. Some authorities questioned the constitutionality of the anti-riot law.

EIGHT DEFENDANTS WERE BROUGHT to trial in Chicago on September 24, 1969, on charges that they crossed state lines to incite, or stir up, the riots at the 1968 Democratic convention in Chicago. The eight were charged with conspiring to start the riots, and also with taking part in them individually. Both charges violated the 1968 anti-riot law. The trial continued for five months, marked by repeated courtroom argument and disorder, and what the prosecution lawyers called "insults to the judge and court."

THE JURY'S VERDICT, returned on February 18, 1970, was that none of the seven defendants still on trial was guilty of conspiracy, but five of them were guilty of individually being leaders of the riots. Federal Judge Julius J. Hoffman sentenced the five ruled guilty of rioting to five years in prison and fined each $5,000. In addition, Judge Hoffman—after the case had gone to the jury—sentenced all seven defendants to contempt of court jail terms ranging from eight months to two years and five months. He also sentenced their lawyers for contempt of court. The eighth defendant, Bobby Seale, a leader of the Black Panthers, had been sentenced earlier for contempt of court and his case declared a mistrial. All of the verdicts were appealed to the higher courts.

NATIONWIDE INTEREST in the trial was built up by daily newspaper and TV-Radio reports of developments. The announcements of the jury's verdict and Judge Hoffman's contempt sentences brought public controversy and many protest demonstrations took place across the country. Police and national guardsmen restored order.

**An AFL-CIO organizing committee,** headed by Cesar Chavez, sought to build up union strength among the Mexican-American farm workers. Some joined, many did not.

TWO GROUPS OF SPANISH DESCENT —the Mexican-Americans and Puerto Rican-Americans—were protected by America's expanding code of civil rights. But in some areas conditions of poverty and slow progress were of much concern to most Americans. In the American West, the Mexican-American problem was most pressing. In some cities of the East, the Puerto Rican problem was increasing as more and more residents of the island took advantage of the commonwealth's right of free entry to the U.S.

GREATER JOB AND EDUCATIONAL opportunities and better housing were the main goals in the fight for a larger share of America's standard of living. In some cities, community action groups were formed to advance the interests of the Mexican-American or Puerto Rican underprivileged neighborhoods. The goals here were to have local government improve conditions of housing and job and school opportunities. Parent groups joined together to help steer their youngsters away from youth gangs. In 1970 elections in California, Mexican-American community groups entered their own candidates for some public offices and attracted much attention with their get-out-the-vote campaigns. Earlier, Puerto Rican groups had won a campaign in New York State to remove voting restrictions on their people based on language problems.

MEXICAN-AMERICAN FARM WORKERS in California became involved in a labor controversy. A United Farm Workers Organizing Committee (AFL-CIO) was formed under the leadership of Cesar Chavez. Some of the Mexican-American workers on grape farms (called Chicanos) joined the union, but many did not. In the long controversy, there was picketing of grape farms and a national boycott against California-grown grapes was attempted in food stores in some cities.

THE NATIONAL LABOR RELATIONS (Wagner) Act did not include farm workers in its union organizing and collective bargaining provisions. California grape growers supported a bill introduced in Congress by Senator George Murphy in 1970 which would create a farm labor relations board. The organizing of farm workers would be governed by rules established under the Department of Agriculture.

PROBLEMS OF FARM WORKERS in the West aroused increasing interest. In June, 1970, college students from campuses throughout California joined Chavez's forces working for a buildup of their union. The students held a weekend assembly in the Coachella Valley near Indio, California. No violence was reported.

# *AMERICANS, SOUTH VIETNAMESE ATTACK BASES IN CAMBODIA*

AMERICAN TROOPS DROVE into Cambodia in May and June, 1970, and struck Communist sanctuaries, or safe retreats, in that country. Ever since the Vietnam War began, Viet Cong and North Vietnamese had made attacks in South Vietnam from across the Cambodian border. Then they would draw back into Cambodia, safe from counter-attacks because U.S. and South Vietnamese troops were not allowed to cross into Cambodia. But on April 30, President Nixon announced that a joint Allied drive into Cambodia had begun—the Communist sanctuaries would be wiped out. This was necessary, the President said, to protect American troops while a scheduled pullout of U.S. servicemen from Vietnam was under way. Nixon said the Cambodian campaign would be ended and all, or nearly all, U.S. troops taken out of Cambodia within two months after the military action began.

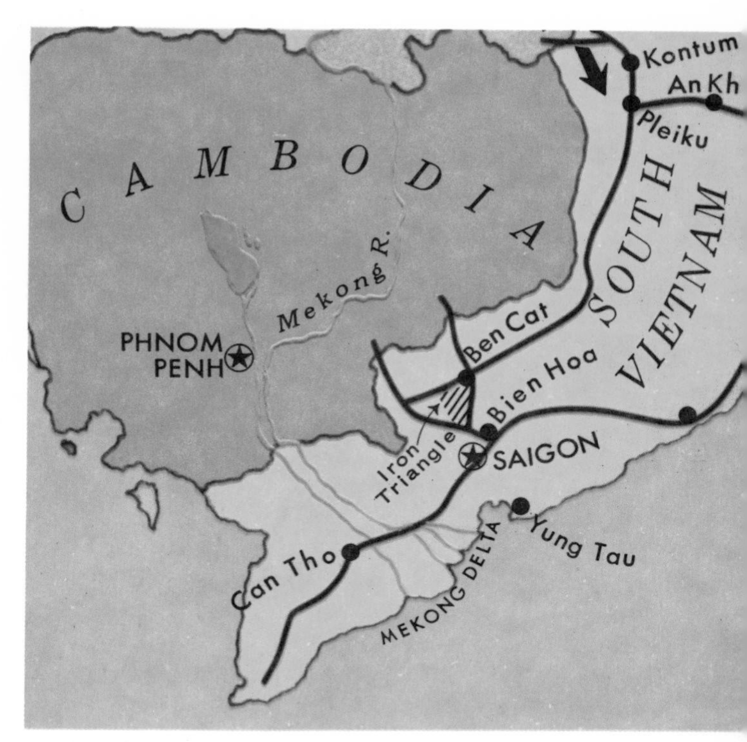


U.S. AND SOUTH VIETNAMESE FORCES attacked on six fronts along 231 miles of the Cambodian border. Their naval units operated on a sixty-mile stretch of the Mekong River to Phnom Penh, Cambodia's capital. Cambodian troops, on their own, fought against Communist attacks around Phnom Penh and Kompong Cham, Cambodia's second largest city, on the Mekong River. U.S. forces in Cambodia were commanded by General Michael S. Davison, under General Creighton W. Abrams, commander of all U.S. forces in Vietnam. The South Vietnamese troops in Cambodia were led by General Do Cao Tri.

A STORM OF PROTEST broke out in the U.S. over Nixon's sending American troops into Cambodia. A move to bar the use of American money, men and arms in further actions in Cambodia after June 30 was led by Senators Mike Mansfield, J. William Fulbright, Frank Church and John Sherman Cooper. Massive student demonstrations took place across the country. On May 4, four students, including two co-eds, were killed when national guardsmen fired on 3,000 student demonstrators at Kent (Ohio) State University. On May 14, two black students were killed when national guards fired on a dormitory at Jackson (Mississippi) State College. At one time, 230 universities and colleges were closed, either briefly or for the remainder of the spring term.

THE CAMBODIAN DRIVE WAS ENDED on schedule and U.S. troops were withdrawn, as Nixon had promised. The President said the troop pullout from Vietnam would continue as planned. After 115,000 troops were withdrawn by April 15, 1970, Nixon had said 150,000 more would be pulled out by spring, 1971—a total of 265,000. The pullout program was based on "Vietnamization" of the war—the South Vietnamese carrying on the fighting alone. U.S. battle deaths in Vietnam by June, 1970, had passed 40,000.

# AMERICA SEEKS HIGHER GOALS IN THE 1970's

Advances were constantly being sought in education, with broader programs and better facilities made available for students of all races. Large sums of money were voted by the government to pay the necessary costs. Courses to be taught spread into new fields of study and knowledge, which were useful to both young and old.

America's standard of living steadily rose to new heights. Inventors provided added comforts and conveniences for the home, and more efficient tools for industry. Giant plants turned out products in ever-increasing amounts, and business expanded with the distribution and sale of the products. America's world trade spread over the sea lanes to new markets.

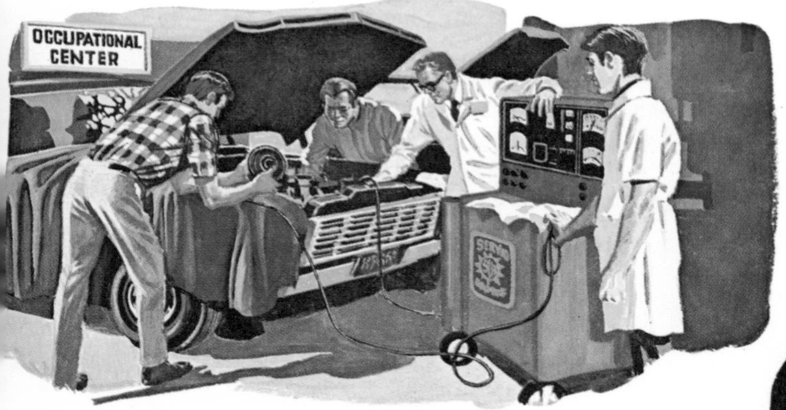


More opportunity and equality in jobs for all Americans were sought. Training programs for unskilled workers to prepare them for better paying jobs were conducted both by the government and industry. More and better housing was sought for the lower-income groups. All efforts and plans were aimed at an even higher standard of living for all Americans.

The nation was determined for its elected leaders to move away from warfare. Peaceful relations were sought with other countries on all continents. The United States and the Soviet Union agreed on the goals of atomic disarmament, halting the spread and possible use of all nuclear weapons. Talks were held on best methods.

# *NORTH VIETNAMESE ACCEPT CEASE-FIRE; WAR ENDS*

**A peace treaty** signed by North Viet Nam's Le Duc Tho and America's Henry Kissinger ended the Viet Nam War after twelve years. American deaths in the war totaled 45,940.

HOPES WERE RISING FOR PEACE in Viet Nam as 1972 began. The number of U.S. troops in the war zone had been cut to just 160,000, down from a peak of 543,000 in 1969. In January, 1972, President Nixon revealed an eight-point peace plan that had been rejected by North Viet Nam's Le Duc Tho at a conference in Paris with Secretary of State Henry Kissinger. On the war front, fighting remained on a fairly low scale, but it was only the lull before the storm.

STRIKING SUDDENLY and swiftly from bases in Laos and Cambodia in April, the North Vietnamese began their strongest offensive of the war, invading South Viet Nam at several points. They struck hard at Quang Tri, northernmost province of South Viet Nam, and also hit the central highlands and as far south as An Loc, 60 miles from Saigon, capital of South Viet Nam. Caught unprepared, the South Vietnamese at first retreated, but managed to halt the invaders.

THE NEXT U.S. STEP was to mine the harbors of North Viet Nam in May, effectively blockading all foreign ships from those areas for the remainder of 1972. Meanwhile, North Viet Nam became more willing to consider a cease-fire. But the talks broke off on December 16 and Kissinger returned to the United States, saying that the North Vietnamese were unwilling to agree on a call for a cease-fire. Two days later, Nixon ordered the heaviest aerial bombardment in the history of warfare. Some 600 B-52's and fighter bombers dropped 4,000 tons of bombs a day on Hanoi, Haiphong, and other industrial targets in North Viet Nam. The damage to that country's industrial and military might was enormous.

ON DECEMBER 30, it was announced that peace talks would resume in Paris. Three weeks later, a cease-fire agreement was signed, to take effect on January 27, 1973. America's longest war was over. It had lasted 12 years and cost 45,940 American lives. The next longest U.S. conflict, the Revolutionary War, lasted nine years.

**Violence broke out** during the first years of forced school busing in large cities. Many whites fled to the suburbs rather than have their children bused to inner city schools.

FORCED BUSING OF PUPILS for the purpose of achieving racial integration remained a source of controversy in many large U.S. cities. The Supreme Court had ruled in 1971 that school busing could be ordered, but many localities chose either to ignore the ruling or to delay its enforcement. They defended their actions by insisting that busing of school children would hasten the flight of whites to the suburbs, weakening the cities' tax base and placing a heavier burden on remaining citizens.

VIOLENCE BROKE OUT in many parts of the country when the first attempts to bus school children were made in the fall of 1971. School buses were burned and many others suffered broken windows, slashed tires, and damaged engines. Parents who opposed forced busing claimed that it was unfair to children to require them to leave neighborhoods familiar to them and ride to unfamiliar, racially mixed schools. Some black parents agreed with white parents, saying it was unfair to their own children as well. School boards objected to forced busing, saying that their budgets could not meet the added expense. President Nixon also opposed the idea, and Governor George Wallace of Alabama told Calhoun County school officials to defy federal orders for busing to all-black Hobson City.

CONTROVERSY OVER THE ISSUE refused to die, and many large cities experienced violence as new school terms began each year. In Chicago, Boston, Cleveland, Louisville, and other localities, opposition to forced busing ranged from outright violence to mere threats. In Louisville, some white parents tried to have their children classified as American Indians, since non-black minorities in Kentucky did not have to take part in the forced busing program. Cleveland did not comply with the Court order because it had no money for buses.

# *SKY LABORATORY OPENS NEW ERA IN SPACE EXPLORATION*

ANOTHER GIANT STEP in America's conquest of space was taken in May, 1973, when an 85-ton laboratory known as *Skylab* was hurled into space from Cape Canaveral. Put in orbit 270 miles from the earth, it was to serve as the base for many scientific experiments and studies by three successive three-man crews of astronauts over a period of 140 days. But the entire project, costing $2.5 billion, came close to disaster when two wing-like panels failed to open at the time of takeoff. The panels were intended to convert sunlight into electrical power, and the mishap left large areas of the craft unprotected from the sun's heat.

UNLESS SOMETHING could be devised to protect the craft from the glare of the sun, the laboratory would be too hot for human tolerance. Space experts on the ground worked around the clock in a crucial attempt to save the valuable project. American ingenuity and daring finally prevailed, and when the first crew—Charles Conrad,

**Members of the second** crew were aboard a rocket that carried them to **Skylab**, the 85-ton space laboratory that was built to determine effects of long space flights.

Joseph Kerwin, and Paul Weitz—reached the crippled craft, they carried with them a device resembling an umbrella. When they entered *Skylab*, the temperature inside was 130 degrees. They forced through an air lock the device they had brought, and it worked as an effective heat shield. The temperature fell overnight to 98 degrees.

A DANGEROUS SPACE WALK later by Kerwin and Conrad enabled the crew to free a solar panel that had become stuck on takeoff and was depriving the laboratory of necessary electrical power. The spacecraft could now operate as planned, and its important experiments began. The crew returned to Earth 28 days later.

SKYLAB'S SECOND CREW stayed aboard for 59 days before returning to Earth. The third and final crew then went aboard and remained in space for a record 84 days.

**Oil shortages in the U.S.** continued despite opening of the Alaska Pipeline. More refineries were needed to process the oil on the West Coast, to which it was shipped.

AN ALARMING SHORTAGE of energy sources plagued the U.S. during the 1970s, adding to ruinous inflation and making the nation more dependent than ever on oil imports. Deeply concerned over the matter, President Carter gave the issue top priority and ordered his newly-created Department of Energy to step up its efforts to locate new sources of energy while conserving current supplies. The most pressing problem, most experts agreed, was the need to drill more oil wells in the United States, both inland and offshore. But the largest American oil companies claimed that they were already doing all they could in that area. Many citizens disbelieved them, insisting that a shortage of oil served to add to their profits.

A SHORTAGE OF NATURAL GAS developed along with the drop in oil supplies. School districts and large industrial plants which used natural gas for heating had to halt or curtail operations. Many Americans were skeptical about the reports of natural gas shortages. They insisted that Congress investigate rumors that gas producers were holding back supplies until federal price controls were lifted on natural gas. The largest producers—most of them large oil companies—denied that they were holding back on gas supplies. But they admitted that they could produce more gas if higher prices were approved. With higher prices, they said, they could afford to search for new sources of natural gas.

THE ENERGY CRISIS had struck America suddenly and hard in November, 1973. Arab nations, angered by U.S. aid to Israel in the Middle East War, imposed an embargo on oil shipments to America. Drastic cuts in fuel oil, gasoline, and electricity had to be made. Automobile travel was reduced, long lines of motorists appeared at filling stations, and many industries were forced to cut back on production and employment. To save fuel, the nation went on daylight saving time the year-round, and heating temperatures in homes and offices were lowered.

THE ALASKA PIPELINE had been expected to solve many of the nation's fuel worries when it began delivering oil in 1977, but it was found in 1978 that refineries on the West Coast to which the oil was shipped did not have the capacity to handle it.

## *WATERGATE BRINGS NIXON'S RESIGNATION; FORD NEW PRESIDENT*

FOR THE FIRST TIME IN U.S. history, a President resigned his high office. Toppled by the ever-widening scandal of Watergate was President Richard M. Nixon, who had been elected in a hard-fought campaign in 1968 and had easily won reelection in 1972. Nixon gave up his post as the nation's chief executive in August, 1974 rather than face impeachment proceedings by the U.S. House of Representatives. Vice-president Gerald R. Ford immediately succeeded him.

NIXON'S FALL FROM POWER began when five persons were arrested in the Democratic party headquarters in the Watergate office building in Washington on the night of June 17, 1972. Investigation revealed that some of the persons connected with the burglary had close ties with officials of the Nixon administration. Although a White House aide tried to dismiss the event as "a third-rate burglary attempt," suspicion grew that high government officials might be involved. Top Nixon aides began a concerted effort to head off any further investigation of the happening, and officials of the Department of Justice and the Federal Bureau of Investigation were even threatened with retaliation if they did not halt their inquiries.

**Facing almost certain impeachment,** President Nixon resigned his high office rather than stand trial before the Senate. Vice-President Gerald Ford succeeded Nixon.

BUT THE SCANDAL REFUSED TO DIE, and despite their denials, officials high in the Nixon administration were indicted one by one. Among those receiving prison sentences from Federal Judge John Sirica for either having knowledge of the break-in or participating in a cover-up of it were former U.S. Attorney General John Mitchell and Nixon's chief White House aides, H. R. Haldeman and John Ehrlichman. Nixon had asked for the resignations of the latter two after they had come under suspicion, but he denied that he himself had any knowledge of either the break-in or of any attempt at a cover-up.

NIXON HAD SECRETLY TAPED all conversations in his White House office over a period of years. This became known, and when the House of Representatives found a tape proving that the President was indeed involved in the cover-up, his closest advisers warned him that he was sure to be impeached by Congress. Rather than face trial before the Senate, he chose to resign. One month later, President Ford pardoned Nixon for any offenses he had committed while President. The act insured that Nixon would not stand trial.

# *U.S. CELEBRATES 200TH BIRTHDAY; SETS NEW NATIONAL GOALS*

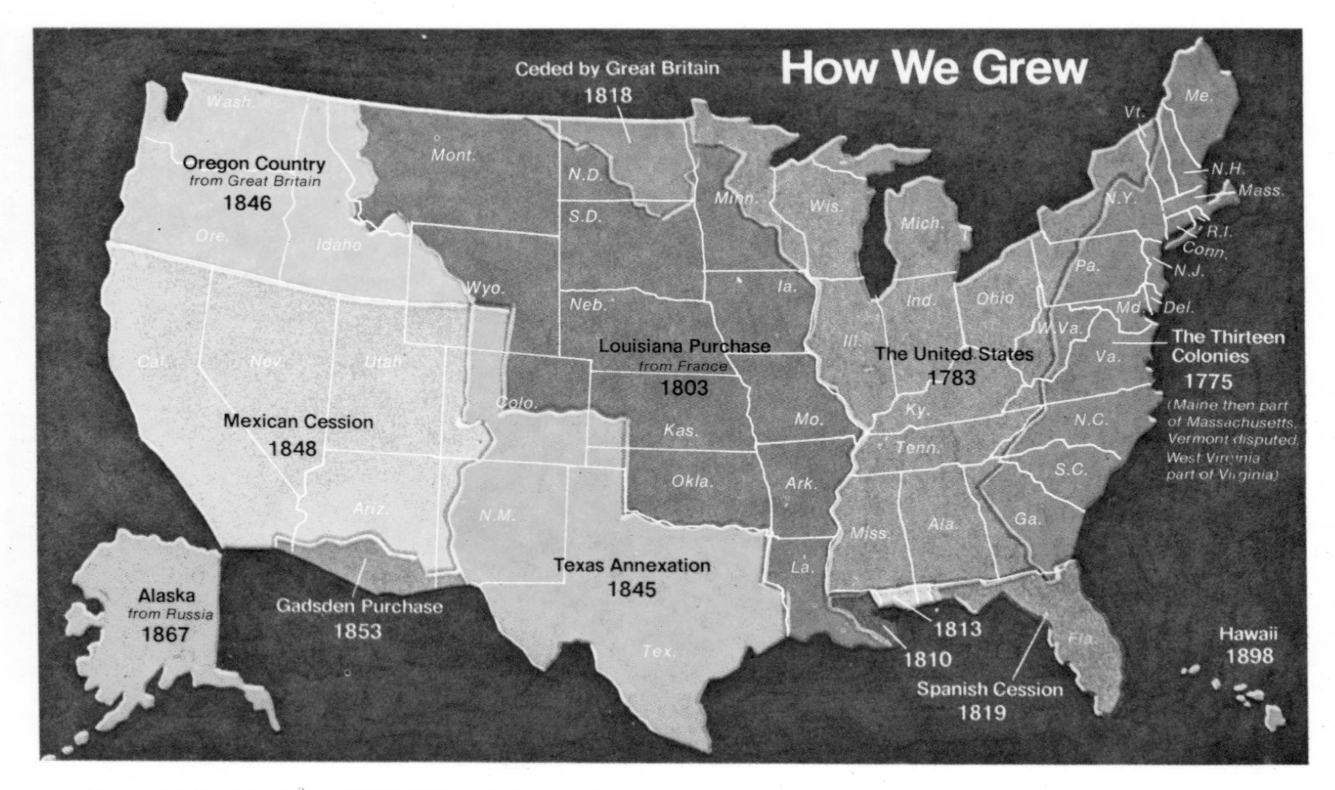


**Growth of the United States** into a major world power in just 200 years was surprisingly fast. Its tremendous increase in size was matched by a great rise in population.

AN ALL-YEAR BIRTHDAY celebration started on January 1, 1976 as the United States saluted the 200th anniversary of its existence. Bicentennial activities included all kinds of pageants, parades, festivals, memorials, and observances as the nation paid tribute to the adoption of the Declaration of Independence in 1776. On the Fourth of July, citizens from Maine to Hawaii and from Alaska to the Gulf of Mexico celebrated the event with dawn-to-dark festivities.

PRESIDENT FORD set the tone for the day when he urged everyone to "break out the flag, strike up the band, light up the sky." Speaking in Independence Hall in Philadelphia where the Declaration of Independence was signed in 1776, Ford warned Americans that "Liberty is a living flame to be fed, not dead ashes to be revered." His words were echoed everywhere across the nation as Americans of all races and creeds joined to make the day memorable.

REENACTMENT OF THE SIGNING of the Declaration of Independence was among the most popular of the Bicentennial observances. In several large cities, thousands of immigrants became American citizens in ceremonies on the Fourth of July.

OVER THE TWO CENTURIES since 1776, the United States had developed into the most powerful and highly respected nation in the world. Its population had increased from 2.5 million to more than 214 million, and it had grown in size from just 880,000 square miles to more than 3,600,000. From the thirteen original states it had expanded to fifty. It had spread from coast to coast and to such distant areas as Hawaii and Alaska. The United States was still "the promised land" to many people throughout the world.

# *WOMEN SEEK EQUAL RIGHTS; ERA RATIFICATION SLOWED*

**American women** stepped up their 130-year fight for equal rights with men. The votes of only three more states were needed for ratification of the Equal Rights Amendment.

THE FIGHT OF AMERICAN WOMEN for equality finished its 130th year in 1978 with victory in sight but the final hurdle proving difficult to clear. An equal rights amendment (ERA) had been passed in 1972 by Congress, but it was still a tantalizing three short of the 38 states needed for ratification. The seven-year deadline for ratification was originally set for March, 1979, but an extension had been voted by Congress, an action that ERA opponents claimed was unconstitutional. The complex matter appeared certain to wind up before the Supreme Court for decision eventually.

THE WOMEN'S RIGHTS MOVEMENT in America began in 1848, when Elizabeth Cady Stanton and Lucretia Mott called the first women's convention at Seneca Falls, New York. In those days, women were not allowed to own property. They could not become doctors or lawyers, and their education in many other fields was severely limited. Mrs. Stanton's demand that women be allowed to vote shocked the assemblage, but she devoted the rest of her life to fighting for that goal. Susan B. Anthony carried on the battle until her own death in 1906. Miss Anthony's co-worker, Carrie Chapman Catt, lived long enough to see their efforts crowned with success in 1920, when the 19th Amendment to the Constitution finally gave women voting rights.

BUT MANY WOMEN INSISTED that even more rights for their sex needed to be spelled out in the Constitution if they were to achieve equal status with men in everyday life. They cited the vast differences existing in wages and promotion opportunities between males and females, and complained that many fields were still closed to them. In 1977, a gathering of the National Women's Conference in Houston, Texas attracted 14,000, and served to closely knit the many different groups which had been competing for power. But many U.S. women still opposed ERA.

**The continuing rise** in the U.S. crime rate posed a threat to citizens' security. Federal law enforcement authorities tested new methods of convicting hardened criminals.

AMERICA'S CRIME RATE rose rapidly during the 1970s, giving rise to fears that law enforcement processes were breaking down. Once confined largely to big cities, serious crime had spread to the suburbs and even to small towns. Prisons everywhere were filled to overflowing, but many criminals still roamed the streets. The cost to U.S. taxpayers was enormous.

THE NATION'S CRIME RATE had risen about 300 percent between 1960 and 1978. In 1977, bank robberies totalled 3,988, despite a number of devices installed to prevent them. The number reached 4,600 in 1978. Burglaries and murders increased as never before. Few streets anywhere were safe after dark, and mugging victims not only lost their valuables but often required expensive medical care as well. If their attackers were caught, they were quickly out on bail.

WHAT COULD HALT THE CRIME RISE? A Massachusetts judge, Walter McLaughlin, gave a clue when he stated that "what criminals fear most is a speedy trial and the certainty of punishment." Confirming his opinion, Lloyd Macdonald, a Boston prosecutor, said that "Defense attorneys are always trying to stall." Agreeing with them, the federal government in 1975 began a systematic war on habitual offenders. The program was devised by Charles Work, a Washington attorney for the Law Enforcement Assistance Administration.

THE LEAA provided federal funds to 24 large cities, enabling them to inaugurate the program, under which career criminals were singled out for close attention. Habitual offenders were carefully catalogued according to their records. One city listed all those with two felony convictions or five arrests. Another city zeroed in on all those who had been charged three times with such crimes as burglary, rape, murder, and armed robbery. For such persons, their next arrest brought quick and decisive action. Their cases were assigned to a special district attorney for prosecution. High bail was asked to keep them in jail, plea bargaining was refused, and a quick trial was sought. Using such techniques, the program sent to jail 5,000 hardened criminals, with terms averaging 14 years. Convictions ranged as high as 94 percent. In New Orleans, 992 convictions of this type were obtained in just two years.

**Elected the thirty-ninth President** of the United States with Walter Mondale as his running mate, Jimmy Carter experienced difficulty in his first White House years.

JIMMY CARTER, A FORMER naval officer and peanut farmer, became the thirty-ninth President of the United States in 1977. The soft-spoken Georgian had surprised the nation and his many opponents when he swept to the Democratic nomination by winning primary elections in many states. He went on to defeat President Gerald R. Ford, 297 electoral votes to 241, and won the popular vote, 40,827,292 to 39,146,127.

IN HIS LOW-KEY INAUGURAL ADDRESS, Carter avoided extravagant promises. He declared that "The bold and brilliant dream which excited the founders of this nation still awaits its consummation. I have no new dream to set forth today, but rather a fresh faith in the old dream." He also said that "We will move this year a step toward our goal—the elimination of all nuclear weapons from this earth."

CARTER WASTED NO TIME in putting into effect some of his pet projects. He created a Department of Energy under James Schlesinger, and instructed Health, Education, and Welfare (HEW) Secretary Joseph Califano to prepare a number of welfare reforms. He also sent Secretary of State Cyrus Vance to the Middle East to begin peace discussions between Egypt and Israel. United Nations Ambassador Andrew Young left to confer with African leaders.

ENORMOUSLY POPULAR when his term of office began, Carter soon ran into major difficulties. The first of these arose when his personal friend and fellow Georgian Bert Lance, whom Carter had appointed director of the Office of Management and Budget, was forced to resign following many allegations of questionable banking habits. Carter had stoutly defended Lance when the investigations began.

THE ADMINISTRATION'S ELATION over a drop in the nation's unemployment rolls was tempered by the ever-growing specter of inflation, which it seemed powerless to arrest. Although personal income was on the rise, rising prices were erasing those gains steadily and adding to the plight of those on fixed incomes. Blacks complained that Carter was going back on his promise to create employment for minorities.

**Landing on the rocky surface** of Mars, the spacecraft Viking I sent back to Earth remarkably clear photos of the Red Planet. There was no sign of animal or plant life.

AMERICA'S CONQUEST OF SPACE advanced another giant step on July 20, 1976 when the U.S. spacecraft *Viking* I landed on Mars. To reach the Red Planet, the 1,300-pound, 3-legged spacecraft had traveled 420 million miles since its launching from Earth on August 20, 1975. After touching down safely, *Viking* began transmitting pictures back to the Jet Propulsion Laboratory in Pasadena, California. The remarkably clear photos it sent to Earth pictured a rust-colored landscape filled with rocks and resembling the wastelands of Arizona and Utah. Sand dunes, rocks, and low ridges were clearly visible. On the horizon was what appeared to be the edge of a crater, with a pinkish sky above.

NO ANIMAL OR PLANT LIFE was apparent in the pictures, although scientists did not entirely rule out that possibility. During the weeks that followed, *Viking* performed various experiments upon commands from Earth. It picked up small quantities of the Martian soil and deposited them in a rotating container inside the spacecraft. After automatically analyzing the samples, it reported its findings to Earth. The soil samples showed the presence of calcium, silicon, titanium, iron, aluminum, and iron oxide.

A SECOND U.S. SPACECRAFT, *Viking* II, landed on Mars on September 3, 1976, and also relayed pictures to Earth. Its landing site appeared to be flatter than *Viking* I's, and was covered with smaller stones of a spongy, porous type—perhaps of volcanic origin. Its later photographs were able to prove that polar caps on Mars were composed of frozen water and not frozen carbon dioxide as some experts had believed.

EVEN GREATER U.S. ACCOMPLISHMENTS in space were just over the horizon. The American spacecraft *Voyager* I, which had been launched on a 400-million-mile journey in mid-1977, was scheduled to fly past the planet Jupiter in March, 1979. It was programmed to photograph not only Jupiter but its 13 moons as well. After completing that assignment, it was to continue on to Saturn, where it would perform a similar chore upon arrival in November, 1980. However, the U.S. spacecraft *Pioneer* II would already have reached Saturn by September of 1979. Scientists were eagerly awaiting first photographs of that planet, 886,000,000 miles from Earth.

# *PANAMA CANAL TREATY; PANAMA NEARS OWNERSHIP*

**Return of the Panama Canal** to Panama by the year 2000 was voted by the U.S. Senate. Completed in 1914, the waterway was too narrow for the newer and wider ships.

OWNERSHIP OF THE PANAMA Canal was to be turned over to Panama in the year 2000 under terms of a treaty approved by the U.S. Senate in 1978. The U.S. also agreed to raise the annual rent it paid Panama from $2.3 million to $10 million, and to loan Panama $275 million for development. The U.S. was to operate the canal until 2000, and retained the right to defend it.

THE TREATY WAS SIGNED after several discussions between President Carter and Panama leader General Omar Torrijos Herrera. Strained relations had existed between the two countries for several years. Americans protesting return of the canal to Panama were told that new U.S. aircraft carriers and giant tankers were too large to pass through the waterway. The canal also would be hard to defend in modern warfare, U.S. officials said.

CONSTRUCTION OF A CANAL in Panama was begun in the 1880s by a French company under an agreement with Colombia, ruler of Panama. It was to save all ships sailing between the Atlantic and Pacific oceans a 7,000-mile trip around Cape Horn at the tip of South America. A Panama canal had been the dream of Frenchman Ferdinand de Lesseps, who completed building the Suez Canal in 1869. But in Panama de Lesseps' company encountered jungles with yellow fever and malaria. More than 20,000 construction workers died. De Lesseps went bankrupt in 1889 and all work on the project was halted.

PRESIDENT THEODORE ROOSEVELT was eager to build a canal in Panama. In 1903, U.S. Secretary of State John Hay offered Colombia $10 million and $250,000 annual rental to allow America to build the waterway. But Colombia refused. Then Philippe Bunau-Varilla, a Frenchman who had worked for the company that had tried to build the canal, went as a Panamanian envoy to Washington. He told U.S. officials that he intended to start a revolution to free Panama from Colombia. Panama would then approve U.S. rights to build the canal. The revolution was a success, and a treaty was signed with the new nation. Building of the canal began in 1904.

# *ILLEGAL ALIENS COSTING AMERICA $13 BILLION A YEAR*

**Crammed into closed vehicles** like cattle and hidden under packing boxes and produce loads, thousands of Mexicans made their way illegally into large U.S. cities.

MILLIONS OF ILLEGAL ALIENS, the great majority of them from Mexico, entered the United States during the 1970s. They settled in many areas, holding some 3,000,000 jobs that American citizens could have filled and adding to a serious unemployment problem. U.S. immigration officials, who employed only 900 persons to investigate the many thousands of aliens who managed to cross the borders, called the situation "a silent invasion." They called for passage of new and tougher federal laws to halt it.

THE TRICKLE OF ILLEGAL ALIENS into the U.S. became a flood during the late 1970s. Smugglers charging fees as high as $400 per person began trucking illegal aliens to large American cities. Crammed into the vehicles like cattle, the immigrants were hidden under packing boxes and crates. The smugglers avoided detection by driving on back roads and country lanes instead of well-traveled highways, and used two-way radios to keep in touch with confederates who warned them of police on their route.

WHEN THE TRUCK reached its big-city destination, usually in an area peopled by Latins where they would be less likely to be noticed, the illegals were hurried off the trucks at night. They usually remained hidden in old buildings until they were able to find a job and support themselves. Some worked for as little as a dollar or less an hour, but others made $150 per week. In 1976, 886,000 illegal aliens were caught, but another 250,000 escaped capture.

SOME AUTHORITIES believed that illegal aliens were costing the U.S. government about $13 billion a year. Many aliens were living in subsidized housing and enjoying welfare, food stamps, and unemployment and medical benefits, all paid for by the American taxpayer.

# *AMERICANS DIE BY HUNDREDS IN GUYANA "DEATH CULT"*

**Fearing a breakup** of his colony, religious cult leader Jim Jones ordered his followers to commit suicide by drinking cyanide that had been poured into cups of soft drinks.

IN A MASS ORGY OF SUICIDE and murder almost too horrifying to be believed, 913 American men, women, and children died in late 1978 in Jonestown, in the South American country of Guyana. All were members of a religious colony, fanatical followers of a cult called the Peoples Temple, led by the Rev. Jim Jones. Although he himself was white, his membership was heavily black.

MADDENED BY THE possibility that his colony might be breaking up, Jones persuaded his followers to commit mass suicide by drinking deadly cyanide that had been put into paper cups containing a purple soft drink. Children and the few adults who resisted Jones' pleas to end their lives were seized by armed guards. Then nurses using syringes squirted fatal mixtures of cyanide down their throats. Jones died of a self-inflicted gunshot.

THE BIZARRE HAPPENING climaxed a day of strange events in Jonestown. Jones, who earlier had established the headquarters of his Peoples Temple in San Francisco, had induced many members to accompany him to his new colony on the edge of a Guyana jungle. There, he ruled with an iron hand and appropriated their properties, money, and even their Social Security checks.

CONGRESSMAN LEO RYAN of San Francisco, concerned about his former constituents, flew to Guyana to investigate the colony after hearing that some members had been prevented from leaving. Along with him were eight newsmen, as well as Mark Lane, attorney for the Peoples Temple, who called Ryan's trip a "witch hunt."

AFTER THEIR PLANES landed on a small airstrip nearby, Ryan and his party drove to the colony. Jones showed him about, and Ryan was favorably impressed until he discovered that the place had many armed guards. When several colony members left to return with Ryan, Jones became enraged. At the airstrip, Ryan's party was fired on, and Ryan and three newsmen were killed. Told of the happening, Jones became hysterical and ordered the suicides.

## *BLACK MAYORS ELECTED, BUT BLACK PROGRESS SLOWS*

**Three large U.S. cities** elected black mayors for the first time. Coleman Young was elected in Detroit, Thomas Bradley in Los Angeles, and Maynard Jackson in Atlanta.

ELECTED BLACK OFFICIALS in the U.S. increased enormously during the 1970s. But their influence failed to lead to the marked improvement in blacks' standard of living that had been expected. At the end of 1978, many blacks felt that the gains they fought so hard to achieve had proved meaningless. They felt frustrated by their failure to increase their share of the job market. They were also conscious of their rating as one of the largest groups of American poor.

WHEN THE VOTING RIGHTS ACT of 1965 was passed, only about 300 black elected officials could be found in the entire United States. By the end of 1978, the number had leaped to more than 4,000, and prospects for even greater representation were bright. Large cities such as Los Angeles, Atlanta, New Orleans, Detroit, and Washington were being governed by black mayors, as were 165 other cities across the nation. But in late 1978, the only black U.S. senator, Edward Brooke of Massachusetts, lost his bid for reelection. His defeat meant that no leadership role or committee chairmanship in Congress would be held by blacks until 1980 at the earliest.

BLACK DISSATISFACTION had been great since mid-1978, following a long-awaited decision by the Supreme Court. It upheld a claim of "reverse discrimination" brought by Allan Bakke, a white, against the regents of the University of California. Bakke said that he had been barred from the university's medical school even though he was better qualified than those of other races who had been accepted. Bakke claimed that he was turned down because he was white and the university was filling its admission lists on a race quota basis. The high court ruled that the university had to accept Bakke. It decided that quotas based on race were forbidden, although it added that race might be taken into account in judging students for admission to universities. Most blacks considered the ruling a blow to civil rights.

EVEN MORE DEPRESSING for blacks than the Bakke decision was their 11.5 percent rate of unemployment, although it had been 14 percent a short time before.

# *U.S., CHINA RESUME RELATIONS; TAIWAN ABANDONED*

**Before a likeness** of China's Deng Xiaoping, President Jimmy Carter and aides Leonard Woodcock and Zbigniew Brzezinski hailed renewal of friendly relations with China.

AMERICA AND COMMUNIST CHINA ended nearly 30 years of estrangement in 1978. In a surprise announcement, the two major world powers said that normal diplomatic relations would be established January 1, 1979. The agreement specified that formal diplomatic relations between the U.S. and Taiwan (Formosa) would end. It also provided that the 1954 mutual defense pact under which the U.S. guaranteed Taiwan's military security would be cancelled. Ambassadors between Washington and Peking would be exchanged on March 1, 1979. The announcement of the agreement was enthusiastically received in China, but the Taiwanese reacted with bitter attacks on the Carter administration for what they termed their abandonment.

ANNOUNCEMENT OF THE AGREEMENT was the climax to nearly seven years of steadily improving relations between the U.S. and China, beginning with the visit of President Richard Nixon to Peking in 1972. Details of the final agreement were worked out during 1978 after President Jimmy Carter sent National Security Adviser Zbigniew Brzezinski to Peking. Through Brzezinski, Carter let it be known that the U.S. had decided to normalize its relations with the Communist Chinese.

CHINA'S VICE PREMIER DENG XIAOPING (pronounced dung sheow ping) was quite pleased, and soon highly secret talks were being held in both China and the U.S. Leonard Woodcock, head of the U.S. Liaison Office in Peking, met with officials of the Chinese foreign ministry on several occasions. Meanwhile, Brzezinski was engaging in frequent secret discussions with Chinese representatives in Washington as well as at his Virginia home. The agreement was finalized in December, 1978.

THE FUTURE OF U.S.-TAIWAN relations was unclear. The ties between the two had their beginning after China's Nationalist Party leader Chiang Kai-shek had lost a long civil war to the Chinese Communists. He moved his government in exile to Taiwan in 1949, and for years America provided him with military and economic aid.

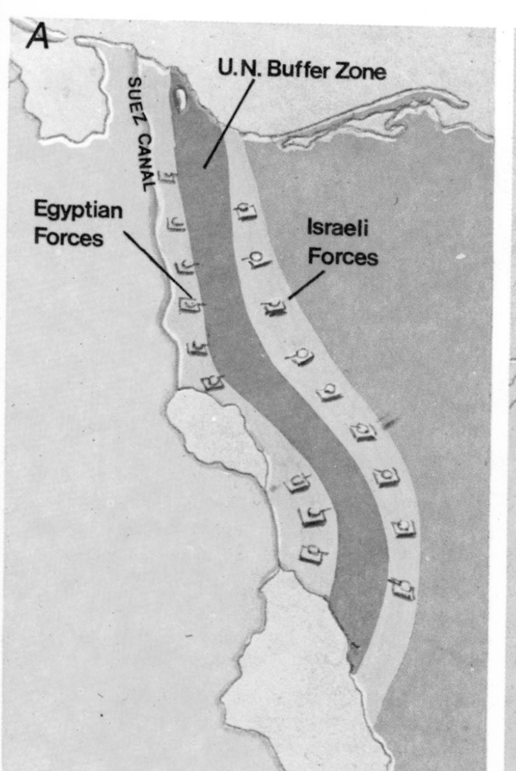


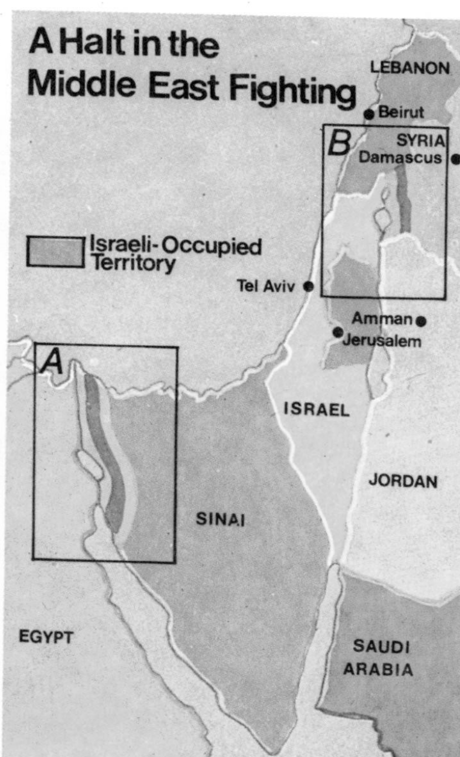


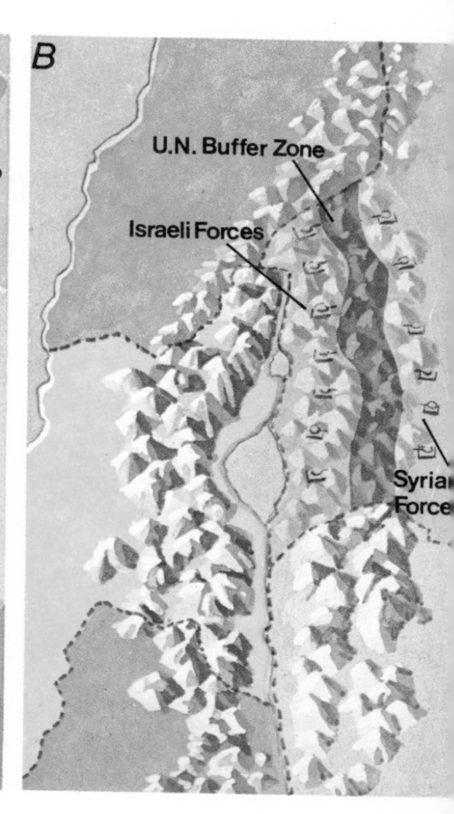


**Buffer zones** set up in 1973 following a cease-fire in the Middle East War were guarded by U.N. troops until 1978, when both sides agreed to sign a peace treaty.

A PEACE TREATY IN THE MIDDLE East War was assured in late 1978 as leaders of both Israel and Egypt agreed to a "framework for peace" suggested by U.S. President Jimmy Carter. Meeting in friendly conferences at Camp David in Maryland, Israeli Premier Menachem Begin and Egyptian President Anwar Sadat signed agreements that pledged both of them to sign a peace treaty just as soon as details of the settlement could be worded to the satisfaction of both nations.

THE LONG-AWAITED AGREEMENT brought to an end more than 30 years of quarreling between Egypt and Israel. It began in 1947, when the United Nations General Assembly withdrew a 1920 League of Nations mandate under which Britain held the right of control over Palestine. The U.N. voted to divide that country between the Jews and Arabs. Although Palestine was the ancient home of the Jews, Arabs also had lived there for centuries and considered the land as their own.

AFTER THE BRITISH WITHDRAWAL in 1948, the Jews proclaimed their section the Independent State of Israel. But the Palestinian Arabs, with backing from other Arab nations, refused to recognize Israel, and invaded it. The Jews won their war for independence, and an armistice was signed in January of 1949.

EGYPT AND SYRIA struck hard at Israel in a surprise attack in 1973. But the Israelis began a counterattack that carried them to within artillery range of Damascus, capital of Syria. They also crossed the Suez Canal and trapped thousands of Egyptian troops in the Sinai Desert with little food or water and without fuel for their 400 tanks. Egypt agreed to accept a cease-fire.

# Rise of Rights and Benefits of the America People

**The dates below are those when the acts were passed or other official actions were taken.**

## BILL OF RIGHTS

**1791** These 10 amendments to the Constitution were ratified and became guarantees of individual rights:

1. Freedom of religion, speech and the press.
2. A militia being necessary, people have the right to keep arms.
3. No soldier, in peacetime, can be quartered in any home unless owner consents.
4. Legal warrants needed for search of homes or seizure of property.
5. Indictment required before bringing a person to trial for a major crime. Nobody has to testify against himself.
6. Fair jury trial required in all criminal cases.
7. Right of jury trial available in all civil suits for more than $20.
8. Excessive bail, fines and cruel punishment are prohibited.
9. Other rights, not listed above, are not denied the people.
10. Powers not given to the federal government, and not prohibited by the Constitution, belong to the states.

## ECONOMIC BENEFITS

**1933** Federal Deposit Insurance Corporation created to guarantee individuals' bank deposits up to $5,000 (later $10,000).

**1935** Social Security provided:

1. Pensions for workers and their wives (or husbands) at age 65.
2. Unemployment compensation, or pay, for workers laid off or losing their jobs.
3. Aid to handicapped or disabled workers, and to needy and dependent aged persons.

**1963** Welfare Administration created to supervise federal programs to aid needy individuals, families, and children. States conduct welfare programs with the federal government sharing in the cost.

**1965** Medicare Amendments to Social Security provided hospital and medical insurance for most aged persons.

## LABOR RIGHTS AND BENEFITS

**1792** First trade union formed by Philadelphia shoemakers. Fight for reforms in hours and wages began.

**1829** Workingmen's Party organized in New York. Fought against use of convicts as laborers.

**1834** National Trades Union was formed in New York. Ten-hour working day was main demand.

**1866** National Labor Union formed in Baltimore. Fought for eight-hour day.

**1869** Knights of Labor formed. Open to all workers, regardless of sex, skill, or race.

**1886** American Federation of Labor formed as first permanent national union.

**1935** National Labor Relations Act guaranteed labor's rights of collective bargaining.

**1938** Wage and Hour Law set minimum on wages and maximum on working hours.

**1938** Congress of Industrial Organizations formed with 4,000,000 members.

**1947** Taft-Hartley Act. "Right to work" clause made union closed-shop illegal.

**1955** A.F. of L. and C.I.O. merged with 15,000,000 members.

## RIGHTS TO VOTE

**1870** Fifteenth Amendment gave blacks the right to vote.

**1920** Nineteenth Amendment gave women full voting rights.

**1964** Twenty-fourth Amendment prohibited poll tax, or registration fee, as a requirement for voting in national elections.

**1965** Voting Rights Law suspended literacy tests as a requirement for voting rights. Federal supervisors were authorized to register black voters. The law banned all poll taxes.

## CIVIL RIGHTS

**1868** Fourteenth Amendment gave blacks equal civil rights and citizenship in the U.S.

**1954** The Supreme Court ruled that school segregation violated the Constitution. Integration was ordered.

**1961** Interstate Commerce Commission prohibited segregated seating in interstate buses.

**1964** New civil rights act ordered equal treatment for all in employment, voting and public services, regardless of race or color. Services included hotels, restaurants, theaters and public transportation.

**1978** The Supreme Court ruled that quotas based on race were forbidden in judging students for admission to universities.

# glossary

**alliance** (al li′ unce), an agreement binding two or more parties to work together.
**armistice** (ar′ ma stis), an agreement to end fighting until a treaty of peace is signed.
**Articles of Confederation** (kon fed′ er a shun), the first written laws for government of the United States.
**assassination** (a sas′ a na shun), the murder of a President or other high official.
**astronauts** (as′ tro nauts), a small group of Americans trained for space exploration.
**authority** (a thor′ i tee), the right to give orders or make decisions.
**Bill of Rights** (rites), the first ten amendments to the Constitution.
**blockade** (blok kade′), the keeping of people or ships from entering a place or port.
**Boston Tea Party,** an incident prior to the Revolution in which citizens of Boston dumped tea into the harbor to protest against taxes.
**canal** (ka nal′), a man-made waterway.
**casualties** (kas′ u al teez), all losses, including dead, wounded and those taken prisoner.
**cavalrymen** (kav′ al ree men), soldiers on horseback.
**census** (sen′ sus), an official counting of all people in the country every ten years.
**charter** (char′ ter), a written plan for the government of a country or area.
**civil rights** (siv′ il, rites), the rights belonging to all Americans, regardless of their race or religion.
**civil service** (siv′ il, sir viss), non-military employment by the government.
**clipper ship** (klip′ per), a very fast sailing vessel.
**collective bargaining** (ka lek′ tiv, bar′ gun ing), meetings between workers and employers to discuss working conditions.
**colonization** (kol a ni za′ shun), the act of settling a new land.
**commander-in-chief** (ka man′ der), the head of the armed forces of a country: in the United States, the President.
**Communism** (kom′ yoo niz um), a system in which the people are ruled by a group called the Communist Party. It is the only legal party.
**compromise** (kom pra mize), a settlement of a dispute in which each side gives up part of what is originally asked.
**confidence** (kon′ fi dense), strong belief or trust in someone or something.
**conglomerate** (kon glam′ er it), a mixed corporation made up of companies doing different businesses.
**consecrate** (kon see krate), to set something aside as holy.
**conservation** (kon ser va′ shun), protection from loss, waste or harm.
**constitution** (kon sta too shun), a written plan for government of a country or state.
**continent** (kon′ ti nent), one of the 7 main large land areas: Africa, Asia, Europe, North America, South America, Antarctica and Australia.
**convention** (kon ven′ shun), a meeting of delegates from various places or organizations.
**cotton gin** (kot′ n, jin), a machine which pulls cotton fiber away from the seeds.
**courageous** (ka ra′ jus), brave.
**Declaration of Independence,** a document setting forth the reasons why the colonies broke away from England.
**dedicate** (ded′ a kate), to set something aside for a special purpose.
**depression** (de pres′ shun), hard times, with many people out of work.
**devotion** (de vo shun), ardent love for something or someone.
**dictator** (dik′ ta ter), a ruler who has complete power over his country.
**disarmament** (dis ar′ ma ment), an agreement between nations to get rid of weapons.
**displaced person,** or D.P. (dis placed′), one who was driven from his home in Europe because of World War II and helped to come to the United States.
**dispute** (dis′ pewt), debate or quarrel.
**elector** (e lek ter), a person who has the authority to vote directly for President.
**Emancipation Proclamation** (e man′ si pa shun, prok la ma shun), a decree by President Lincoln declaring the South's slaves free.
**emperor** (em′ per or), the ruler of a large country.
**equal opportunity,** giving equal chances to all, such as in obtaining jobs.
**execute** (ek si kute), to carry out or do something.
**exports** (ek′ sport), merchandise leaving a country to be sold in a foreign land.
**extinction** (ek stingk′ shun), dying out.
**Free States,** those states which did not allow slavery.

# glossary

**frontier** (frun′ teer), the edge or end of a settled country.

**galleon** (gal′ e un), a 16th century Spanish ship.

**generous** (jen′ er us), liberal.

**guilders** (gil′ ders), the basic money of the Netherlands.

**gunboat** (gun′ bote), a small armed ship.

**Hessians** (hesh′ anz), German soldiers paid by England to serve in the Revolutionary War.

**House of Burgesses** (ber′ jis says), the assembly of the colony of Virginia.

**House of Representatives** (rep re zen′ ta tivz), the lower branch of Congress, whose members are elected according to population.

**immigrants** (im′ a grants), those people coming to America from other countries.

**impeachment** (im peach′ ment), congressional action accusing an officer of the United States government of wrongful conduct.

**imperialism** (im pir′ i al izm), the practice of creating an empire by conquering other countries or forming colonies in other lands.

**imports** (im′ ports), merchandise brought into a country.

**impotence** (im pa′ tens), helplessness, without power.

**incandescent** (in kan des′ nt), glowing with heat.

**influence** (in′ floo ens), power over persons or things.

**injunction** (in jungk′ shun), court order against some action or practice.

**inseparable** (in sep′ ar a bl), that which cannot be separated or divided.

**insurrection** (in′ sa rek′ shun), a revolt or rebellion.

**integration** (in ta gra′ shun), giving all persons the same services in the same places, regardless or race or color.

**international** (in ter na′ shun al), between or among nations.

**interstate commerce** (kom′ ers), the shipment of goods between the states.

**invader** (in vay′ der), one who enters a country or area with an army to conquer it.

**inventor** (in ven′ ter), one who develops a new idea or product.

**ironclad** (iron′ klad), a wooden ship covered with iron sheets for protection.

**Iron Curtain** (ker tun), the imaginary wall set up by the Communists to block off their countries from the rest of the world.

**isthmus** (is′ mus), a narrow strip of land with water on each side, joining two larger bodies of land.

**"Jim Crow" laws** (jim croe lawz), laws passed by some states to keep Negroes from exercising their rights.

**Ku Klux Klan** (koo), a secret organization in the South to keep Negroes down.

**land battleship** (bat′ tl ship), an armed tank.

**League of Nations** (leeg, uv, nay′ shunz), an organization set up after World War I to keep world peace.

**lunar module** (lu′ nar, ma′ dule), a small scale spacecraft used in landing on the moon.

**Manifest Destiny** (man′ a fest des′ ti nee), the obvious certainty of America expanding and becoming a great nation.

**Medal of Honor** (med′ l, on′ er), the highest award for bravery given by the United States military services.

**Minutemen** (min′ it men), colonial patriots.

**monopoly** (ma nop′ a lee), a business establishment so large that it can control prices of the products it makes and sells.

**Monroe Doctrine** (mun′ roe, dok trin), a foreign policy announced by President Monroe to keep European nations out of the Americas.

**NATO** (nay′ toe), an agreement among certain Western nations to help one another in case of attack.

**neutral** (noo′ trul), one who does not take part in a war or argument.

**New Deal** (deel), a series of laws sponsored by President Roosevelt to help end the depression of the 1930's.

**organize** (or′ gan ize), to arrange or place according to a system.

**Pan-American Exposition** (ek′ spa zish′ un), a fair in New York at which President McKinley was assassinated in 1901.

**paralysis** (pa ral′ a sis), the loss of power to move or feel.

**parliament** (par′ lah ment), the lawmaking body in some countries, as in Canada and England.

**patriotism** (pa′ tree ut izm), great love and loyalty for one's own country.

**permanent** (per′ ma nent), something which can, or is meant to, last a long time.

**police regulations** (pa leese′, reg′ yoo lay′ shunz), rules established by the police for the protection of a community.

# glossary

**pollution** (pa loo′ shun), making air or water impure by putting impure matter in it.
**Pony Express** (eks press′), a system for delivering mails, using fast ponies.
**portrait painter** (pore′ trit), an artist who specializes in painting pictures of people.
**protectorate** (pro tek′ tar it), a country guaranteed protection in return for some favor.
**raiders** (rayd′ erz), pirates.
**ratified** (rat′ a fyed), approved.
**reaper** (reep′ er), a machine for harvesting grain.
**rebellion** (re bell′ yun), a revolt or revolution.
**recognized** (rek′ ug nized), accepted as a new state or government.
**reconstruction** (re kon struk′ shun), the period in which the South was rebuilt after the Civil War.
**Redcoats** (red′ cotes), British soldiers during the Revolutionary War.
**relief** (ree leef′), support by the government.
**reparations** (rep a ra′ shuns), money damages claimed by the Allies from Germany after World War I.
**reservation** (rez er va′ shun), a large tract of land set aside as a home for Indians.
**restored** (ree stored′), brought back to its original condition.
**scandal** (skan′ dl), a public shame or disgrace.
**sculptor** (skulp′ tir), an artist who works in clay, wood, stone or other 3-dimensional materials.
**seamanship** (see′ man ship), skill as a sailor.
**SEATO** (see′ toe), a treaty binding certain nations, including the U.S., to joint action in Southeast Asia.
**secede** (see seed′), to withdraw from membership in a group or nation.
**sedition** (see di′ shun), stirring up of a rebellion against a government.
**segregation** (seg′ re ga′ shun), keeping white and non-white persons separate in public places, such as schools.
**seizure** (seez′ your), to take something suddenly by force.
**self-government** (guv′ ern ment), independence or democracy in government.
**senator** (sen′ a ter), a member of the upper house of Congress, one of two such men elected from each state.
**Social Security** (sew′ shall, see cure′ i tee), a system of government insurance for making payments to the aged, unemployed, widows, etc.
**Stars and Stripes** (starz), the American flag.
**strike** (stryke), an action in which workers refuse to work until their demands are met.
**supplication** (sup la kay′ shun), the act of asking someone very humbly to do something.
**supply station** (sa ply′, stay′ shun), a port at which warships or military groups can put in for food, weapons and other needed items.
**Supreme Court** (sa preme′), the highest court in our country.
**surrendered** (sa ren′ derred), gave up.
**territory** (ter′ a tory), land ruled by a nation or state.
**throng,** a large number of people.
**Tom Thumb** (thum), the name given the first railroad steam engine in our country.
**treason** (tree′ zn), the crime of helping the enemies of one's own country.
**triumvirate** (tree um′ ver it), government by a group of three men.
**unconscious** (un kon′shus), not able to feel or think.
**unconstitutional** (un kon sti two′ shun l), illegal because it is against the Constitution.
**underground,** an organization of patriots who fight secretly for the freedom of a country.
**Underground Railroad,** a system by which slaves in the South were secretly helped to travel to the North and freedom.
**United Nations,** or UN (nay′ shunz), an organization set up after World War II to keep world peace.
**veto** (vee′ toe), refusal to approve something.
**vulcanizing** (vul′ kan eyes ing), a process of heating rubber to make it stronger.
**volunteer** (vol un teer′), one who offers to do something of his own free will.
**War between the States,** the Civil War.
**War Hawk,** one who favors war.
**warmonger** (wor′ mong er), one who seeks to start a war.
**warrant** (wor′ ant), an official paper giving the right to do something.
**"white primaries"** (pri′ mare eez), elections in which blacks were not allowed to vote.
**wrought** (rawt), shaped or formed.
**XYZ Affair,** an incident in which a high official of France demanded a large bribe for France to remain peaceful with the U.S.
**yellow fever** (fee′ ver), a serious disease caused by certain tropical mosquitoes.

# index

# index

# index

# index

Alaska
the 49th state
1959
Oregon
Territory
opened
Migration
of the Mormons 1847
Settlement
of California
Spanish
missions
First atomic
bomb exploded
1945
Santa Fe
under four flags
MEXICO
Hawaii
the 50th state
1959